Postfeminist War

War Culture

Edited by Daniel Leonard Bernardi

Books in this series address the myriad ways in which warfare informs diverse cultural practices, as well as the way cultural practices—from cinema to social media—inform the practice of warfare. They illuminate the insights and limitations of critical theories that describe, explain, and politicize the phenomena of war culture. Traversing both national and intellectual borders, authors from a wide range of fields and disciplines collectively examine the articulation of war, its everyday practices, and its impact on individuals and societies throughout modern history.

Tanine Allison, *Destructive Sublime: World War II in American Film and Media*

Brenda M. Boyle and Jeehyun Lim, eds., *Looking Back on the Vietnam War: Twenty-First-Century Perspectives*

Jonna Eagle, *Imperial Affects: Sensational Melodrama and the Attractions of American Cinema*

H. Bruce Franklin, *Crash Course: From the Good War to the Forever War*

Aaron Michael Kerner, *Torture Porn in the Wake of 9/11: Horror, Exploitation, and the Cinema of Sensation*

David Kieran and Edwin A. Martini, eds., *At War: The Military and American Culture in the Twentieth Century and Beyond*

Delia Malia Caparoso Konzett, *Hollywood's Hawaii: Race, Nation, and War*

Nan Levinson, *War Is Not a Game: The New Antiwar Soldiers and the Movement They Built*

Matt Sienkiewicz, *The Other Air Force: U.S. Efforts to Reshape Middle Eastern Media Since 9/11*

Jon Simons and John Louis Lucaites, eds., *In/visible War: The Culture of War in Twenty-First-Century America*

Roger Stahl, *Through the Crosshairs: The Weapon's Eye in Public War Culture*

Mary Douglas Vavrus, *Postfeminist War: Women and the Media-Military-Industrial Complex*

Simon Wendt, ed., *Warring over Valor: How Race and Gender Shaped American Military Heroism in the Twentieth and Twenty-First Centuries*

Postfeminist War

Women and the Media-Military-Industrial Complex

MARY DOUGLAS VAVRUS

Rutgers University Press

New Brunswick, Camden, and Newark, New Jersey, and London

Library of Congress Cataloging-in-Publication Data
Names: Vavrus, Mary Douglas, author.
Title: Post-feminist war : women and the media-military-industrial complex /
Mary Douglas Vavrus.
Description: New Brunswick : Rutgers University Press, [2018] | Series: War culture |
Includes bibliographical references and index.
Identifiers: LCCN 2018012685 | ISBN 9780813576824 (cloth) | ISBN 9780813576817 (pbk.)
Subjects: LCSH: Women soldiers in mass media. | Women soldiers—United States. |
Women and the military—United States. | Militarism—United States. | Mass media and
war—United States. | Feminism and mass media—United States.
Classification: LCC P96.W352 U5583 2018 | DDC 355.0082—dc23
LC record available at https://nao1.safelinks.protection.outlook.
com/?url=https%3A%2F%2Flccn.loc.gov%2F2018012685&data=02%7C01%7Cjfb131%40pr
ess.rutgers.edu%7C819609289b2d43afbc4b08d58f1ed580%7Cb92d2b234d35447093ff69aca6
632ffe%7C1%7C0%7C636572284977302442&sdata=a2KMMNxY6VkkGcC1h3yBKkIuk%
2FPDV4FBwiIq8VCKLUE%3D&reserved=0

A British Cataloging-in-Publication record for this book is available from the British Library.

∞ The paper used in this publication meets the requirements of the American National
Standard for Information Sciences—Permanence of Paper for Printed Library Materials,
ANSI Z39.48-1992.

www.rutgersuniversitypress.org

Manufactured in the United States of America

Dedicated to my loving parents, Hallie and Gus Vavrus

Contents

Introduction   I

1   Lifetime's *Army Wives*, or, I Married the
Media-Military-Industrial Complex   29

2   Counterintuitive Mothering in the
Media-Military-Industrial Complex   63

3   "No Longer Women, but Soldiers":
The Warrior Women of Television News   101

4   "This Wasn't the Intended Sacrifice":
Warrior Women and Sexual Violence   140

Conclusion: Banality's Fatalities   178

Acknowledgments   195
Notes   199
References   207
Index   227

Postfeminist War

Introduction

On a gorgeous summer day in the not-at-all-distant past, I set out on my bike to ride for as long as was necessary to organize the thoughts swirling in my head as I wrote this book. As I have so many times, I headed to Fort Snelling State Park in St. Paul, Minnesota, and soon was cruising fast down the hill that skirts the base of the bluffs where the old fort sits. I rode blissfully for over a half hour before being struck by what should have been obvious: I was surrounded by a site for everyday militarism. Fort Snelling is not just any old military site; it had seen the deaths of hundreds of Dakota Indians, interned there during the U.S.-Dakota war of the 1860s. Even after making this ride over a hundred times, I had not previously contemplated how the violent and martial history of the park could be easily subsumed by the recreational activities it offers for dog walkers, kayakers, and cyclists like me. It is telling that this feat of history denial was possible even while I was writing a book about militarism and how common media sites can reproduce it with content that blends into otherwise-mundane life activities. Returning after this somewhat-humiliating epiphany, my route home took me by an American Legion post, on whose western exterior wall is a faded mural depicting a white man in military uniform pinning a medal onto the uniform of a white woman, apparently signaling this as one spot where military veterans regardless of gender can eat, drink, and socialize. Again, I was struck by how even in a war-weary country, as the United States appears to be, sites across our cultural landscapes allow us to participate in some degree of militarism, perhaps without a second thought. As this book argues, it becomes even easier to give tacit support to militarism and all it entails when women are involved.

Women's involvement in militarism and war is not new to this post-9/11 moment. For over a century in the United States, women have been on and behind war's front lines and have played supporting roles as military spouses and mothers and as contract personnel and sex workers on domestic and international bases (see Enloe 2000). What is different now and therefore worth examining is how U.S. women are used in public discourse produced by an ostensibly independent media system to sell war and the militarism that accompanies it.[1] With no end in sight after sixteen years of war and occupation in Afghanistan and fourteen of the same in Iraq, maintaining public support for these and other military interventions has become a marketing project— one with which U.S. media outlets have become enthusiastically engaged. Historically, women have proved difficult to convince of the wisdom of particular wars, and these twenty-first-century conflicts as part of the Global War on Terror (GWOT) are no exception. *Postfeminist War* addresses how, since September 11, 2001, select hybrid,[2] news, and documentary media have worked to bring women into public conversations about war and, in the process, succeed in marketing militarism to viewers, listeners, and readers of these texts. For war makers and supporters alike, this is an ongoing project necessitated largely by the all-volunteer military forces (AVF) that rely on a positive image of the military and war to recruit and maintain adequate staffing levels.

But despite such intensive and concerted marketing efforts, public support for post-9/11 military operations is waning. For example, a poll conducted in 2017 for the Committee for a Responsible Foreign Policy revealed that a majority of those who were queried expressed skepticism about U.S. military interventions abroad, wishing to see reductions in both aid and military "physical involvement" in conflicts around the globe as well as reflecting a strong desire for Congress to reestablish authority over military actions (Carden 2018). This poll and another cited by James Carden (2018) reveal that a "wide bipartisan majority . . . seeks an American foreign policy of realism and restraint." In a similar effort, pollsters surveyed U.S. residents in 2014 for their feelings about whether they believed the wars in Afghanistan and Iraq had been worth fighting. Gallup discovered that for the first time since 2001, respondents were evenly divided about the war in Afghanistan, whereas in years prior, a majority supported war there (Newport 2014). A poll conducted by NBC News, the *Wall Street Journal*, and the Annenberg Public Policy Center several months later revealed that 71 percent of adults in the United States believe that the war in Iraq was "not worth the cost"—a significant increase over the 59 percent who reported they felt the same way in a similar poll conducted a year and a half prior (Sakuma 2014). These post hoc regrets came eleven years after the Iraq invasion as news media once again covered heated debates about the prudence of U.S. involvement in Iraq, as Iraq's government struggled to beat back the advances of Islamic State in Iraq and Syria (ISIS) and President Obama was ordering airstrikes against ISIS in Northern Iraq and Syria. Old talking points were rehashed, and familiar figures such as the former vice president

Dick Cheney, the pundit William Kristol, and the former *New York Times* reporter Judith Miller reappeared to offer their advice to return combat troops to Iraq; despite their efforts, the polls reflected a war weariness evidently felt by a wide swath of the U.S. public—fatigue routinely dismissed by lawmakers and the Pentagon.

President Trump's administration revealed its fundamental bellicosity early on through an astonishingly large defense spending request for 2018 (an increase of $54 billion, for a total request of $603 billion [Sahadi 2017]); by awarding hefty contracts to Boeing, Raytheon, and Lockheed Martin that boosted the stock prices of these weapons contractors (Hartung 2018); and by conducting bombings, such as dropping the Mother of All Bombs, or MOAB, on Afghanistan in April 2017. A bird's-eye-view image of the crater produced by the MOAB prompted a *Fox & Friends* host to declare, "That's what free-dom looks like. That's the red, white, and blue!" Brian Williams of NBC, along with other pundits, expressed enchantment with the massive explosion as well. Surely the disjuncture between these issues—the remorse reflected in the 2014 and 2017 poll results and now the Trump administration's and Penta-gon's plans for what Andrew Bacevich (2008) has predicted will be "frequent, protracted, perhaps perpetual" wars—can be traced to how the Afghanistan and Iraq wars have been represented by U.S. media outlets since September 11, 2001, when war became a central part of the twenty-four-hour news cycle.

Managing disjunctures between public opinion and war policy necessitates public relations work as tactical as it is invisible. Although the success of such campaigns is far from guaranteed, they are neither difficult to implement nor difficult to hide in the current media environment, dominated as it is by tac-tics associated with perception management. The Pew Research Center, for example, reports that today PR workers outnumber traditional journalists five to one, making them virtually ubiquitous (Williams 2014). Their work is made easier by the well-developed, extensive Pentagon PR machine acting in con-cert with that within each branch of the military, documented by Nick Turse (2008). Sarah Maltby (2012) has detailed how the British military strategically manages media in the United Kingdom in a fashion identical to what we have seen in the United States. Thus, it is not a stretch to suggest that perception management is an important part of military PR efforts. These days, the goal of such efforts is to normalize support for war and other military interven-tions, casting it as a commonsense, inarguable position that equates to forti-fying the home front against terrorists. Signifying this political construction as nonpolitical or outside the realm of public contestation is a feat of media orchestration that has been documented by a number of works, such as Scott Bonn's *Mass Deception* (2010), Anthony DiMaggio's *When Media Goes to War* (2009), Tanner Mirrlees's *Hearts and Mines* (2016), Bill Moyers's documentary film *Buying the War* (2007), and many others (e.g., Bloch-Elkon and Nacos

2014; Hoskins and O'Loughlin 2010; Kellner 2004, 2010; Maltby 2012; and McLaren and Martin 2004).

None of these accounts, however, addresses the role that women play in such postpolitical media constructions after 9/11, despite the ubiquity of women in these representations. To remedy this omission, the research I have compiled in the chapters of *Postfeminist War* reveals the multiple discursive strategies used in hybrid, news, and documentary media to normalize militarism using constructions of women in various military-related roles. These media discourses serve different purposes, three of which are most germane to this book. First, they illustrate a growing recognition of women's value to a military dependent on the AVF; second, they legitimate both war and militarism in and through narratives about women; and third, they reveal how meanings around gender in military life may be discursively constructed, intensively managed, and negotiated in and through media.

For a variety of reasons, U.S. media generally avoid regressive or explicitly antifeminist accounts of gender; instead, about issues historically associated with women, mainstream media typically utilize postfeminist framing and ideology (see Vavrus 2002, 2012). I titled this book *Postfeminist War* because my research shows that since 2001, war- and military-themed media exhibit a mixture of resistance *and* capitulation to racialized patriarchy as they work to naturalize women's support for martial values and actions. In this context, narratives about women use feminism selectively to focus on gender equality as they preclude examination of structural problems that differentially disadvantage women both inside and outside the military: chiefly racism, economic inequality, and misogyny. In so doing, such discourses advance what I call *martial postfeminism*, an ideology that both pushes military solutions for an array of problems that women and girls face and endorses war by either glorifying or obscuring the forms of violence it entails. *Postfeminist War* thus argues that martial postfeminism discourages critical investigation of the military as an institution, the wars U.S. troops fight, and the military-industrial complex that both drives and profits from war.

Media discourses have played a significant role in informing cultural practices and beliefs about warfare and in providing the civilian public with cultural sites on which to negotiate meaning around both warfare and the military. As Robin Andersen argues, war is "understood and interpreted, justified and judged through the images and narratives that tell the stories of war. Most civilians experience military conflict through the signs and symbols of its depiction, their impressions derived not from battles in distant lands but from the manner they are rendered at home" (2006, xvi). Especially since the 1991 Persian Gulf War, such signs and symbols have depicted women in relationship to the military: as troops, spouses, mothers, and intelligence officers.

With the end of male conscription in 1973, the number of service women of all races has risen steadily, albeit slowly, and includes those serving as officers. Today about 14 percent of enlisted forces and 16 percent of commissioned officers are women (Patten and Parker 2011, 4), and "minority women" constitute 55.4 percent of enlisted women and 38 percent of women officers (Women's Research and Education Institute 2013, 17) (see chapter 3 for a discussion of the implications of these demographics in news coverage of women in combat). For the enlistment trend to continue in this direction, as numerous military spokespersons claim to want, the patriarchal values that suffuse military service must be suppressed in order to convey the message that the military is safe for women and their families.

It is noteworthy that one of the examples of banal militarism that I spied on my bike ride—at the typically conservative American Legion—would prominently feature a woman soldier as the face of that organization. For a military that relies on the AVF, including women at every level is necessary to keep functioning, particularly at a moment in which the military is employing more "soft power" tactics—historically gendered as feminine—than ever before (Hajjar 2014).[3] Rosa Brooks lists some of the less-well-known but typical soft-power activities of "modern military personnel":

> They analyze lines of computer code in Virginia office buildings, build isolation wards in Ebola-ravaged Liberia, operate health clinics in rural Malaysian villages, launch agricultural reform programs and small business development projects in Africa, train Afghan judges and parliamentarians, develop television soap operas for Iraqi audiences and conduct antipiracy patrols off the Somali coast. They monitor global email and telephone communications, pilot weaponized drones from simulated airplane cockpits thousands of miles away, and help develop and plan for high-tech new modes of warfare.... These and a thousand other activities now performed by the U.S. military are intended to "shape the battlespace," prevent and deter future conflict, and disrupt or destroy the capabilities of potential adversaries, whoever—and wherever—they may be. (2016b, 13–14)

But practical needs and legal mandates to include women as either soft- or hard-power personnel do not always translate into a warm welcome for them, especially from a masculinist organization such as the U.S. military. Nevertheless, maintaining women's support for military endeavors in a time of wavering public commitment to overseas interventions and high levels of military spending is essential. Mainstream civilian media in the United States have done just that, as the following chapters will show using examples of media representations intended for civilian audiences that have appeared over the course of fifteen years after September 11, 2001—a protracted period of war making that has yet to see an end.

• • •

After September 11, 2001, when more and more women were making appearances in war reporting and military-themed media, I became curious about how they were being depicted and in whose interests. As a media studies researcher, I knew that none of what was presented to the public to view, read, and hear was there by accident, so I began studying some of the sites featuring militarized women to try and understand how commercial media outlets might be employing them. Over time, the informal morphed into a systematic examination—one that has made me realize how crucial militarized women are to a post-9/11, martial regime of representation. This book is the result of my investigation and chiefly addresses two interrelated issues. First, I consider how the discursive construction of women in civilian media produces what Stuart Hall labels a "regime of representation" (2001, 328)—in this case, a regime concerning war and military life after 9/11. With varying degrees of success, this regime attempts to manufacture general public consent to war making and intensifying militarism by depicting various ways in which *women* consent to these; the chapters that follow this one illustrate different discursive strategies used to accomplish this depiction. Second, I illuminate the media political economy, or what I refer to as the *media-military-industrial complex* (MMIC), underlying this regime's manufacture of public consent to war and militarism. Specifically, I examine some of the commercial relationships that aim to shape the meanings that emerge from this martial regime of representation and gain the status of "truth." On the basis of this analysis, I argue throughout the book that news, hybrid, and documentary media representations discursively articulating (linking) women to the military at this historical moment construct martial postfeminist subjects suitable to serve in or support the military and its geopolitical objectives. By introducing the subjects of each of *Postfeminist War*'s chapters, the following sections detail the elements of the theoretical framework I use to identify and understand this post-9/11 representational regime.

Discourses of Militarism

Since September 11, 2001, militarism has become a predominant force in producing what Lawrence Grossberg labels a cultural context of life, or a matrix composed of "discursive practices [that] are inextricably involved in the organization of relations of power" (2010, 8). The discursive practices I focus on in *Postfeminist War* are those that produce media representations of women in and around the military and constitute meanings around them. Theoretical work involved with interrogating the articulations that produce contexts of life, necessarily include identifying "the basic processes of the production of reality, of the production of context and power. . . . It is the transformative practice or work of making, unmaking, and remaking relations and contexts, of establishing new relations out of old relations or non-relations, of drawing lines and mapping connections" (Grossberg 2010, 21). What results, he continues, is a "sense of context [that] is always of a complex, overdetermined, and contingent unity" (21). Media discourses that I examine in the book have worked together over the course of fifteen years to produce a militarized context of life—one that instructs media audiences in how they should regard women within its specific realms. To my mind, one of the most significant aspects of this discursive context is the truths it produces about war, the military, and women's involvement in them both. I therefore draw on Michel Foucault's concept of a regime of truth in combination with Stuart Hall's notion of a regime of representation to track media discourses that have worked together to legitimate some subject positions and views of war as they subordinate others or leave them unaddressed altogether.

Foucault's concept rests on the argument that truths are historically contingent, discursive constructs linked to particular bodies of knowledge—a process that endows them with disciplinary power at specific historical moments. Beliefs about women's suitability for combat that change drastically over the course of a few decades after the end of conscription in 1973 exemplify the ways in which statements can gain and then lose their status as truth. Objective, capital-T Truths are not the central concern in this theoretical framework; rather, it is the process by which small-t truths are produced and circulated socially that is of interest: Foucault describes this as "a system of ordered procedures for the production, regulation, distribution and circulation of statements" on a particular subject. A set of statements gains status as truth by being "linked by a circular relation to systems of power which produce it and sustain it, and to effects of power which it induces and which redirect it" (1977, 14). Understanding this system, Paula Treichler argues, necessitates a view of truth *as* power; thus, "we can forget the fight for or against a particular truth and instead interrogate the rules at work in a society that distinguishes 'true' representations from 'false' ones" (1999, 139).

A regime of truth influences social experience and knowledge production, and about war this is no exception: it guides and sculpts audience perceptions of what are real and accurate accounts of war and military service, as well as about those populations that the United States targets for war. (For example, see Scott Bonn's *Mass Deception* [2010] for an analysis of how media representations constructed Iraqis, and especially Saddam Hussein, as weapons-of-mass-destruction-hoarding folk devils and thus stoked a moral panic resulting in public support for war.). At the very least, regimes of truth regulate public support for military spending and the enormous defense budgets for which there appears to be no upper limit (Lewis 2008; R. Thorpe 2014). But more importantly, perhaps, regimes of truth potentially garner public support for the military recruitment and martial values that virtually guarantee warfare in perpetuity.

Discourses that operate within a regime of truth at this historical moment are likely to be media representations, an aggregation of which Hall refers to as a regime of representation. In this regime, historically specific signification practices of media producers and users imbue media representations with particular meanings, which in some contexts can become truths. A representational regime is thus composed of media constructions linked intertextually, which accumulate "meanings across different texts, where one image refers to another, or has its meaning altered by being 'read' in the context of other images," resulting in a "whole repertoire of imagery and visual effects through which 'difference' is represented at any one historical moment" (Hall 2001, 328). Although Hall specifies images, I broaden his conception of regime to consider the words that accompany images, which together manage difference in media representations of women in and around the military after 9/11. Media representations that a regime comprises are not simply reflections or re-presentations of the object(s) in a domain, Hall (1997) explains; rather, they discursively constitute the meanings of these objects, in part by persistently articulating specific meanings to an object or object domain, thus normalizing those meanings as truths. *Army Wives*, for example, features women mainly engaging in family- and warrior-supporting activities that express Army-approved truths. To wit, Officer Joan Burton praises to a potential recruit ROTC and the Army together for offering her a route out of her childhood poverty and a means to realize her skills as a warrior and leader. Army wives Pamela and Roxy grudgingly endure their spouses' long deployments because they believe the men are fighting in Iraq to protect them and their children on the home front. As I argue in chapter 1, performances such as these attempted to renegotiate meaning around women, war, and the military at a time when public support for the war in Iraq, especially, was waning as skepticism about the upcoming troop surge there was on the rise. The truths constructed in these representations work to counter such public unease by both humanizing soldiers and Army families and highlighting good works they engage in while deployed to Iraq.

A representational regime is valuable to the extent that it produces truths resonant with the experiences of media audiences. Achieving such verisimilitude rests on how a regime regulates its constituent representations' affective registers using interpretive frameworks: "What we feel is in part conditioned by how we interpret the world around us; [and] how we interpret what we feel actually can and does alter the feeling itself," as Judith Butler explains

(2010, 41). She observes, moreover, that media representations of war act as trajectories of affect; as such, they orient audiences to understand, sympathize, and even empathize with their subjects in particular ways. Two other, interrelated, concepts from Butler's scholarship on war—recognizability and grievability—explain how representations may produce empathetic responses in media audiences. To Butler, recognizability does not come about simply because we realize that another human is within our field of perception but only when we fully comprehend or apprehend that life's vulnerability, its precariousness. In this context, precariousness is not only inherent to human life; it "implies living socially, that is, the fact that one's life is always in some sense in the hands of the other. . . . Reciprocally, it implies being impinged upon by the exposure and dependency of others, most of whom remain anonymous" (2010, 14).

Grievability works in tandem with precariousness and operates in a form that Butler refers to as the "future anterior," or the understanding that, projecting into the future, we will mourn the loss of a life with which we have come in contact. "Without grievability," Butler explains, "there is no life, or, rather, there is something living that is other than life. . . . The apprehension of grievability precedes and makes possible the apprehension of precarious life" (2010, 15). How women achieve recognizability and, therefore, grievability particularly as warriors in this post-9/11 regime of representation is a subject I address at length in chapters 3 and 4, where I delve into the discursive practices that constitute that portion of the regime I call Warrior Women.

Social Identities of Militarism

The social identities of the individuals involved in warfare, those fighting or victimized by it, are integral to constituting meaning around them, militarism, and war. For example, feminist critics of the war in Afghanistan point to the problematic, Orientalist optics of male Army troops storming rural Afghan villages, intimidating brown-skinned women and children as part of the U.S. mission to root out Al-Qaeda and "liberate" the country from the Taliban (Zine 2006). To enhance the optics (but not eliminate the practice), the Department of Defense (DoD) devised Female Engagement Teams (FETs) and Cultural Support Teams (CSTs), assigning them to interact with Afghan and Iraqi women, both to gather intelligence from them and to gain their trust in these occupying forces. The film *Lioness* (2008) poignantly documents the experiences of one FET, and the book *Ashley's War* (Lemmon 2015) follows the training and deployment of one CST. At one point in the film, Army Captain Anastasia Breslow, a member of Team Lioness, reads an entry in the diary she kept when deployed as a Lioness: "We kill for peace. We kill for each other." Breslow's conflicted assertion captures media sentiments surrounding women warriors in this discursive regime: that while they symbolize kinder and gentler warfare, they also act as vehicles for banal and spectacular militarism.

Lioness and *Ashley's War* are two among many stories about women's experiences in warfare and the military that, since 9/11, have constituted an emerging media niche I discuss in chapter 3. Two important academic contributions to this niche are by Kelly Oliver (2007) and Yvonne Tasker (2011). Oliver has examined mainstream media coverage of women associated with the war on Iraq, and she argues that the use of a pornographic gaze focused on women in images of Abu Ghraib torture, Army Private Jessica Lynch (whose media treatment I discuss in chapter 3), and Palestinian women suicide bombers normalizes a link between violence and sex in war media. In this context, the gaze regards its object "for its own pleasure or as a spectacle for its own enjoyment without regard for the subjectivity or subject position of those looked at. The pornographic way of looking reinforces the power and agency of the looker while erasing or debasing the power and agency of the looked-at" (Oliver 2007, 2). Although Oliver does not use the term *postfeminism*, she argues that media and military sources justify war and paper over more troubling moments by evoking feminism selectively to create the illusion that the United States places women's rights at the forefront of policy making of all kinds (50). To guard against accepting such an illusion, Oliver encourages media audiences to adopt a politically informed perspective that she calls "ethical witnessing." By this, she means a clear examination of "the horrors of the war, torture, abuse, and oppression. This sense of witnessing not only involves testifying to the events observed, the historical facts, . . . but also to the meaning of those events, which goes beyond what the eyes can see" (161).

Whereas Oliver's focus is on images of women in the context of the war on Iraq, Tasker's is on film and TV images and narratives about military women between World War II and the war on Iraq. "At times normalized, at times deviant, often peripheral, and typically controversial when she takes center stage, the military woman is a contradictory icon of modernity and continuity," she argues (2011, 3). And although media representations of military women in TV and film are "culturally troubling" because they disrupt the naturalized link between masculinity and military service, they are not "inherently transgressive or subversive. . . . It is clear that to a large extent a place appears for military women as and when their labor is required. In our current historical context of open-ended war and ongoing military interventions, that labor has been integral to American assertions of military authority" (15). While Oliver's and Tasker's ideas inform my project, *Postfeminist War* departs from theirs in examining how discursive constructions of raced, classed women work to market militarism, as it were, through civilian media and in illuminating the political economy that undergirds those constructions.

Whether part of this niche or in general coverage, much media content about war and the military after 9/11 centralizes women and issues historically associated with them: parenting, marriage, and sexual assault, for example. The chapters that follow this one critically examine such representations using feminist analysis, the chief goal of which is "to understand and theorize power as it pertains not only to women, but also to other groups marginalized on the basis of their race, class, sexuality, religious background, ethnicity, age, dis/ability, etc.," as Ellen Riordan explains (2002, 13n1). When applied to media representations and political economy, feminist theory enables us not only to map relations between gender constructions and power but to push inquiry into how commercial relations between media and other corporations influence the meanings that representations consist of and why they appear when and as they do.

Throughout this book, I examine martial gender performances as the outcome of particular social practices. Using this same approach, Candace West and Don Zimmerman, for example, theorize gender as an ongoing, lifelong project, a "doing" that involves "a complex of socially guided perceptual, interactional, and micropolitical activities that cast particular pursuits as expression of masculine and feminine 'natures'": "Rather than as a property of individuals, we conceive of gender as an emergent feature of social situations: both as an outcome of and a rationale for various social arrangements and as a means of legitimating one of the most fundamental divisions of society" (1987, 126). They conclude by observing that gender is a "powerful ideological device, which produces, reproduces, and legitimates the choices and limits that are predicated as sex category"; this ideological process gets an assist from powerful social institutions such as media, which associate a "sense of 'naturalness' and 'rightness'" to those practices that they deem gender appropriate, while they cast others as deviant and discipline them accordingly (147). Representations that I examine in this book accomplish this gender project in different and at times aesthetically complex ways, while they persistently privilege heteronormative doings of gender.

Like West and Zimmerman's theory, Judith Butler's *Gender Trouble* maintains that "gender proves to be performative—that is, constituting the identity it is purported to be. In this sense, gender is always a doing, though not a doing by a subject who might be said to preexist the deed" (1990, 24–25). In later work, Butler emphasizes social context or the "sociality of gender," arguing that "one does not 'do' one's gender alone. One is always 'doing' with or for another even if the other is only imaginary. What I call my 'own' gender appears perhaps at times as something that I author or, indeed, own. But the terms that make up one's gender are, from the start, outside oneself, beyond oneself in a sociality that has no single author (and that radically contests the notion of authorship itself)" (2004b, 1). Media discourses construct social contexts for doing gender, as West and Zimmerman and Butler have concep-tualized the process. Thus, building on these theorists, van Zoonen argues that gender is a discourse that describes and prescribes performances of difference and sexuality. In this discursive constitution, media act as "(social) technolo-gies of gender, accommodating, modifying, reconstructing and producing disciplining and contradictory cultural outlooks of sexual difference" (van Zoonen 1994, 41). Butler adds that this mutually constitutive process endows gender performances with the "appearance of substance, of a natural sort of being" (1990, 33). As I show in the chapters following this one, military-themed media representations naturalize performances of gender that buttress both the military and the martial goals of the executive branch, pushing them to become accepted as cultural truths.

Although I may use the term *gender* by itself, I understand it as always already intersecting with other identity categories, such as race, class, sexual-ity, and ability. As Kimberlé Crenshaw lays out her pathbreaking theory of intersectionality, she argues that women of color are "differently situated in the economic, social, and political worlds. When reform efforts undertaken on behalf of women neglect this fact, women of color are less likely to have their needs met than women who are racially privileged" (1991, 1250). She therefore urges feminist and critical race scholars researching media represen-tations to "include both the ways in which . . . images are produced through a confluence of prevalent narratives of race and gender, as well as a recognition of how contemporary critiques of racist and sexist representation marginalize women of color" (1283). Doing so, Crenshaw argues, allows scholars to gain a more complete understanding of how these representations work politically to obscure oppression. Building on Crenshaw's work, Patricia Hill Collins and Sirma Bilge tease apart the interpersonal, disciplinary, cultural, and struc-tural as four "distinctive yet interconnected domains of power" within which intersectionality works to situate individuals and institutions differentially to one another and to systems of power (2016, 7). The cultural and structural domains are those on which I concentrate my analysis: media culture, in par-ticular, and how gendered militarism is produced within it through structural relations between media corporations, public relations organizations, think tanks, governmental institutions, defense industries, and the military. Chap-ters 1 through 4 illustrate discursive constitutions of women of color and white women that work to depoliticize military life and war, giving them the appearance of a "natural sort of being."

Posts of Race and Gender

Whereas feminists theorize intersections of race and gender in terms of how they situate individuals and groups in differential relationships to social, political, and economic power, many public, and especially media, discourses fail to recognize intersectionality. Rather than exploring oppression, mainstream media discourses tend to both deny its existence and obscure important lessons about racial and gender discrimination from the civil rights, Black Lives Matter, and feminist movements, among others. The result is media discourses that produce and reproduce ahistorical, postracial, and postfeminist ideologies. Such public discourses on race reproduce what Catherine Squires refers to as a "post-racial mystique," a condition "conjured by the disjuncture between the entrenched effects of institutional racism and the media texts that deny—or purport to resolve—racial inequalities" (2014, 5). "Post-racial discourses," she continues, "obfuscate institutional racism and blame continuing racial inequalities on individuals who make poor choices for themselves of their families. Post-racial discourses resonate with neoliberal discourses because of their shared investment in individual-level analysis and concern with individual freedoms" (6).

Squires's analysis of this mystique shows that it operates in a range of media sites, from news to TV serial dramas to blogs; to her list, I would add *Army Wives*, as well as news and documentary accounts of the military topics that I examine in this book. Unlike the discourses that Squires analyzes, however, those I consider do not explicitly address the roles that race or racism may play in the lives of military women. Instead, while the texts in *Postfeminist War* are straightforward in their invocations of so-called women's issues, such as the combat-exclusion policy, parenthood, marriage and family life, and sexual violence, they render racial oppression invisible; they include no discussion of how, even in the military—a purportedly racially egalitarian institution—race intersects with gender to disadvantage women of color relative to their white peers, especially men. This is in spite of evidence indicating that various branches of the military operate within a racialized, gendered hierarchy that is stubbornly resistant to more than minor, incremental change.

For example, one recent survey of "senior military elites"—that is, from the rank of lieutenant colonel / commander through brigadier general / rear admiral—reveals that 94 percent are male, 89 percent are Caucasian, and 95 percent are Christian. These respondents, who were students at the National Defense University, "foreshadow the composition of those who will lead the military in the coming decade. The answer is overwhelmingly white, Christian, men" (Bryant and Swaney 2017).[4] Such a homogeneous officer corps surely affects governance of the divisions they lead, which are increasingly multiracial and gender mixed (although 68.8 percent of active-duty members are white and 84.5 percent identify as male, these numbers are declining as women of all races enlist and rise through the ranks [Dao 2011]). Intensifying the military's homogeneity is its reliance on intergenerational enlistees largely drawn from the southern United States, a de facto selection practice that over decades has seen the same families from the same geographic regions in military service. Further separating service members from civilians and their communities, the practice reproduces a white, male "warrior caste" (Schafer 2017).

Discourses I interrogate in this book reflect this racialized, gendered hierarchy but work to obscure both its power and its very existence with postracial and postfeminist representations that suggest that women of all races have achieved equality in the armed forces. In this way, they take up gender in much the same way as postfeminist media discourses do in civilian contexts, which includes moving solipsistically to generalize to all who identify as women the concerns of white, hetero, middle-class women; offering, at best, only cautious and partial analyses of gender and power; mostly refusing to consider structural, institutional oppression; and suggesting that women have achieved equality "in order to install a whole repertoire of new meanings which emphasize that [feminism] is no longer needed, it is a spent force," as Angela McRobbie puts it (2009, 12). Postfeminist discourses thus work to depoliticize the subjects and subject matter they construct, moving them outside the realm of public debate and contestation. But I maintain that these discourses are post- rather than antifeminist because instead of being "antithetical to feminism," they produce and reproduce "an ideology constructed, in part, from various aspects of both first- and second-wave feminism. However, at the same time, [they] reject these feminisms' more provocative challenges, such as those grounded in critiques of capitalism and class privilege" (Vavrus 2002, 22). What I term *martial postfeminism* works discursively as McRobbie and I have explained and goes further to reject critiques of racial inequality or racism directed at the military, militaristic cultural practices, or war policy making. I distinguish martial from other forms of postfeminism to illuminate the ways in which it subtly pushes militarism as common sense: a nonpolitical, prowoman ideology that paves the way for civilians to accept and integrate it as a worldview.

Marouf Hasian's analysis of the film *Zero Dark Thirty* expresses some of these concerns. A fictional account of actual events, the film features tough, smart CIA agent Maya as she prepares for the 2011 raid that killed Osama bin Laden and his family. Hasian argues that one of the film's most troubling messages is that because a female agent can ascend to a high level of responsibility, the CIA is a quasi-feminist organization; he therefore urges feminist scholars to critique "hijacked and appropriated" feminist ideologies such as those found in *Zero Dark Thirty*, which "normalize the belief that all types of harsh wartime measures are not only legal, but culturally acceptable ways of acting in the 21st century" (2013, 325). Hasian contends further that the film's appropriation of feminism enables it to be marketed as a "patriotic commodity, firmly convinced that women can act in empowering ways that take-for-granted the fruits of activism without any continued engagement with any lingering structural inequalities. . . . Yet what all of this focus on individual accomplishment hides are the structural barriers that inhibit radical feminism while contributing to the death and destruction of many foreign others" (337). Analysis of the much-broader post-9/11 discursive terrain found in *Postfeminist War* comports with Hasian's, and I would add that the danger of martial postfeminism is both in its deference to postracial militarism as a net positive for women and in its deflection from scrutiny of either the violence, trauma, and death it incurs—particularly for civilians—or its negative impacts on civil and human rights. Martial postfeminism is thus an exemplary ideology for advancing the economic and social interests of the military-industrial complex.

The Political Economy of Militarism

Militarism permeates twenty-first-century media cultures owing in part to the corporate media system's numerous ties to the military-industrial complex. In Dwight D. Eisenhower's last speech as president in 1961, he warned listeners and viewers about the military-industrial complex—a set of collusive relationships between the military and businesses that profit from war—and how its "unwarranted influence" and "misplaced power" would prove disastrous to "our liberties or democratic processes" (15). Decades before Eisenhower's warning about the social and political dangers of a permanent war economy came one from the decorated World War I Marine Corps major general Smedley D. Butler. After his retirement from the Marine Corps in 1931, Butler toured the United States giving his "War Is a Racket" speech to alert the U.S. public to "war millionaires," whose fortunes are made in payments to a deadly bill: "And what is this bill? This bill renders a horrible accounting. Newly placed gravestones. Mangled bodies. Shattered minds. Broken hearts and homes. Economic instability. Depression and all its attendant miseries. Back-breaking taxation for generations and generations" (2013, 5). Like Eisenhower, Butler was disturbed by war profiteering and its continuation, even as he recognized signs of a war brewing in Europe. Among the World War I profiteers he identified was the Du Pont family for making gun powder, a decision that caused company profits to increase by more than 950 percent during the war's four-year duration (11). Many other manufacturers—of copper, steel, leather, and more—saw similar profit margins, according to Butler. Twentysome years after Butler's warning and eight years prior to Eisenhower's well-known farewell address, Eisenhower voiced concerns about the ramifications of war-economy priorities persisting during peacetime. In a 1953 speech to the American Society of Newspaper Editors laying out the social consequences of perpetual preparation for war, Eisenhower encouraged his audience to opt for butter over guns, telling them, "Every gun that is made, every warship launched, every rocket fired signifies, in the final sense, a theft from those who hunger and are not fed, those who are cold and are not clothed. . . . [The] cost of one modern heavy bomber is this: a modern brick school in more than 30 cities. . . . We pay for a single fighter with a half million bushels of wheat. We pay for a single destroyer with new homes that could have housed more than 8,000 people" (quoted in Bacevich 2011).

Despite Eisenhower's and Butler's warnings, since World War II, the U.S. economy has been driven by what Bacevich refers to as "Military Keynesianism," or "the belief that the production of guns could underwrite an endless supply of butter" (2011). Military Keynesianism has intensified greatly since the Eisenhower era: spending to support the United States' seventeen intelligence agencies is more than $80 billion annually, according to Bacevich (2011). The Costs of War Project figures that through 2017, military spending by the U.S. government on post-9/11 wars (which includes payments to veterans) will be around $4.8 trillion (2017). The U.S. military budget is much larger than that of any other country in the world and according to the National Priorities Project is about the size of the next seven countries' military budgets—China, Saudi Arabia, Russia, the United Kingdom, India, France, and Japan—*combined* (Koshgarian 2017). The Pentagon alone receives about $700 billion for its annual budget (Hartung 2017), and that is not the only eye-popping figure here: other defense-related spending occurs through the Departments of Homeland Security and Veterans Affairs and, along with others, approaches a total of $1 trillion *each year* (Brooks 2016b, 9). Sustaining this stratospheric level of military spending requires a public that is supportive of (or ignorant about) such a diversion of resources, and Bacevich observes cynically that "what worked during the Cold War still works today: to get Americans on board with your military policy scare the hell out of them" (2011)—an imperative that the U.S. media system has dutifully obeyed.

However much Americans might like to believe they exert influence on military spending, the U.S. populace has almost no place in decision-making about defense budgets. Rebecca Thorpe shows that today members of Congress are most influential on defense spending and especially when they represent rural, "economically homogeneous" districts. Thus, regardless of defense funds' utility for national security, Congress members who represent defense-dependent constituencies "work especially hard to promote more military spending" (2014, 184). Thorpe argues that there is little resistance to such arrangements because of the benefits they confer to congressional constituencies across the country. William Hartung adds that lobbyists for weapons manufacturers see to it that Congress and the White House work together to funnel funding to corporations such as Raytheon, Lockheed, and Boeing by promoting defense systems whose specs claim that they are tailored to meet the threat du jour. The most public of these threats currently comes from North Korea, against whose saber rattling several large contractors are testing drones fitted with lasers meant to shoot intercontinental ballistic missiles (Hartung 2018). But even as some congressional districts experience short-term benefits from military spending in their communities, this arms race has many downsides. Since World War II and the end of conscription, Thorpe shows that its social costs have been shifted "onto political minorities who volunteer to fight, foreign populations where US wars take place, and ultimately, future generations of taxpayers" (2014, 11).

Further, investments in defense are neither gender nor race neutral. As they divert much-needed spending away from the social welfare programs, schools, and health care that benefit people of color and white women particularly, they are directed instead toward weapons manufacturing, increased incarceration, immigration enforcement, and militarization of police forces across the country—a trend that disproportionately disadvantages immigrants of color and African American girls, for example (African American Policy Forum, n.d.). Such expenditures come to 64 percent of annual discretionary spending, resulting in what the National Priorities Project (2017) refers to as the militarization of the federal budget. In a report produced for Brown University's Costs of War Project, Heidi Garrett-Peltier concludes that "by spending trillions of dollars on wars since 2001, the US lost the opportunity to create millions of jobs in other sectors, and further lost the opportunity to create a healthier, more educated and more economically secure nation" (2017, 5).

• • •

Growth in the military-industrial complex is enabled by the United States' corporate media system, or what the late Ben Bagdikian more than three decades ago warned was a "media-industrial complex" (1983). Like the complex that Eisenhower identified, the media-industrial complex exerts influence over U.S. government agencies and politicians to ensure that its constituent corporations remain profitable—a goal whose achievement affects content as well as the economic and political alliances of media outlets. Tactics by which the media-industrial complex reproduces itself and expands include interlocked directorates, synergy, market monopolies, political lobbying, and campaign contributions. These activities are evident today more than ever, as Robert W. McChesney explains: "Media have exploded in prominence in the past century; as their social importance has increased, so have media industries become an increasingly important part of capitalism. They have become very profitable. This has undermined the media system's ability to serve democratic values and practices; it cannot serve two gods" (2015, xxxvii). The corporate media system's antidemocratic tendencies have contributed to the "great political crisis of our time," McChesney argues: the "governing system is in thrall to corporate interests that are hostile to participatory democracy and impervious to the problems faced by most of the population" (2015, liv).

What I call the *media-military-industrial complex* is assembled from mutually constitutive actors, practices, and discourses that profit in myriad ways from the military and from war. The *New York Times* reporter David Barstow identifies one of the practices that this complex comprises in the collusion[5] of retired military officers and TV news media in war reporting on Iraq and Afghanistan (2008a, 2008b). Each entity in this partnership profits from not disclosing conflicts of interest: retired military officers provide expert commentary to news media and also serve on the boards of directors of various defense contractors; media corporations are commercially and institutionally interlocked with—or, in the case of NBC and General Electric, partially owned by—defense contractors. None of the parties in this collusion reveals that encouraging the war effort (as Barstow shows they have) allows them to profit financially and professionally. Lee Fang's research reveals that this aspect of the complex is still very much in evidence in reporting on the Islamic State. For example, as retired generals Anthony Zinni and Jack Keane were making numerous appearances to advocate across various cable-TV and print media outlets for the United States to go to war against the Islamic State during 2014, their roles as director on the board of the defense contractor General Dynamics (Keane) and advisers to various investment firms that specialize in defense-contractor holdings (Keane and Zinni), for example, were never disclosed. Yet the financial rewards they receive as consultants and directors are great: in 2013, General Dynamics paid Keane $258,006 (Fang 2014). Keeping advisers with conflicts of interest on the payroll is but one means by which media corporations link up with the military through their news divisions.

An additional form that DoD influence takes comes from psychological operations, or psy-ops, the practices of which have been honed especially since World War II, when the DoD established its Psychological Warfare Branch and was praised effusively for its work by General Dwight Eisenhower. According to Tanner Mirrlees, psy-ops activities in the early post-9/11 period, when the Bush administration was gearing up for wars in Afghanistan and Iraq, included "everything from black propaganda (official lies planted in the foreign press to embellish US foreign policy aims) to white propaganda (the manipulation of foreign journalists and news organization to bias their reporting to US goals)" (2016, 140). Since then, "information operations," or IO, has replaced the psy-ops label, though its goals and strategies remain much the same: "IO encompasses the DOD's sourcing of the news media and manipulation of media sources to persuade US and foreign publics to support US war policy; it also involves the DOD's manipulation, censorship, or destruction of news-media sources that are perceived as threats to the United States' ability to win the media war" (Mirrlees 2016, 143). To secure the public's support for the United States' controversial preemptive war on Iraq, DoD personnel working with the Bush administration successfully employed IO strategies, which included making prowar military experts available to news outlets far and wide (as I discussed earlier); designating some journalists as "embeds," which allowed them to accompany deployed combat units and be privy to "DOD-provisioned information, photo ops, and protection" (147); providing video news releases (VNRs) to TV news outlets to manage information flowing from sites in Iraq; and creating "pseudo-events" that would "make US citizens feel good about the war," such as *Saving Private Lynch*, a docudrama that I discuss in chapter 3 (150).

Integral to war-promoting IO operations were other activities meant to damage the reputations and physically harm those who did not fall in line to support war on Iraq. Reporters who conveyed critical views on the war, such as those who worked for Al Jazeera, were publicly discredited by Defense Secretary Donald Rumsfeld and other DoD elites; some were even put in the crosshairs themselves by Iraqi and U.S. forces. In April 2003, for example, a Reuters camera operator was killed by U.S. tank fire on the Palestine Hotel in Baghdad, where he and other journalists were staying. Soon thereafter, Al Jazeera's Baghdad office was bombed by a U.S. A-10 Warthog, killing the correspondent Tariq Ayyoub (Mirrlees 2016, 154–155). Speech-chilling techniques such as these serve to discipline the press and act as object lessons for any who might stray from the party line on war.

Alongside these top-down IO operations is another means of pushing the military-industrial complex "deeper into American lives and the American psyche than Eisenhower could ever have imagined" (Turse 2008, 2): through an extensive range of consumer products and services for civilians. Produced by corporations with large DoD contracts and advertised across media outlets of all kinds, everyday products such as Coffee Mate and Dawn dishwashing liquid also serve to further banalize militarism for consumers of these items. Such relationships between military contractors and all realms of life are so numerous now that the military reporter Nick Turse uses "The Complex" to refer to its contemporary incarnation as the "military-industrial-techno-logical-entertainment-academic-scientific-media-intelligence-homeland security-surveillance-national security-corporate complex" (2008, 4). Tracing its expansion and influence, he argues that The Complex "uses all the tools of the modern corporation: publicity departments, slick advertising campaigns, and public relations efforts to build up the armed forces, which are, of course its *raison d'etre*. With an all-volunteer military embroiled in two disastrous wars in Afghanistan and Iraq, the armed forces have had to ramp up advertising, marketing, and product-placement efforts to attract ever more reluctant recruits" (18).

James Der Derian's (2009) acronym is "MIME-NET" for the military-industrial-media-entertainment network, which indicates its spatial vastness and temporal persistence, its multidimensional production of social reality, and the partnerships between its producers and the DoD (for example, the University of Southern California's Institute for Creative Technologies). The Pentagon, for its part, maintains control of entertainment media content through its Entertainment Office. In a post on the *Armed with Science* blog, the office's current director, Phil Strub, explains that producers "still very much want U.S. military production support—even though it comes with strings attached": "For example, filmmakers must also send us the[ir] scripts. These ultimately have to present a reasonably realistic portrayal of the military. . . . If filmmakers are willing to negotiate with us to resolve our script concerns, usually we'll reach an agreement. If not filmmakers are free to press on without military assistance" (2010). So that the military can accomplish its ideological work and lend martial verisimilitude to different productions, each branch as well as the CIA maintains an Entertainment Liaison Office. Tom Secker and Matthew Alford have created an extensive database of such DoD and CIA support for recent films and TV shows, compiled after three years of making Freedom of Information Act (FOIA) requests. They found 814 films and 1,133 TV programs that received DoD or CIA support (mostly DoD); 977 of the TV programs were produced since 2004, a steep increase that reflects the DoD's decision to extend its influence to reality TV (Secker and Alford 2017, 3). Further, both organizations now engage with film and TV production "from the earliest stages of the creative process" in order to, the Army explains, "help shape the topics before they are finalized by studio executives" (Secker and Alford 2017, 11). *Army Wives* is one such program, and in chapter 1, I illuminate connections between the Army and the Lifetime Network in producing *Army Wives'* Pentagon-approved gender performances. Secker and Alford's research shows that the "CIA and DoD are primarily and explicitly concerned with promoting a positive self-image and propagating a useful version of history and politics where they play a critical and benevolent role" (2017, 6–7). *Army Wives* proves to be exemplary in crafting such a positive image for the Army and its families.

What the examples in the foregoing sections reveal is that far from fading into obsolescence as Eisenhower had hoped, the military-industrial complex has grown into a multinational behemoth with ever more numerous means of and financial reasons for influencing media content, surveillance, and technology development. And although the mutually constitutive relations between the DoD and all manner of media are profitable, they are not particularly healthy for civil society. "The casualty of these complexes," Mirrlees reminds us, "is a media [*sic*] that serves democracy and mainstream cultural products that contest and forward alternatives to war as a way of life" (2016, 241). I share

Mirrlees's concern. As the chapters of *Postfeminist War* show, alternatives to war and militarism are either absent from the martial regime of representation that I interrogate or overwhelmed by rally-round-the-flag sentiments that cast critical views of war in a negative light and suggest that those who hold them are unpatriotic or working against women's interests.

Political Economy and Media Militarism

Militarism, a concept central to the argument of *Postfeminist War* and one product of the MMIC, has been an issue of concern to scholars and peace activists for well over a century. The Bush administration's bellicose response to 9/11, in particular, has inspired an enormous body of research on the topic. Henry Giroux, for example, argues that the GWOT has pushed militarism into all facets of civilian life, "further sanction[ing] a military that has assumed a central role in American society influencing everything from markets, education, popular culture, and fashion." At this point in time, Giroux argues, evidence abounds of U.S. culture being "shaped by military power, values, and interests" with the goal of "producing militarized subjects and a permanent war economy" (2013, 261). Appearing prior to the 9/11 attacks yet still applicable, the feminist international relations scholar Cynthia Enloe's description of militarization is that it is a "step-by-step process by which a person or a thing gradually comes to be controlled by the military or comes to depend for its well-being on militaristic ideas. The more militarization transforms an individual or a society, the more that individual or society comes to imagine military needs and militaristic presumptions to be not only valuable but also normal. Militarization, that is, involves cultural as well as institutional, ideological, and economic transformations" (2000, 3). Following Enloe, Jody Berland and Blake Fitzpatrick emphasize that militarization is "not just something that happens in war zones; when our government invests billions of dollars in war planes, prisons and the 'digital economy,' while starving resources in social justice, education, the environment and culture we are living the consequences of global militarization" (2010, 9). Militarization should concern feminists, Enloe argues, for its gendered power differential: women experience militarization differently than do men and sustain persistent gender-specific damages from it—military sexual trauma, for example (a subject I address at length in chapter 4). Francine D'Amico adds that militarization is always already gendered because the process relies on principles used in military training, "the essence of [which] consists of the subordination of the individual to the institution, a desensitization to violence, and a dehumanization of the potential opponent. For male recruits, it also includes a process of masculinization where female and feminine are defined as 'other' and as unworthy" (1998, 123).

As D'Amico suggests, militarization originates not only from the military proper but also from the ideas and practices that the military comprises as well as those that sustain and legitimate it. Chapter 2 on militarizing motherhood homes in on this process in an analysis of news-media constructions of "Security Moms": civilian women once known as Soccer Moms but who, by 2004 news reports claimed, had been transformed into fearful, security-obsessed mothers supportive of GWOT-related security measures, such as phone and internet surveillance and increased airport security. News reports from this time construct Security Moms to embody and legitimate militarism, a term that connotes acceptance of the ideological and material practices brought about by the process of militarization—what Catherine Lutz notes is a "marked social emphasis on martial values" (forthcoming). Militarization, in other words, produces and circulates militarism, a process that the civilian media system has fully participated in, as the Security Mom example and many others in *Postfeminist War* will attest.

Neil Balan argues that a more accurate understanding of militarism is as an ongoing process to convince populations that their military fights wars whose objective "is not necessarily 'killing scumbags' but securing the people's ways of life" (2010, 156). Citing Foucault, he continues, "the object of life itself—the life of the individual, the population, the people as a 'society to be defended'—becomes a focal point for the art of government, the object mediated by prescriptive and always-pedagogical missives about the routine and the common sense, linking the politics of living with life itself" (159). Throughout *Postfeminist War*, I show that since 2001, numerous media accounts of women in and around the military intensify, feminize, and extend militarism culturally through postfeminist constructions that link the "politics of living with life itself." Military mothers whose representations I also discuss in chapter 2, for example, are constructed in such a way as to articulate them to right-wing, prowar policies in the name of securing the freedom of the homeland, even when it means sacrificing the children to whom they gave life—a poignant example of "linking the politics of living with life itself."

To illustrate the politics of living and its links to militarization, I utilize the concept of "banal militarism," which Tonja Thomas and Fabian Virchow derive from Michael Billig's (1995) notion of "banal nationalism." "Banal militarism" refers to the myriad ways in which everyday life practices—and particularly those represented in popular culture—legitimate militarization and the military itself. Thomas and Virchow define it as the "mechanisms and procedures by which the military, its necessity, and its demands for financial assets are (re)produced in a society." Referencing Hannah Arendt's warning about the banality of evil, they emphasize that " 'banal' does not necessarily mean innocuous or without consequences" (2005, 27). In later work, Thomas expands the definition to include "the wide range of public discourses, media activities and political courses of events, which imply the existence of armed forces, their visibility in public, the spending of relevant amounts of money for military purposes, and the acceptance of war as a means to resolve conflict" (2009, 97). Banal militarism, she adds, encourages civilian acceptance of the "existence and mission of the military" and the "normalization of military force as state-organized and politically legitimized approach to conflicts" (99). Postfeminism works here as a means of further banalizing militarism in media discourses that deploy feminist messages about soft power, family security, and career benefits of military life while they obscure such issues as military violence and imperialism that have been subject to sharp feminist criticism for decades.

My own use of "banal militarism" is not always as literal as Thomas and Virchow's; for example, as chapter 2 documents, Security Moms are civilians, yet their construction attempts to mobilize mothers to both accept the militarization of daily life and support then President Bush's war efforts in Afghanistan and Iraq. And although I use the term "militarism," I do so advisedly: as Balan points out, the "militarization thesis" that he criticizes posits that, especially since September 11, 2001, militarism has encroached on formerly pristine realms of culture, politics, and social life and thus "reinscribes a binary opposition between 'military' and 'civil,' confining military organs and activities to some vacuum as if they exist independent of the very discursive and material processes that produce military organs themselves" (2010, 149). This thesis is problematic because at the very least, justifications for a standing army and a well-funded national defense have been woven into the fabric of national politics—and the U.S. communications system—for at least a century.

Dan Schiller even argues that after World War II, the "nation's political economy was rebuilt as an armamentarium with communications at its center" (2011, 266). Today, as a result of symbiotic partnerships between military agencies and telecommunication and media corporations, an "offensive arsenal is being fashioned around and through [communications] networks," he cautions (272). Similarly, John Bellamy Foster and Robert McChesney's extensive historical examination of the military-surveillance complex reveals martial uses for giant digital media corporations' user data, which they continually gather and sell to other entities. Google, for example, advances surveillance practices developed by the Army during the Vietnam War era and has used the resulting technologies to branch out into aerial-drone manufacturing as well (Foster and McChesney 2014). For all intents and purposes, then, there are no such things as demilitarized zones in contemporary communications and media systems.

Pairing a structural examination of militarism with an analysis of its discursive production illuminates how the militarization process unfolds, moving beyond denotative boundaries to include cultural ideologies and practices that do not necessarily emanate from the Pentagon. Of course, the bulk of this book does, in fact, interrogate literal militarism, and I do not wish to obscure this issue. However, the point of recognizing *banal* militarism is to illuminate the everydayness of those gendered discursive practices that constitute the meaning of war and military service today. Roger Stahl's interrogation of militainment and its proliferation through everyday cultural practices explicates the political and personal stakes of banal militarism. He argues that U.S. media audiences' interactions with such offerings as sporting events and reality TV draw them further into martial cultural practices that rewire their relationship to war and turn them into citizen-soldiers (Stahl 2010).

We can see banal militarism as well in the military's seemingly egalitarian and diverse employment opportunities, which appear in a wide variety of advertising, marketing, and other media content. Women's growing presence in the military since the end of conscription in 1973 has necessitated a dramatic change in military recruitment and marketing. This includes the branches (with the possible exception of the Marines) representing themselves as "promoting racial diversity and gender (most recently lesbian, gay, bisexual, transgender, and queer) inclusion, as means to signify that the institution works as a generator of not only self-esteem and secure employment but also social equity," as Beatrice Jauregui observes (2015, 464). Mia Fischer adds that "the military remains the nation's largest employer and job program for poor and working class people, . . . oftentimes the only means for access to better living standards" (2016, 104–5). To maximize public support for war and military service when relying on the AVF and fighting unpopular wars, military branches must appeal to the broadest pool of potential recruits to constitute an adequate force; this has required a multifaceted marketing campaign that promotes military duty to a broad array of women and men and that uses media of all kinds to equate military service to heroism—a campaign whose processes I examine in the following chapters.

Interrogating Media Representations

Using feminist and cultural studies theories and methods, I have tracked and interrogated civilian media discourses about war and military life as a means of understanding our contemporary, militarized context of life and the "circular relations between truth and systems of [media-military] power" at work in these discourses (Foucault 1977, 14). To interrogate media representations, I use Foucauldian discourse analysis, which understands discourse as collections of signs and symbols that together operate as a source for social knowledge. Stuart Hall adds that Foucault's notion of discourse is "about language and practices. . . . Discourse . . . constructs the topic. It defines and produces the objects of our knowledge. It governs the way that a topic can be meaningfully talked about and reasoned about. It also influences how ideas are put into practices and used to regulate the conduct of others" (1997, 44). Discourses I examine in *Postfeminist War* are produced by mainstream media outlets mostly between September 11, 2001, and December 31, 2016, and refer to the wars in Afghanistan and Iraq, the troops deployed to fight them, home-front activities intended to show support for them, and, even more specifically, the actions of women vis-à-vis all of these topics. As I have explained, the entire collection of media discourses works in concert as a regime, or what Foucault calls a "discursive formation": "Whenever one can describe, between a number of statements . . . a system of dispersion, whenever, between objects, types of statement, concepts, or thematic choices, one can define a regularity (an order, correlations, positions and functionings, transformations) we will say, for the sake of convenience, that we are dealing with a *discursive formation*" ([1972] 2010, 38; italics in original).

The militarized, post-9/11 discursive formation that I examine across the following chapters constitutes a regime that articulates women to warfare and the military in particular, historically specific ways. Each chapter illustrates how various media represent women in relation to four different military topics: marriage and family life, motherhood, combat service, and sexual violence. One of the assumptions that informs *Postfeminist War* is that discourse matters: how media discourse is constructed and edited, where and when it is circulated, and the audiences for whom it is intended all make a difference not only in how the civilian public comes to regard wars and the rationales proffered for the United States initiating and fighting them but also in how the public regards the military and service to it as well.

Given the voluminous media output that the wars in Afghanistan and Iraq have inspired since 2001, it would be impossible to analyze all of it. Even limiting myself to four topical object domains poses a challenge, as each of these has generated an enormous number of representations. To do justice to each topic, I thus either examine the entirety of a production (for example, all seven seasons of *Army Wives*) or track over time a representative sample of local and national news stories along with relevant documentaries. Tracking discourses is an inductive, interpretive process that examines those themes and patterns in media representations that coalesce around specific topics over a period of time, formats, and subjects (Altheide 2000, 292). The fifteen-year period through which I track discourses starts with the month following the 9/11 Al-Qaeda attacks and ends in December 2016. Discourses I examine are hybrid, news, and documentary media representations from easily accessed legacy outlets: mainly broadcast and cable-TV news programs (including some local affiliates), the *New York Times*, the *Washington Post*, some local newspapers, and National Public Radio (NPR). According to the Pew Research Center, broadcast and cable-TV news was the source that news consumers turned to most to get their news during this period, despite increasing competition from digital and social media; thus, I draw a large sample of stories from TV news for the analysis in chapters 3 and 4 and part of chapter 2. Together, all these sources generate most of the news to which the public is exposed, whether it is reposted, recirculated on social media platforms, or blogged about (A. Mitchell 2014). Additionally, I consult think-tank reports and white papers that deal with the book's subject matter, such as the Rand Corporation's report on military sexual harassment and assault, to flesh out my understanding of military issues.

To ensure that I worked with as complete a set of discourses as possible, I viewed multiple times the 117 episodes of *Army Wives'* seven seasons as well as the bonus material that accompanied each season's set of DVDs. As chapter 1 explains, DoD-friendly themes about military marriage and family life emerged readily from this set of representations. Discourses that serve as the basis for chapters 2 through 4 run the gamut from local newspapers to national news magazines to NPR, and in each chapter, I explain my rationale for choosing the sources I do. To generate the material in these chapters' analyses, I input relevant search terms—"Security Moms" or "military mothers," for example—into the LexisNexis database. Because each of the topics that these chapters address has generated voluminous amounts of coverage, I narrowed search results by word count and reviewed only those texts with five hundred or more words. This mainly eliminated teasers, bumpers, and other short promotional segments, while it yielded a set of hundreds of news stories and transcripts to work with for each chapter; I narrowed further by examining only different, distinct stories and not the numerous reruns that networks play over the course of a day or more. Wherever possible, I viewed video segments alongside TV news transcripts to get a fuller sense of how the elements in each representation work together to construct women within the context that each chapter addresses. In addition to these hybrid and news representations, I reference at length *The Invisible War*, a documentary film that significantly influenced news coverage of military sexual violence.

Absences in this regime are meaningful, as well. For example, none of the media texts I examine gives civilian deaths more than fleeting attention. Critics of the wars in Afghanistan and Iraq are similarly invisible until Cindy Sheehan—a military mother mourning her son Casey, killed in Iraq—appeared in 2004. Further, TV news reports were virtually silent on the topic of rampant sexual assault of military women until the release of *The Invisible War* made it impossible to ignore, something I discuss at length in chapter 4. I argue that, taken together, what is absent *and* manifest in these representations intensifies and feminizes a militaristic regime that, in addition to minimizing the horrors of war and the dangers of a patriarchal military, casts troops as heroic, military families as their indispensable supporters, women as equal to men in combat capabilities, and sexual assault as incidental to military service (when it is recognized at all). Because practices historically associated with women have become focal points in war reporting, documentary film, and hybrid serial drama since 9/11, I examine salient examples of them in the following chapters to gain insight into how they contribute to a martial regime of representation that has been prominent in our cultural landscape for over a decade and a half now.

Because *Army Wives* was successful by so many measures—including serving as a vehicle for Army propaganda—I start with its constructions of military marriage and family life in chapter 1, then examine strategic alliances between the Lifetime Network, its commercial partners, and the DoD to consider how they mutually constitute meaning around military life and war for an audience of women. Entertainment media, along with their news counterparts, have historically played an important role in the reproduction and construction of promilitary, prowar ideology (Alford 2016; Boggs and Pollard 2007; Kellner 2010; Robb 2004; Secker and Alford 2017; Stahl 2010). *Army Wives* is an example of this process, albeit a hybridized and somewhat more nuanced one than those found in many news stories.

News constructions of motherhood are the subject of chapter 2, specifically Security Moms and military mothers (those with children serving in Afghanistan or Iraq). This chapter draws from a broad array of news discourses: national as well as local TV and print sources, along with NPR. Because numerous stories about military mothers focus on local women and what they do within their respective communities to cope with their children's absences, I turn to local outlets and affiliates, where these formulaic stories appear with regularity. These constructions of motherhood have ties to national organizations, however, so I examine as well politically conservative front groups that feed information to the press about military and security mothering. Cindy Sheehan became a prominent critic of both President Bush and the Iraq War, and news stories employed discursive disciplinary tactics attempting to silence Sheehan's protests even as they legitimated her grief. Such a maneuver is tricky, to say the least, and as I discuss in chapter 2, it serves as an object lesson for news audiences about the treatment that media outlets believe should be meted out to women who transgress the discursive bounds of proper military motherhood.

Chapters 3 and 4 shift gears away from depictions of women in service-member support networks to focus specifically on military women and two issues pertinent to their service: performing combat duties and being victims of sexual violence by peers and commanders. The discourses in these chapters work together, I argue, to ascribe meaning to women—specifically as capable fighters—so I have labeled it the Warrior Women regime. Warrior Women is not stand-alone, however; its constituent representations work intertextually with those from chapters 1 and 2 as well as those in the larger representational context of post-9/11 war reporting to form cultural sites on which to negotiate our understandings of women in a militarized milieu. Chapter 3 deals specifically with how TV news coverage wrestles with whether women are suitable to serve in combat, both before and after the combat-exclusion policy was eliminated in 2015. A combination of war correspondents, commentators and anchors, and politicians together overwhelmingly affirm women as rightful warriors as they glorify ongoing war efforts. Building on this theme, chapter 4 asks how TV news outlets address a serious problem besetting thousands of women warriors: rampant sexual violence in the military's branches and service academies. What emerges is a series of missed opportunities for reporters and commentators to confront the military's rape culture and the misogyny and patriarchy that fuel it. Instead, they mostly cede that work to the makers of *The Invisible War* and support organizations tasked with remedying military sexual trauma.

The final chapter ties up the conceptual threads that weave through chapters 1 through 4 and addresses the implications of *Postfeminist War*—for my field of feminist media studies, specifically, as well as for a more general media-literacy practice around representations of war and the military. Given the militarism of the Trump administration as well as the current president's proclivity for alarmingly bellicose rhetoric (exhibit A: the threat to meet North Korea's missile program with perhaps nuclear "fire and fury"), decoding military media representations is more necessary than ever. Women veterans who have begun to run for and win public office on the basis of their military expertise offer another reason to understand martially postfeminist media representations.

Postfeminist War illuminates how media have participated in escalating militarism since September 11, 2001, by integrating women into representational regimes of truth about the military and war. And much as Treichler (1999) explains how and why we need to "have theory in an epidemic" as she analyzes cultural constructions of AIDS as a long war, I believe we need to theorize gendered media constructions of military life in order to understand the intensification, even to epidemic levels, of militarism in the post-9/11 United States.

1

Lifetime's *Army Wives*, or, I Married the Media-Military-Industrial Complex

In the second season of the Lifetime Network's *Army Wives*, Pamela Moran hosts a popular call-in radio show about the travails of being an Army wife. During one episode, a listener calls to complain that she has not been able to find a job and blames Army life—the constant moves and her husband's deployments—for the problem. Pamela replies impatiently, "You're an Army wife. I'm an Army wife. And that means you're always going to be playing second fiddle career-wise while your spouse is in the military.... In the Army, your husband is always going to be the senior partner." The caller responds with, "But I have a life, too!" Pamela counters, "You married a soldier. And a soldier gets sent off to war to defend our country, ... and we just accept it, move on, and quit complaining" ("Last Minute Changes" 2008). Pamela's exchange encapsulates the tension at the heart of *Army Wives'* narratives and the relationships between its characters: negotiating marital and family relationships amid the Army's exertion of control over the lives of its soldiers and their families.[1]

When *Army Wives* premiered in the summer of 2007—only months after the beginning of the troop surge in Iraq—the public had been given precious few means by which it could either encourage the troops beyond "Support Our Troops" yellow ribbons or gain insight into their family lives. Enter *Army Wives*, which accomplishes this and, I believe, a great deal more. Through its sympathetic portrayal of Army family and military life on the fictional Fort Marshall Army post in Charleston, South Carolina, the program illuminates a microcosm that is probably unfamiliar to many viewers and one freighted with great contemporary political and social significance. *Army Wives* is another in the corpus of propaganda texts rolled out since 2001 to both mobilize public support for U.S. military interventions in Afghanistan and Iraq and burnish the image of the Army. But unlike the standard news-media fare in this corpus, *Army Wives* produces gendered military propaganda using the conventions of soap opera and serial drama—genres usually intended for female audiences— in an attempt to fix meanings around Army family life. I argue that this works via *Army Wives'* constitution of two different marriages: the first weds individuals to the Army (including its regime of gender politics) to achieve homeland defense; and the second weds the Lifetime network to the military-industrial complex through partnerships and strategic alliances that extend Lifetime's brand and construct verisimilitude about contemporary military life.

As a hybrid program, *Army Wives* played an important role in amplifying, reiterating, and even reshaping propaganda that has proliferated in news media from 2001 onward. It worked in concert with these news discourses to constitute meaning around military family life at a juncture when polls showed diminishing public support for the wars in Afghanistan and Iraq (e.g., Keeter 2007) and President Bush was attempting to rally the public behind the troop surge he promised would translate into a U.S. victory in Iraq. By presenting identifiable story lines performed by an appealing cast, over the course of the show's 2007–2013 run, Lifetime's *Army Wives* promoted an image of military life that transcends the clearly political machinations of war making and discouraged its viewers from interpreting various issues, and even the military itself, as political. This perspective on military life owes largely, I believe, to creative and executive producer Katherine Fugate's vision of the program.

Writing in *Television Week*, Fugate explains why the program has broad appeal: "At its core, 'Army Wives' is about love: love of our families, our friends, our country. . . . America's presence in Iraq is controversial. Some might wonder how a show can thrive against that backdrop. But our show isn't about Iraq. It's about relationships and people who make sacrifices" (2008, 12). The relationships that Fugate references here are not simply those friend, family, and romantic relationships that form the core of the program; she also implicitly references the relationship between the program's producers and the Pentagon, a type of strategic alliance characteristic of Lifetime. Such alliances have had a mixed record overall for Lifetime, but its partnership with the DoD, and specifically the Army's Entertainment Liaison Office, was integral to the success of this program, which, during its seven-season run, brought Lifetime its highest ratings.

The Banality of Militarism

One could contend that any program titled *Army Wives* would glorify military life. However, this is not the gist of the program; instead, its central role, I argue, is to naturalize and normalize historically specific ideologies about Army gender politics and the wars in Iraq and Afghanistan. With its family-focused content, popularity, generic conventions, and place in the media universe, the program produces banal militarism. Rather than glorifying war, *Army Wives* instead legitimizes militarism in its showcasing of the families of Fort Marshall, largely *because* it features family relationships rather than directly addressing the politics of war. Family relations and the domestic sphere in general have long been considered women's domain; this domain is also, and importantly for this chapter, where life is sustained and reproduced through mundane practices such as nurturing children, for example. *Army Wives* and Lifetime enhance banality in this construction of militarism by depicting quotidian, heterosexual family concerns—identifiable to many civilian viewers—intermingled with those specific to life on an Army post. This admixture of sympathetic depictions and familiar, gender-specific situations likely enhances viewers' affinity for *Army Wives* while reducing their resistance to its militaristic and propagandistic content.

Military, U.S. foreign policy, and media corporate interests infuse *Army Wives* narratives, and the propaganda performed on behalf of these interests is much as West and Zimmerman (1987) have theorized gender as an ongoing practice, a doing. In this chapter and in chapter 2, on martial motherhood, I draw from West and Zimmerman's theory of doing gender and Judith Butler's theory of gender performance to illustrate how gendered performances of marriage and motherhood articulate to particular aspects of war and military propaganda prevalent in the United States since September 11, 2001. Like West and Zimmerman, Butler argues that gender is "performatively constituted by the very 'expressions' that are said to be its results" (1990, 25). *Army Wives'* performative constitution of propaganda thus naturalizes historically and institutionally specific discourses concerning both gender and militarism. Additionally, the program's typically heteronormative gender performance occurs in a mutually constitutive relationship with that of propaganda concerning the rightness and naturalness of Army politics, which makes it an especially rich venue for discursively normalizing both Army-specific gender *and* militarism. For example, the program takes as a given that the U.S. military presence in Afghanistan and Iraq is accomplishing positive things for the people there, just as it naturalizes heterosexual nuclear families,[2] thereby obscuring the discursive production of both these military missions and this gender- and historically specific organization of family.

A seamless fusion of militarism with the generic conventions of serial dramas and soaps[3]—including gorgeous, Antebellum settings and conventionally attractive, even glamorous, cast members—makes *Army Wives* a standout hybrid program in a network whose success is staked on its lineup of hybrids (Byars and Meehan 1994–1995; Lotz 2006; and Meehan and Byars 2000). This allows the program to shift its attention from warfare, the reason for the program's existence and its verisimilitude, to the personal lives and problems of the cast. Focusing on family life apparently resonates with Lifetime's audiences and corporate partners, who, as I will explain shortly, enthusiastically support this extension into militainment of Lifetime's brand of television for women.

The Banality of Lifetime

Lifetime boasts that it offers "the highest quality entertainment and information programming content that celebrates, entertains and supports women" (n.d.-a). Over the course of thirty years, Lifetime has stayed "true to its most famous slogan, 'Television for Women,'" Emily Newman and Emily Witsell argue (2016, 2). "Tackling tough subjects like domestic abuse, sexual assault, eating disorders and addiction," they continue, "Lifetime has worked to tell often-silenced stories of women. Each film is accompanied by information that can provide access to help, be it 24-hour access hotlines or therapeutic resources" (3). To further support women, Lifetime strives to hire female film directors, an effort that has resulted in women directing about half of its films. Lifetime has also launched the Broad Focus initiative, which materially supports "female creative talent (writers, developers, producers, and directors)" and encourages "content dedicated to women's experiences" (Newman and Witsell 2016, 3).

Based on an ethnographic and political-economy analysis of Lifetime, Eileen Meehan and Jackie Byars (2000) characterize its programming as "telefeminist," intended to appeal to upscale women *and* men. Lifetime distinguishes itself from conventional networks with programs that hybridize "male-identified genres" such as "buddy cop shows" with female-identified ones such as soaps (Byars and Meehan 1994–1995, 24); this strategy aims to avoid alienating male viewers while simultaneously appealing to women. Lifetime envisions its audience as being composed mainly of "working women" who are "as economically independent, but not as emotionally independent from men"; thus, Byars and Meehan argue that Lifetime's programming should be considered "feminine but never feminist" (1994–1995, 25). *Army Wives* hews to the formula that Byars and Meehan identify by repeatedly validating Army patriarchy as well as that structuring the marriages of the wives to their soldier-spouses.

But *Army Wives* features somewhat-untraditional gendered story lines, too: Pamela Moran, for example, returns to the wage-labor force as a Charleston city cop once she divorces Chase, and Roland Burton takes on the role of state-side primary parent—proving to be a more competent parent than his wife, Joan, the ambitious, skilled warrior. These examples are more postfeminist than feminist, however, in that they represent deviations from the program's gender-essentialist norm—a legitimation of traditional gender performance and meritocracy that renders feminism apparently unnecessary (Vavrus 2002).[4] In story lines such as those that tout joining the Army as a smart career move for women, particularly those of color; that obscure racism in either the Army or in South Carolina, Fort Marshall's home state; that promote the GI Bill as a life-enhancing benefit for service women; that reward military men when they eschew patriarchal behavior and embrace women as their equals; and that illuminate the problem of gender violence while obscuring the power relations that underpin it, *Army Wives'* regime of representation constructs a postracial, postfeminist Army as it encourages military solutions to resolve problems faced by women and girls.

Army Wives is based on a book by Tanya Biank (2006), originally titled *Under the Sabers: The Unwritten Code of Army Wives* and republished in 2007 as *Army Wives: The Unwritten Code of Military Marriage*. Biank, formerly a reporter for North Carolina's *Fayetteville Observer*, wrote the book after covering North Carolina's Fort Bragg, where Army personnel committed five murders between 2002 and 2003. Biank writes, "Even without sensational murders, the lives of Army wives are the stuff of drama. These women play roles that are bound by convention in circumstances that are sometimes precarious, frequently close-knit, and too often heartrending. Yet what life is really like for Army wives has never been closely examined" (2006, xi). To bring those lives to light, Biank's book thus follows the lives of four women—married to Army men and living at or near Fort Bragg—and their families from late 2000 until 2003, as they navigate the challenges of Army life. With the book's success, Biank has become an unofficial spokesperson for Army families, having written an Erma Bombeck–esque syndicated column about military life for *Operation Homefront Online*, among other sites, and a book about the experiences of four service women, titled *Undaunted: The Real Story of America's Servicewomen in Today's Military* (2014).[5] A self-professed Army brat, an Army wife, and a writer and consultant to the *Army Wives* program, Biank presents herself as a voice for Army families, whose unique needs and problems she believes are insufficiently addressed by policy makers and the military itself. Judging from comments on fan pages, *Army Wives*, too, has offered discursive support to viewers who live with extreme stress anticipating injury or death befalling deployed family members. The need for social and institutional support and compassion in these circumstances, incomprehensible to many of us, is indisputable, and *Army Wives*, commendably, illuminates many concerns of military families. But the illumination is selective; throughout its run, the program is silent on the human toll that U.S. wars and occupation have had on Afghan and Iraqi families, the politics of war, the military-industrial complex, or any number of problems experienced by service women, particularly rampant sexual harassment and abuse.

Army Wives has the distinction of having been Lifetime's most popular program, regularly attracting TV's most sought-after viewers: eighteen- to forty-nine-year-old women ("Lifetime's 'Army Wives'" 2011). At different times, it was cable TV's most viewed drama among this same group of women ("Lifetime Orders More 'Army Wives'" 2009) and the top program on Lifetime among college students, ages eighteen to twenty-four ("Big Show on Campus" 2009). During its fifth season, viewership ranged from a high of 4.8 million to a low of 3.5 million viewers (Gorman 2011); its sixth season saw a drop to an average of 3.08 million viewers (*"Army Wives*: Season Six Ratings" 2012), a trend that, along with troop reductions in Iraq and Afghanistan, ultimately led to its cancellation in 2013. The program's popularity with women attracted the interest of Senators John McCain and Barack Obama while on the presidential campaign trail in 2008, when each candidate recorded a thirty-second bumper praising military families that aired just before the second season's premiere episode (Eggerton 2008).

Along with attracting Obama's and McCain's notice, *Army Wives*' ratings appealed to the U.S. Army's Entertainment Liaison Office (ELO), which became involved with the program after its first season and maintained support throughout the life of the program. Weekly reports by the Army ELO's Western division (Office of the Chief of Public Affairs, or OCPA-West) reflect its interest in ratings and suggest that OCPA-West's involvement with *Army Wives* was fueled both by these numbers and the program's ideological support for themes that the ELO wished to emphasize. One entry among the weekly OCPA-West reports assesses the program positively as the liaison officer considered whether to support a fifth season. The entry noted that seasons 1 through 4 had seen weekly audience numbers of four-million-plus viewers and "specifically target[ed] centers of influence in the 25–50 year old female demographic." The liaison officer recommended continuing OCPA-West's support of *Army Wives* for "realistic story lines that showcase the day-to-day life of Army spouses and the Soldiers they support," as well as for how the program "Broadens Understanding and Advocacy"[6] (U.S. Army 2015, 30).

From the program's inception, *Army Wives* wove together actual and fictionalized events and people to enhance its verisimilitude. For example, with the ostensibly nonpolitical "support the troops and their families" mantra, the program has featured Jill Biden, the former vice president's spouse, giving a brief speech advocating for military families;[7] the (now former) governor of

South Carolina Nikki Haley, mingling at a post soiree as a means of showing support for Fort Marshall's green initiatives; and presidential candidates John McCain and Barack Obama in 2008, appearing in the segments mentioned earlier. With such intertextual weaving of fictional and nonfictional worlds, *Army Wives* expanded the number of sites available to negotiate meaning about military family life and U.S. missions in Iraq and Afghanistan—beyond news media and into serial drama, to reach in real time audiences of women who were perhaps unfamiliar with the program's premise. This appeal is what Katherine Fugate was hoping to achieve, a goal affirmed by military families she met while touring Army posts with Tanya Biank: "A young Army wife told us she watches each new episode with her husband, who was severely burned from the waist up, as she sits on the edge of his hospital bed. A newly widowed woman, who lost her husband to a sniper attack, told us the series has 'saved her life.' Other wives told us the camaraderie on the show gets them through the long months when their husbands are deployed and they become single mothers, running a household on their own" (Fugate 2008, 12). Army wives at Fort Drum watching the program with a *New York Times* reporter echoed Fugate's account; although the Fort Drum viewers quibbled over some details, the group "mostly found 'Army Wives' entertaining, well acted and able to shed some light on their real lives." Explaining the stakes of the program, one of these wives laments, "People don't understand what our lives are like. . . . I guess that's why we want this show to get it right. We take this so personally" (Lee 2007, E8). And although military-focused TV programs such as *China Beach*, *JAG*, and *M*A*S*H* have had successful runs, they focused neither on military family life nor on wars occurring at the time the programs aired. *Army Wives*, on the other hand, drew from contemporary topics for its story lines. OCPA-West noted, for example, that in season 5, the program was slated to deal with "difficult, yet relevant topics, . . . keeping it fresh while realistic" (U.S. Army 2015, 30). Such fresh realism and sympathetic narrative commentary about the current wars' impacts on families allowed the program to garner further support from partnerships with brick-and-mortar support organizations, corporations, and individuals.

Since 2001, tomes have been written about relations between the military and the media during the Afghanistan and Iraq conflicts; such research tends to focus on news media, gaming, and film to analyze the extent to which these have circulated prowar propaganda (e.g., Kellner 2004, 2010; McLaren and Martin 2004; *Buying the War* 2007) and, to a lesser extent, exemplified militainment (Singer 2010; Stahl 2010). But because *Army Wives* is a military soap opera that, I argue, feminizes militainment, it also serves as a vehicle for propaganda: it circulates familiar, albeit contested, maxims about the wars in Iraq and Afghanistan as it simultaneously burnishes the Army's credentials as a compassionate organization that unfailingly aids soldiers and their families.

From its ratings apex at Lifetime, *Army Wives* offered the Army—the branch of the military that has historically recruited more women and offered more employment to women than any other (M. Brown 2006; Bailey 2009; Mittelstadt 2012)—an entertainment platform from which to promote its interests. That *Army Wives'* audiences are predominantly female should not be underestimated: women are at once more resistant to such messages, historically speaking, and yet seldom the subjects of them in any form (Elder and Greene 2007; Enloe 2000; Turse 2008).

This chapter's feminist analysis of *Army Wives* has two parts: an examination of both the discursive production of gender and militarism through the propaganda themes that run through its multiple episodes and an examination of the program's political economy. And although instances of gendered propaganda performance abound in the program, the examples I include here are representative of the forms these performances take, some of which also compose significant plots and subplots that span episodes and even seasons. I argue that *Army Wives* employs marriage as a framing device for the military missions in Iraq and Afghanistan that encourages acquiescence to these missions' continually shifting ends: for example, instead of searching for weapons of mass destruction (WMD) in Iraq (the stated purpose of the invasion of 2003), the troops of *Army Wives* can be seen engaging in "soft power" activities typically associated with a feminine approach to diplomacy and foreign policy (Nye 2008), such as building schools, rescuing dogs, and ensuring that Iraqi children get needed medical care.

Pamela Moran's exhortation to her caller to "accept," "move on," and "quit complaining," is writ large in *Army Wives*, which encourages viewers to do the very same about military policy; indeed, viewers are regularly treated to object lessons suggesting that criticizing Army policy is tantamount to becoming the "complaining" wife represented by Pamela's caller. Historically, downgrading structural critique to "complaint" is a method used to diminish feminist criticism of patriarchal power, effectively disarticulating the political from the personal.[8] Although *Army Wives* is only one TV program (which inspired a short-lived spin-off, *Coming Home*), its clear and direct support of these wars and their shifting missions—alongside Lifetime's strategic partnerships and synergistic relationships—links it to news media, as well as brick-and-mortar life practices and institutions that multiply its message, reinforce its connections to the military-industrial complex, and produce banal militarism.

Married to the Army

The marriage that *Army Wives* showcases most visibly is that between soldiers and their spouses and the Army—its gender politics figuring prominently throughout. The excerpt from Pamela Moran's radio show in this chapter's introduction is a particularly illustrative segment. Just as Pamela does in her radio advice, many other *Army Wives* episodes include references to soldiers' deployments having the most virtuous of goals: protecting the United States. Because the official rationale for waging and staying in the wars in Afghanistan and Iraq has been controversial, to say the least, and the connection between far-away battles and defense of the United States unclear, that many *Army Wives* episodes include such references, and seemingly to reinforce the rationale for staying in a *marriage*, is significant. Constructing soldiers as ever heroic and self-sacrificing, *Army Wives*' not-so subtle message is that both warriors and the Army deserve vigorous defense as partial compensation for soldiers' sacrifices; to question their mission is to betray profound, even unforgivable selfishness.

This message accords with what Roger Stahl argues about "support-the-troops" rhetoric, which has proliferated across numerous cultural sites since the 1991 Persian Gulf War: it directs "civic attention away from debates about legitimacy and toward the war machine itself, . . . extolling mindfulness and gratitude for those volunteer servicemen and women who have been ordered into harm's way" (2010, 29). The "choice" on offer here is thus to "either stand with official policy or stand against the soldier" (30). To Stahl's reading, I would add that war critics since Vietnam have nuanced their message to more clearly support the humans involved in war—troops included—while arguing against the bellicose mind-set and policies that make war possible; for example, through many years, front yards in my community sported yard signs with the imperative to "support the troops—bring them home now."[9] Although *Army Wives* expresses no such criticism of war, in every episode it foregrounds the concerns of soldiers and their families in situations that appear to be outside of politics (and discourse), thus making support for the troops apparently natural, uncontroversial, and even foreordained.

Army Wives weaves troop-supporting rhetoric into virtually every episode, at times using a heavy hand to drench scenes in patriotic symbolism while at others utilizing more subtle devices, which are clear in message nevertheless. In an episode from the first season, for example, Fort Marshall is holding its annual Fourth of July picnic in a large park on post, where soldiers quietly sneak out for their deployments; while their families strain to enjoy the event, the music from "America the Beautiful" plays, and sunlight filters gently through the leaves on the tree branches above them. The post commander's wife, Claudia Joy Holden, addresses the picnicking group. She lauds the heroism of the U.S. military, telling the crowd that it is "still protecting the rights guaranteed by our forefathers . . . every minute of every day." Soldiers' "battles go beyond religion, race, or gender," she tells them. "They're the defenders of us all. They're the defenders of our differences. . . . Together we [soldiers and their families] fight for our freedom. . . . I am proud of the role we play in maintaining peace . . . in our country and throughout the world. I am proud to call myself an Army wife" ("Independence Day" 2007).

Other references to homeland defense are embedded in story lines in which they could easily go unnoticed. Season 3, for example, sees Pamela growing increasingly unhappy about her Delta Force husband Chase's long absences on missions that come with no warning, require immediate departure, and are accompanied by enforced silences about his work. However, his success with Delta has meant that the family is eligible to move into a larger house. Because Pamela's two children are increasingly restive sharing a bedroom in their too-small house, she jumps at the chance to move—though Chase is deployed when this happens. In one scene, Roxy LeBlanc and Pamela walk through Pamela's front door as they bring boxes into the new house. Pamela complains about Chase's absence for yet another of their moves: "that man is useless." Roxy retorts sarcastically, "Right, just when you need him he's off risking his life for our country!" Pamela, realizing the trivializing nature of Roxy's comment, sighs, "Exactly, . . . dereliction of domestic duty" ("Incoming" 2009). Any complaints from Pamela about the difficulty of moving without her husband's help are swiftly buried under Roxy's retort, which tells Pamela she must not assert her own needs but should suppress them in a show of respect for her husband, who represents both the Delta Force mission and the Army. These two scenes defend at least two commonsense notions, both about war and gendered labor: first, that soldiers are fighting over *there* to protect us, over *here*—an arguable point that foreign policy and military experts have debated since the U.S. assault on Afghanistan began in 2001 (e.g., Johnson 2008, 2009); and, second, that wives properly bear responsibility for the home front while their husbands are deployed to other lands.

Performing Propaganda

Efforts to mobilize populations both to accede to the necessity of war (often by demonizing opponents) and to engage in home-front support for it fall into the category of propaganda, which has been integral to modern military campaigns since World War I (Andersen 2006). Nancy Snow defines propaganda as "systematic and deliberate attempts to sway mass public opinion in favor of the objectives of the institutions (usually state or corporate) sending the propaganda messages" (2002, 21). Gerald Sussman posits that "the point of propaganda is not necessarily to deceive but rather to internalize or reinforce in the audience deference to the authoritative status of a particular advocacy bearing a clear or implicit rationale or policy prescription that on some level requires the audience's participation or consent. . . . Propaganda implies a relationship of asymmetrical power between the interest that the propagandist represents and the audience to whom the message is addressed" (2010, 117–118). Jacques

Ellul adds that the aim of propaganda is "orthopraxy," which is "the active or passive participation in its actions of a mass of individuals" (1965, 61). Propaganda campaigns since the GWOT began in 2001—in the attempt to rout Al-Qaeda from Afghanistan and when the Bush administration convinced the U.S. public that Iraq sponsored the Al-Qaeda attacks on the Pentagon and World Trade Center—have focused on gaining and maintaining public support for these wars using news media. During this same period, media researchers and journalists alike reached consensus that the U.S. news media played a vital role in circulating numerous uncritical stories that later proved false, their sources planted by Bush administration officials to create a seeming necessity and urgency for war (e.g., Andersen 2006; Bonn 2010; DiMaggio 2009; Kellner 2004; McLaren and Martin 2004; and *Buying the War* 2007).

Army Wives played a role in extending this propaganda campaign by casting it into soap-opera form and timing it propitiously: it premiered in 2007, well after the first stages of these wars but just after the so-called surge of troops to Iraq was rolled out. At this time, the wars in Afghanistan and Iraq had been going on for six and four years, respectively, and according to numerous polls conducted nationally, they had been losing the support of the public, troubled by the thousands of casualties and injuries these wars had incurred (Keeter 2007; Pew Research Center 2008). *Army Wives* propaganda thus served slightly different (yet no less important) functions than that appearing earlier: first, to maintain acceptance of the surge and the ongoing campaign in Afghanistan by illustrating Army life's heroic possibilities and Army goodwill projects—particularly those enacted by women on behalf of women—and, second, to promote Army gender politics, all situated in a soap opera, the most banal of TV genres. Early in season 1, for instance, Trevor is at the swimming pool on post with his sons, TJ and Finn, when the five p.m. bugle begins to blow "Taps." Along with everyone else at the pool, Trevor stands up, places his hand on his heart, and faces the flag for the duration. TJ and Finn, playing, fail to observe this ritual; immediately after the last note of "Taps," and in a clear fusion of patriarchy and patriotism, Trevor explains sternly to them both that they must salute the flag with hands over hearts each day at five when they are on post: "In doing that, you're honoring your country, the Army, and me, your father" ("Who We Are" 2007).

For the mothers and spouses on the program, standing in the way of either their children or their deploying husbands and wives—even to complain or worry visibly—is to prevent children and spouses from reaching the heroic self-actualization that awaits each soldier in theater (the program is suffused with references to heroes and heroism, used routinely to describe soldiers). Numerous episodes—about Joan Burton, Trevor LeBlanc, and Chase Moran, for example—include dialogue about and between characters whose core identities are defined entirely by being soldiers. During season 3, the newly promoted General Michael Holden offers Joan Burton (the mother of an infant) the opportunity to be his second in command at Fort Marshall and therefore remain close to her baby. But because she is thriving as a combat strategist and commander, Joan is conflicted about whether to stay on post and be an involved parent or to lead her brigade in Iraq; after thinking it over, she calmly tells the general, "Sir, I respectfully request the privilege to deploy" ("Incoming" 2009). Later she leads her troops out of a firefight to safety, sustaining a facial wound and traumatic brain injury in the process. In response to Roxy's complaints about her husband Trevor's upcoming deployment, her friend Betty notes tartly, "The Army's his identity; take it away and what's he got?" ("Who We Are" 2007). Following this observation, in season 2, Trevor spots and kills a sniper in a crowded bazaar in Baghdad before the sniper can shoot anyone. He earns a Silver Star and hero's welcome upon his return, thus demonstrating that submitting to Roxy's concerns would have resulted in grave consequences.

To enhance the program's verisimilitude, many *Army Wives* episodes reference and reframe events that have occurred in the brick-and-mortar world to cast the Army in a favorable light. The episode in which the Fourth of July picnic scene appears (mentioned earlier) serves both purposes, as its primary plot revolves around the issue of "friendly fire," an Orwellian term used for accidental attacks by and on a military unit's own troops. The former St. Louis Rams football player Pat Tillman was perhaps the most well-known victim of friendly fire in these current wars, and the incident's treatment in the press casts the Army in a less-than-flattering light: commanding officers appeared eager to cover up rather than investigate his death (Krakauer 2009). In the *Army Wives* friendly fire episode, Hannah White, whose husband is killed in battle and who is an old friend of Claudia Joy Holden, appears for a visit just as news emerges that she plans to testify in front of a congressional committee to challenge the Army's account of her husband's death and bring to the committee evidence showing that her husband had been killed by friendly fire. Word of Hannah's plans spreads quickly through the Fort Marshall grapevine and causes great dissension as the wives line up to support or disparage Hannah. Denise Sherwood is adamantly opposed to Hannah's testimony, exclaiming, "We are at war! Mistakes like this happen. We need to support our troops. The last thing we need is a wife testifying in front of Congress! . . . Nothing she says to Congress is going to bring her husband back" ("Dirty Laundry" 2007).

Those who believe Hannah should testify maintain that she is doing so to get to the bottom of her husband's death, while those opposed believe her appearance is a publicity-seeking effort that dishonors her husband and has no merit—once the Army has rendered its verdict, the case should be closed. In the Holden household, Michael tells Claudia Joy that their houseguest

Hannah must leave because he cannot be seen with a critic of the Army. Claudia Joy agrees, reluctantly, telling Michael, "You're right. We have an obligation to the Army." When she tells Hannah that she must leave their house, Hannah becomes upset and justifies her actions: "I think they're lying to me, Claudia Joy. Can't you understand that?" Claudia Joy replies, "Yes, I do. But I have to support my husband." "And I have to support mine," Hannah retorts. In this way, the much larger and more troublesome problem of friendly fire, which includes the Army's record of covering up such incidents, is reduced to preserving the stature of husbands, even posthumously. The scenes in this narrative also suggest that criticism of the Army, and not friendly fire, poses the more serious threat to troops.

This episode ends with Hannah beginning her testimony before Congress: "My name is Hannah White. I was an Army wife for twenty-two years. I want you to know that I believe in the U.S. Army and all that it stands for" ("Dirty Laundry" 2007). Hannah's and Claudia Joy's responses divert attention from the Army's response with the suggestion that even if the Army had covered up the death of Hannah's husband, she remains a supporter of it "and all that it stands for." This episode also serves to illustrate the subtitle of Biank's book, *The Unwritten Code of Army Wives*—a code that guides the program's debates and interpersonal conflicts. Whereas most problems are resolved by swearing undying fealty to one's spouse (usually husband), Hannah White's conflict is more complicated as it tests both marital and Army fidelity. When Hannah eventually assures her congressional audience that her belief in the Army is unshaken despite its treatment of her husband's death, she upholds her commitment to both marriages. Notably, this episode aired during the troop surge in Iraq. The program's sympathetic portrayal of the Army and its families' support of it and "all that it stands for" presents a pro-Army position as it poses a strong refutation of waning public support for military intervention. After all, if the war widow Hannah White remains supportive of (and married to) the Army, shouldn't civilians too?

Pride-worthy actions of the Army are numerous on this program, but they are not usually about fighting and dying honorably;[10] rather, they concern the Army's benevolence through soft-power acts that ultimately replaced the goal of seizing WMD, the original justification for getting into a preemptive war with Iraq. In a narrative arc that spans seasons 3 and 4, Joan Burton is injured by an improvised explosive device (IED) blast in Iraq as she heroically leads her troops out of a firefight, leading to her temporary blindness. Once she recovers her sight, Joan is sent to a location where a school is being shoddily built by corrupt contractors. Her orders are to intervene and hire trustworthy workers to build the school correctly, a task she excels at despite the Iraqi men's discomfort with taking orders from a woman. Joan and her troops clean up the mess, get the project back on track, and are rewarded by being sent home.

Season 3 also includes the story of Haneen, an Iraqi girl who needs hand surgery as a result of an injury incurred in a battle between U.S. and Iraqi troops in her home that kills everyone else in her family. Haneen comes to the attention of Roland Burton, at that time a psychiatrist working at Fort Marshall's Mercer Hospital. Roland persuades Claudia Joy and Michael Holden to take in Haneen while she undergoes and recuperates from the delicate surgery at Mercer. Claudia Joy and her daughter Emmalin tend to Haneen, preparing Iraqi food and placing a prayer rug in her bedroom. Haneen is hesitant to have the surgery, questioning why she was spared while the rest of her family was killed. Roland assures her that her family would want her to be alive, and Haneen reluctantly agrees, never blaming the United States or the Army for what has befallen her family; instead, she blames the Iraqis—"my people"— and is profoundly grateful to the Holdens and the U.S. Army for repairing her hand and then returning her to Iraq ("Onward Christian Soldier" 2009). Similarly, after season 1, the Army does the right thing in aiding soldiers experiencing posttraumatic stress disorder (PTSD), suicidal depression, and painkiller addictions and then refusing to locate a toxic-waste dump at Fort Marshall and risk contaminating homes and residents. On *Army Wives*, the Army's mission is always already an upstanding one—much as gendered identities appear to "preexist the deed" of their performance, in Butler's words.

These characters and plots, dominated by women, construct a virtuous Army, perhaps as a response to criticisms of the military when these problems have occurred in the brick-and-mortar world.[11] Outside U.S borders, the Army acts as a responsible world citizen, aiding Iraqis in their quest to get good health care and helping to rebuild the country's schools. (That the schools would not need rebuilding if the United States had not bombed them goes without remark.) Such acts of feminized "soft power" offer a stark contrast to the aggressive and violent tactics of masculinized "hard power," with which the military has been historically associated. *Army Wives* thus performs gendered propaganda by embracing the military mission as it morphs into a feminized form over time and by casting the Army in the most favorable light. These explicit and subtle performances normalize and naturalize support for the Army and its use of soft power as they wed soldiers and their families to the Army: a somewhat flawed but ultimately redeeming spouse. And while this marriage is depicted as far from perfect—the Army spouse making unreasonable and even life-threatening demands—its participants repeatedly renew their vows to it throughout the seasons of *Army Wives*.

Married to The Complex

Entertainment media have historically played an important role, along with their news counterparts, in the reproduction and construction of promilitary, prowar ideology (Boggs and Pollard 2007; Kellner 2010; Robb 2004; Stahl 2010). Although the *Army Wives* title suggests that it, too, may do this, what may be less obvious is how the program's characters and narratives manifest efforts by the Pentagon to influence everyday domestic life through banal militarism. This is the basis of what I assert is *Army Wives'* second marriage: that between Lifetime and the military-industrial complex.

With *Army Wives* allied with the Pentagon Entertainment Office since its second season, the program's scripts must receive Pentagon approval via OCPA-West's liaison staff in order to, among other benefits, use Charleston's Air Force base as a backdrop for filming on-post scenes and for employing its Air Force reservists as extras (O'Connor 2008). The city of Charleston has also bestowed *Army Wives* with tax breaks in order to maintain the program's base in Charleston, a controversial practice continued by the South Carolina legislature after members of the cast lobbied in favor of it (Cieply 2011; T. Smith 2010). As season 5 was concluding, OCPA-West reports indicate that the future of the program rested on whether the legislature would maintain this program: "They will not know if they are getting a Season 6 until Mid July after the South Carolina government votes on tax incentives for the industry" (U.S. Army 2015, 641).

For *Army Wives* to sustain its standing in South Carolina and maintain militaristic realism, it could be expected to pull its punches at times and self-censor, just as the Pentagon entertainment liaison chief Phil Strub insists film producers must if they want military cooperation with the program. OCPA-West entries reveal that *Army Wives* production staff did, in fact, modify scripts to adhere to Army dictates. About two episodes that were aired successively during season 4, meant to represent "Afghanistan-specific deployment scenarios," for example, a liaison officer notes that the first "caused for a great deal of pre-production involvement" to make the episode a proper "tribute [to] soldiers downrange." The episode that followed this one apparently required intervention as well, but the "writers were willing to change a good deal of the script to make sure that the Army didn't come across as the villain" (U.S. Army 2015, 270). Numerous other entries in OCPA-West's weekly reports indicate that its staff worked at the *development* stage of production as well as at the more well-known script-approval stage. Secker and Alford's (2017) research on ELO involvement in film productions documents numerous instances of intervention at this point as well.

Along with Secker and Alford's work, DoD influence on the film industry has been documented extensively in David Robb's *Operation Hollywood* (2004), which enumerates examples starting in 1927 of filmmakers calling for military assistance to make their films more realistic—and getting that assistance only after modifying their scripts to adhere to strict rules about casting the military in a positive light. Robb refers to these arrangements as quid pro quo and in an interview asserts that all concerned—even the Writer's Guild—believe this arrangement to be a mutually beneficial one. However, he cautions that in this "chronic sanitization of the military and what war is," the losers are "the American people. They're being saturated with military propaganda in their mainstream movies and TV shows, and they don't even know" (quoted in Fleischer 2004). Alford (2016) and Secker and Alford (2017) concur.

What results from *Army Wives'* submission to ELO influence is a program that both epitomizes and feminizes a media genre known as "militainment." This is a move that pushes the genre beyond its characteristically masculine content and intended audiences, such as those for military-themed video games, in order to appeal to influential/affluential women between the ages of twenty-five and fifty (a key group for TV advertisers). What is militainment? In describing *America's Army*, a video game developed by the Pentagon to recruit and train soldiers, P. W. Singer notes that militainment signals a cultural "transformation [that] has taken place over the last decade—largely escaping public scrutiny, at modest cost relative to the enormous sums spent elsewhere in the Pentagon budget, and with little planning but enormous consequences" (2010, 91). The term "militainment" was "first coined to describe any public entertainment that celebrated the military, but today it could be redefined to mean the fascinating, but also worrisome, blurring of the line between entertainment and war," Singer explains (92). Stahl examines a diverse array of popular culture produced since September 11, 2001, such as video games, films, reality TV, and even children's toys that fit a definition of militainment. Each of these products, Stahl reveals, translates "state violence . . . into an object of pleasurable consumption," making such violence "not of the abstract, distant, or historical variety but rather an impending or current use of force, one directly relevant to the citizen's current political life" (2010, 6). Most of these products are interactive in one way or another, a feature that Stahl believes to be crucial for pushing the "discourses of militainment" to burrow "deeper into the capillaries of the subject, working internally to intensify a prescribed posture toward state violence and thereby widen the 'coalition of the willing'" (210, 140).

Producing militainment is a carefully orchestrated process benefiting both the Pentagon and media industries. Robb traces it back to the beginning of the film industry in the United States, calling it out as "Hollywood's dirtiest little secret, . . . a devil's bargain that's a good deal for both sides" (2004, 25). Film and TV producers generally like the arrangement because "millions of dollars can be shaved off a film's budget if the military agrees to lend its equipment and assistance. And all a producer has to do to get that assistance is submit five copies of the script to the Pentagon for approval; make whatever script changes the Pentagon suggests; film the script exactly as approved by the Pentagon; and prescreen the finished product for Pentagon officials before it's shown to the public" (Robb 2004, 25). For the military, the ultimate goal of such "mutual exploitation" (Bennett 2012) is spelled out in *A Producer's Guide to U.S. Army Cooperation with the Entertainment Industry*: to "aid in the recruiting and retention of personnel" (Robb 2004, 26). On PBS's *NewsHour*, a liaison officer underscored the important role these productions play in recruiting, noting that a Youth Attitude Tracking Survey conducted twice by the Pentagon "found that young men of recruiting age cited movies and television as the primary source of their impressions about the military. So it's very important [for showing] what the possibilities are and to see what being a soldier would be like" (PBS 2006). Today all branches of the military, the FBI, and the CIA actively shape military-themed media productions; along with the DoD, each branch maintains a liaison office in Los Angeles, while the DoD's main entertainment media division operates from the Pentagon (S. Smith 2006). The Pentagon's liaison chief since 1989, Phil Strub, has claimed that Pentagon influence has begun to wane in Hollywood as a result of Special Forces operations increasing while "big combat arms are being pared down" (Bennett 2012).

In addition to OCPA-West notations that praise *Army Wives'* depictions of military life with an abundance of superlatives, the program's alliance with the DoD is confirmed and celebrated in a bonus feature from the season 2 DVD set, "Operational Intelligence: Getting the Army's Support." This eight-minute segment features executive producers and cast members alike gushing with gratitude for the "realism," "plausibility," and "authenticity" that DoD support brings to the program. In one clip, for example, the actor who plays General Michael Holden, Brian McNamara, asserts confidently that military authenticity allows *Army Wives* to "honor the people we're portraying." ELO staff likewise appreciate *Army Wives'* representation of military life: project officer Master Sergeant Kanessa Trent explains that Army ELO staff approached the program's producers about providing support once they realized the program "was touching hearts, that people were watching it."

Paralleling Sergeant Trent's assessment, notations made by OCPA-West officers between 2010 and 2015 document not only that *Army Wives* was wildly successful by ELO standards but also that its ability to maintain an enthusiastic, pro-Army viewership encouraged the DoD to support other, similar types of programs. Secker and Alford note that around 2005, the DoD began to focus on reality TV (2017, 3), yet they do not speculate as to why this might be so. OCPA-West reports, however, provide insight into the DoD's turn to reality programming in numerous entries that highlight themes that the DoD encourages in its supported reality and dramatic TV programs. ELO staff notes indicate that "building resiliency," "restoring balance," "broadening understanding and advocacy," and "strength of the Army family," for example, can be woven effectively into programming projected to air on select woman-focused networks: Lifetime and the Oprah Winfrey Network (OWN), in particular. The *Army Wives* spin-off *Coming Home* is one such program. As the project was being developed for Lifetime by the creators of *Extreme Makeover: Home Edition*, ELO staff predicted that *Coming Home* would build resiliency for its four to six million viewers, as a result of witnessing each episode's featured service person making a "spectacular homecoming." "In every episode, the show will follow one bigger-than-life surprise intercut with real documentary homecomings that are happening at schools, ball games, and airports, and elsewhere in the USA. It's the best of both worlds—a combination of a big network production and the raw emotional real stories that make this concept so relatable" (U.S. Army 2015, 517).

Resembling *Army Wives* even more than *Coming Home* and an obvious attempt to capitalize on its success was *Army Wives of Alaska*: a docuseries pitched to OPCA-West in 2011 to appear on the Oprah Winfrey Network. Intended to "tell the story of 'the sisterhood of Army spouses' stationed in Alaska" and overseen by the executive producer Stephanie Drachkovitch—"the daughter of a career Army officer [who] has a deep affinity for Army personnel and their lifestyle"—the program was approved, its eight episodes airing in 2012 as *Married to the Army: Alaska*. ELO staff support appears to hinge on the program's "favorable depiction of Army lifestyle," a portrayal that staff believed would also "serve to further connect the American public to their Army" (U.S. Army 2015, 677). Once filming had been completed, the liaison officer supervising the production deemed it a success for being thoroughly "complimentary to Army units and operations" (U.S. Army 2015, 714).

ELO endorsements were not always forthcoming, however, as the experience of another OWN-proposed docuseries, *Homefront*, reveals. Pitched as a "'realistic, compelling and inspiring' documentary series" that would follow a "select group of 6–8 wives and girlfriends, representing all ranks and levels of experience, through 'the challenges and rewards of day-to-day living they encounter as the spouse or significant other of a U.S. Army soldier,'" the program would appear to satisfy ELO dictates. But neither this characterization nor *Homefront*'s proposed focus on "core beliefs of strength, sacrifice, and sisterhood, as well as family and community," prevented it from being viewed with suspicion. OCPA-West staff expressed concern that despite these factors and several others that weighed in the program's favor, *Homefront* "risks being a 'Real Housewives of the Army' series," given its production company's role in producing *Real Housewives of Atlanta* (U.S. Army 2015, 781–82). *Real Housewives*' branding of family life being one that the ELO wants to distance itself from is revealing. Despite the franchise's high ratings and loyal viewership, ELO concern that its supported reality programming might drift into *Real Housewives* territory suggests that the franchise's rendering of family would fail to properly represent themes that the Army requires to be in the constructed versions of reality it agrees to underwrite.

Projects the OPCA-West has endorsed, along with the language that staff use to describe the programs it will support, express an apparent desire to brand the Army experience as a lifestyle—a term typically used in conjunction with reality programs focused on domestic activities such as cooking and home remodeling. Casting martial experience as lifestyle entertainment, as OPCA-West does in its reports, is a method for obscuring its uniquely morbid, violent, and dangerous aspects, perhaps making it more appealing to potential recruits and their families. Pursuing a military lifestyle in Alaska or some other spot appears much less life-threatening than does being deployed to war zones (a more realistic outcome of Army enlistment). ELO reports such as those I am drawing from exemplify Jonathan Burston's point that "it is no longer always productive to think about cultural power and military power separately. . . . With the advent of militainment, the intricate relationships between popular cultural forms and military technology have all become rather difficult and confused" (2013, 93). Given the DoD's support for the program, it is thus no surprise that *Army Wives* operates as militainment. Its very premise blurs the line between entertainment and war, while its sexualized, conventionally attractive cast members and lush sets populated with real military equipment and personnel all aid in the process of translating state violence into an object of pleasurable consumption.

Army Wives' arrangement with the DoD enhances its military verisimilitude, but to succeed commercially, it must possess other attributes as well. In order to retain its premier spot on a cable network, it must continue to resonate with sponsors and audiences and enrich Lifetime's brand. In turn, Lifetime's ability to thrive as a media corporation in today's economy also depends on strengthening its brand through strategic alliances with its sibling divisions and other corporations to create synergy. As Carolyn Bronstein (1994–1995) and Newman and Witsell (2016) point out, Lifetime has been quite successful at achieving this. Lifetime's current owner is A&E Television Networks—a joint venture between the Hearst Corporation, Disney-ABC Television Group, and NBC-Universal (Wikipedia, n.d.), each of which has a successful track record making strategic alliances and coordinating them synergistically.

In promotional segments aired during *Army Wives'* fifth season, Lifetime highlighted these alliances. Perhaps the network's most valuable alliance is with Outback Steakhouse: a national restaurant chain whose president states, "The sacrifices that our troops and their families make so that we can enjoy the freedoms we have in the United States is something Outback employees have recognized and appreciated since we opened our doors 22 years ago" (Outback Steakhouse 2010). For one month during spring 2011, Outback offered a special "Red, White, and Bloomin'" menu, whose $1 million in proceeds were directed to Operation Homefront (Outback Steakhouse 2011a). As part of this promotion, Outback bused in Army spouses from nearby Fort Stewart to be fêted at a thank-you luncheon at the Outback Steakhouse in Savannah, Georgia, hosted by Brian McNamara, the actor who played General Michael Holden on *Army Wives*. In the advertisement for this event (airing between *Army Wives* segments), McNamara exclaims to these Army spouses, "We are incredibly honored to be telling your stories, considering what you do for us and what you do for the troops" (Outback Steakhouse 2011b). Following his speech, McNamara presented Operation Homefront with a $10,000 check from the *Army Wives* program.

Lifetime initiated other promotions for Army wives through its *"Army Wives* Give Back" program, in which cast members teamed up with viewers to visit Army posts and provide Army families with donations and gifts. Each of these segments acted as a two-minute "branded content segment meant to pay tribute to military wives" (Tanklefsky 2009). Cast members also paired up with actual Army wives to visit wounded soldiers at Walter Reed Army Hospital (Lifetime 2008), and the program hosted contests for military spouses in which the winner received a makeover from *Project Runway* (another Lifetime program) or a pink Ford Mustang identical to one featured in an episode that boosted breast cancer awareness. In addition to these promotions, Lifetime secured partnerships with Proctor and Gamble, Hallmark, and Ford Motor Company, which allowed Lifetime to integrate their products—the pink-racing-striped "Warriors in Pink" edition of the Ford Mustang, for example—noticeably into various episodes (Lafayette 2008). With such integrated marketing and extratextual practices, *Army Wives* has stamped a Lifetime-specific brand (Lotz 2006) on its rendering of military life while simultaneously feminizing militainment and the MMIC.

Attempting to seize on *Army Wives'* commercial momentum, in 2011 Lifetime spun off *Coming Home*, which in its first season immediately followed *Army Wives* on the Sunday-evening lineup (*Coming Home* ran just two seasons). *Coming Home* featured homecomings of military personnel in staged venues to surprise their family members. One episode, "Daddy's Little Girl," was described this way: "We surprise a 12-year-old girl with the Navy father she hasn't seen in months at the violin concert of her dreams—and there isn't a dry eye in the house" (Lifetime, n.d.-b). On the *Coming Home* webpage—next to an ad for *Army Wives*—one could view full or partial episodes, see real-life homecoming videos, and learn more about "special military organizations," such as the Red Cross, USO, and Operation Homefront.

Incorporating this type of issue advocacy and support into dramas is a long-standing strategy at Lifetime. In 1999, the network executive Carol Black explained that she envisioned Lifetime being a "support network intended to empower women"; Black's vision was for Lifetime to be "not only about entertaining and informing, but advocacy and support as well": "I want us to have the best shows, but we also have a unique opportunity to make women's lives better" (quoted in Hundley 2002, 178). Marketing research by Lifetime's top programmer during Black's tenure, Dawn Tarnofsky-Ostroff, revealed that viewers loved such programming: "These women identify with drama. The [heroines] are women who overcome obstacles, and I think women love to see women triumph" (quoted in Hundley 2002, 180). Andrea Wong, who took over Lifetime's leadership just prior to *Army Wives'* debut, observed that the success of the program owed to how it "really connected with women, really resonated with women. . . . It's obviously the right time for a show like Army Wives"; echoing Katherine Fugate's vision of the program, Wong averred, "Our show is more than just entertainment. We believe that on a higher level, we are embracing the stories of real people, of real sacrifice" ("Wong Polishes Lifetime's Brand" 2008, 23). Embodied by *Army Wives*, the formula was again successful. Soon after Wong's arrival and owing mainly to the success of *Army Wives*, Lifetime achieved the distinction of being the top cable network of 2007 in two prized demographic groups of women: ages eighteen to forty-nine and twenty-five to fifty-four (Lafayette 2007). Strong ratings during *Army Wives'* first season demonstrated that it could attract female eyeballs— some of recruitment age—and keep them trained on the program.

One organization absent from *Army Wives'* extensive list of links is Military Families Speak Out (MFSO), a group with a different view of how best to support the troops. The MFSO website explains that it is an "organization of over 4,000 families across the US and around the world who are opposed to the wars in Iraq and Afghanistan and have a loved one currently serving in the military, who has served in the military since 9/11 or who has died as a result of the wars in Iraq and Afghanistan": "As people with loved ones in the military, we have both a special need and a unique role to play in speaking out. It is our loved ones who are, have been, or will be on the battlefront" (Military Families Speak Out, n.d.). Another group with similar objectives was the Cindy Sheehan–founded Gold Star Families for Peace (now apparently inactive), which worked to end the wars in Iraq and Afghanistan and was composed of members "who [had] lost a member of their family in the Iraq War" (Gold Star Families for Peace, n.d.).

MFSO and Gold Star Families for Peace explicitly question the Army's mission in Afghanistan and Iraq. Conversely, Lifetime portrays Army life as if it were sculpted by Army PR (which it was); in *Army Wives'* mise-en-scène, Army wives maintain steadfast support for the Army despite the unimaginable pressures it exerts on their lives—and even after a spouse's death by friendly fire is covered up or a child is killed in battle. Toward the end of the Hannah White friendly fire episode, for example, the community of Fort Marshall wives tries to mend fences ("Dirty Laundry" 2007). Roxy, the newest Army spouse, seizes the microphone at an event to assemble care packages for the troops and shouts that this situation is their worst nightmare: "So why're we fightin'? We're in this together!" Pamela, who has been one of the most vocal supporters of Hannah's testimony before Congress, takes this message to heart and goes to Mercer Hospital to find nurse Denise, with whom Pamela fought while defending Hannah's testimony to the other wives. Apologetic, Pamela tells Denise, "Look, I'm opinionated and I've got a big mouth." Pamela trivializes her opposition to the Army as just her opinion, personalizing and subordinating it in favor of her friendship with Denise. She is an Army wife who learned her place and internalized the "unwritten code" first documented by Tanya Biank and then performed in each episode of *Army Wives*.

This incident is noteworthy not only for the role it plays in performing Army propaganda but also for the way in which it typifies Lifetime's rendering of female characters, interpersonal conflict, and narrative formulas: while as a soap *Army Wives* was ideal for producing banal militarism, it was also a boon to Lifetime, whose brand benefited from both its high ratings and simultaneous reinforcement and extension of its signature qualities (Lotz 2006). This fusion of propaganda and brand ensured that both the Lifetime network and *Army Wives* received a positive reception from a group of women prized mainly as consumers. Thus, among the program's many advertisements, for example, was a pitch for "Kraft, the *American* cheese" (emphasis in original). Another ad, for Outback Steakhouse, featured a female combat-helicopter pilot who explains how she thrives in her job and enjoys a meal at Outback after a tour of duty.

The consumer orientation is crucial to consider here, as securing this demographic group's eyeballs is vital to the continued success of Lifetime. The words of the former NBC Universal president and CEO Jeff Zucker reveal that the goal of women's programming for that network is to establish synergies among its subsidiary properties. Although he was talking about a different network, Zucker's assertion applies to Lifetime as well (particularly with NBC Universal's ownership stake in Lifetime): "When we go to market, we're selling young women and affluent women in a way that virtually no one else can when you look over our properties. We go to market with a suite of assets that is unmatched in the female demographic." The women being trafficked in this audience market are "upscale, educated . . . 'affluencers'" (Becker 2007), a group whose eyeballs Lifetime captured to the satisfaction of the Department of Defense.

Appealing to affluential consumers is central to Lifetime's programming decisions: as Bronstein demonstrates, Lifetime designs programs that "create profitable synergies among their divisions" and "generally follows programming practices that serve its corporate and advertisers' interests first" (1994–1995, 216, 234). In the case of *Army Wives* (and *Coming Home*), those sponsors include the Army and its multiplicity of sanctioned support organizations, Outback Steakhouse, USAA insurance, Lifetime's subsidiaries and sibling organizations, and the many advertisers that found the audience of *Army Wives* to be a loyal group of affluencers. And although Lifetime suggests that its fare is for all women, it, like most media corporations, has a narrow conception of the category: most of the women appearing in Lifetime programming continue to be "white, heterosexual, thin, young, and financially secure" (Bronstein 1994–1995, 234).

The Postpolitics of *Army Wives*

By constructing Fort Marshall as a world apart from vexing problems of geo- and identity politics, the program serves as an attractive venue for both airing promilitary sentiments and securing commercial sponsorship. To achieve its distance from what Kent Ono refers to as "icky historical abominations" (2010, 227), the program manages different oppressions by not invoking them (in the case of racism), by constituting them to suggest that they are mainly irrelevant and no longer require attention from the political movements historically associated with them (in the case of sexism and homophobia),[12] or by discrediting actions of those characters who hold explicit political positions (in the case of antiwar and Black Power activism). Postpolitics thus enables *Army Wives* to serve as a Pentagon public relations campaign to recruit women and girls while it counters criticism of the military and the wars in Iraq and Afghanistan. In this way, the program works much as Marouf Hasian believes the film *Zero Dark Thirty* does, which I have noted in the introduction to this book.

Like other Lifetime fare, *Army Wives'* featured protagonists are often "terrorized, abused, or threatened" (Hundley 2002, 180). To make it Army specific, the program integrates intertextually "real-life, ripped-from-the-headlines scenarios" (U.S. Army 2015, 62–63), political figures, and organizations and reconstitutes them as postpolitical. Intertextuality such as this offers one more means by which viewers can negotiate the meaning of military life throughout a tumultuous period for the wars in Afghanistan and Iraq. Over the course of the program's life, *Army Wives* addressed such issues as sexual assault (not, however, that perpetrated by Army personnel on other Army personnel), domestic violence, torture (enacted *on* Pamela Moran's Delta Force husband, Chase, but not *by* him or any other member of the military—an especially unrealistic scenario given the findings of the 2014 Senate torture report), suicide, sexual harassment, breast cancer and the pink-ribbon campaign, PTSD, Don't Ask Don't Tell (DADT), and child adoption by a lesbian couple.

Many of these intertextual activities are commercial in nature, a factor allowing cross-pollination between the military and *Army Wives'* corporate sponsors. This is an environment ideal for postpolitics, which typically privilege consumerism over political activism, and specifically for postfeminism: a "revision of feminism that encourages women's private, consumer lifestyles rather than cultivating a desire for public life and political activism" (Vavrus 2002, 2). Catherine Squires defines the "post-racial mystique" similarly, as a reduction of the "social and political aspirations" of the civil rights movement, "to consumer and individual choice [and] . . . market-oriented freedoms rather than a transformation of the society and common understandings of our humanity, our relations with each other, our responsibilities to each other, regardless of race, color, or creed" (2014, 15). The consumer orientation of postracial/postracist and postfeminist regimes of representation thus makes them ideal for Lifetime and the DoD, particularly as they combine to together produce a view of the military cleansed of the racism and sexism that, in reality, persist in both the military and the world in which it is situated.

Postfeminist Army

Although examples abound of *Army Wives'* "postfeminist sensibility" (Gill 2007, 254), I want to examine what I believe are the two most prevalent means by which it "posts" feminism: by personalizing systemic gender violence such as domestic abuse and rape and by rendering invisible the military's own epidemic of sexual violence, *Army Wives* deflects attention from patriarchal power and misogyny that legitimate and perpetuate such violence—and at a moment when the prevalence of domestic and sexual violence by military personnel was just coming to light. By the program's final season, newspapers, film, and Capitol Hill lawmakers were all publicizing the military's sexual assault problem; within *Army Wives'* mise-en-scène, however, the issue was conspicuously absent.

A soldier abusing his wife or another family member is the typical formula for writing domestic violence into *Army Wives* episodes. Such narrative arcs in *Army Wives'* seven seasons include Denise being abused by her son, Jeremy, and learning from Roxy how and why to fight back against him; Army wife Marilyn being abused and finally killed by her husband, who also kills Claudia Joy and Michael Holden's daughter Amanda when he blows up the popular Hump Bar; Pamela Moran (formerly a police officer) being stalked by a listener to her radio program; and in an episode featuring Wynonna Judd (which included a contest to win Wynonna prize packages), Army wife Marisol reveals that her husband is abusing her, prompting the wives to help her escape.

In response to these scenarios, *Army Wives* offers domestic-violence remedies that comprise fighting back by acquiring self-defense skills, jailing abusers, and contacting organizations that help domestic-violence survivors. All of these strategies are important for dealing with domestic violence, and all derive from feminist principles and activism. But the episodes that advance such remedies neither identify gender violence as an expression of patriarchal power nor challenge men to stop it. And although the program treats violence survivors sensitively, viewers should not "mistake concern for victims with the political will to change the conditions that led to their victimization in the first place" (J. Katz 2006, 6). Instead of shouldering women with the responsibility for remedying the violence they experience, Jackson Katz believes we must challenge "those aspects of male culture—especially male-peer culture—that provide active or tacit support for some men's abusive behavior" (2006, 7). Such a critique of patriarchal power is absent from the military's policies dealing with sexual assault, according to the documentary film *The Invisible War*, and it is unlikely to appear on Lifetime, which, since its beginning, has relied on "telefeminist programming formulae that defuse any basic structural challenges to patriarchy and its institutions," according to Meehan and Byars (2000, 34).

Refusal to confront "patriarchy and its institutions" occurs clearly in a story line spanning two episodes—"Safe Havens" and "Payback"—which features the attempted rape of Claudia Joy Holden by a family friend, the visiting Chilean diplomat Paolo Ruiz. Paolo holds the key to negotiating a lease on land that the Pentagon seeks in order to expand a strategically important Army post. Paolo explains to Michael Holden that Chile's president is reluctant to renew the lease, concerned that it might affect his popularity. But Paolo's wife, Maria, belongs to a family that owns the corporation providing goods to the Army for Fort Marshall's residents, and if Michael could influence the Pentagon in favor of Maria's company continuing to serve the post, then Paolo would be willing to push for an extension of the lease. Throughout "Safe Havens," Paolo works on Michael and his Pentagon contacts as he flirts overtly with Claudia Joy, exclaiming numerous times about her beauty. As the episode progresses, Paolo becomes increasingly daring and attempts to rape Claudia Joy on a sofa in the Holdens' home. When he finds her home alone, Paolo announces happily that his president has renewed the lease agreement; Paolo suggests they celebrate with the wine he has brought with him into the room. Claudia Joy declines to drink, then Paolo starts to attack her. As Paolo tears at her clothes, she struggles against him, eventually reaching around for the wine bottle beside the couch and breaking it over his head. The episode ends with a brief scene of a determined-looking Pamela at the shooting range, aiming her gun at the camera as she prepares to take on her stalker ("Safe Havens" 2009).

"Payback" begins with a sequence of Paolo lying unconscious on the floor, Claudia Joy calling the military police officers (MPs), and an ambulance taking Paolo away as Michael storms into the home and through the MPs stationed outside. When Claudia Joy tells Michael what has happened, he is incensed and tells her that he wants to prosecute. Cleaning up the broken glass and ice on the floor, Claudia Joy tells him, "It's over. Let it be over." She assures him that the attack did not go "far at all" and urges him to drop his pursuit of Paolo: in addition to Paolo being "connected" and having diplomatic immunity, she says, "We're in the middle of a very sensitive lease negotiation. We need them more than they need us. . . . The only punishment this bastard is going to get is a champagne bottle to the head." Michael protests to Claudia Joy that she should forgo such stoicism: "You're not a soldier!" "I became one the day I married you!" she shouts in return.

Michael's frustration grows as he realizes that the situation is untenable; he must satisfy the Pentagon—which has sent explicit instructions for him not to press charges and to attend the lease-signing ceremony, as per Paolo's mandate—yet he feels the need to avenge the attack on Claudia Joy. Deciding that he must act, Michael confronts Paolo in a dark, shadowy room at the jail where three MPs stand guard. Michael stands in front of the table where Paolo sits and casts a long shadow; Paolo, his head bandaged, calmly insists, "Michael, this is all a misunderstanding. Claudia Joy was being so friendly. It was a mistake." Michael corrects him: "It was an attack. On my wife." Invoking a pernicious rape myth, Paolo replies, "Sometimes signals are not what they seem. Occasionally no means something else." Michael walks toward Paolo, looking menacing as he shouts, "My wife!" Paolo pulls back, telling him, "Nothing happened. I got what I deserved. I will go home, confess to my wife, and get even worse. . . . Okay? You have my word." He also reports that his president would "like this kept quiet." Michael says, "And you just walk away, like nothing ever happened." Paolo returns with, "That's how it is sometimes in world politics." As he starts to walk away, Michael responds ominously, "Not in my world," as he stalks out of the room.

Further into "Payback," Pamela, Roxy, Claudia Joy, and Denise sit on Claudia Joy's porch discussing their various experiences being threatened and attacked. Claudia Joy ruminates on what would have happened if she had not been able to reach the champagne bottle: "I would not have been able to defend myself." Roxy reveals that she, too, had been attacked once: "Thank God he was drunk because that was the only way I got outta there. And I started kickboxing class the next day!" Pamela, a former police officer still dealing with a stalker who is becoming increasingly threatening, says, "Well, I know how to defend myself, and it doesn't always help. That's why I got a gun."

The last sequence of the episode's scenes starts with Claudia Joy trying to help a resistant Michael dress for the lease-signing ceremony. After Michael tells her that he does not want to go and give Paolo the benefit of seeing him there, Claudia Joy tells him, "Even generals have to take orders when they come from the Pentagon!" Michael follows this with an observation that she is still suffering, and Claudia Joy turns to face him: "Okay, you're right! I'm not okay! I'm mad as hell. I'm ashamed, and I didn't do anything wrong. But we can't let him know that! We can't give him the satisfaction of thinking what he did is going to change the way we live our lives. That's what he wants. That's what rape—even attempted rape—is about: power. I need you to go because I don't want him to hold any power over us. . . . The Army needs that land in San Pasqual, and they're not going to lose it because of what he did to me."

At the ceremony, Paolo signs the lease, surrounded by military and diplomatic staff; he tells the crowd what a happy day this is for relations between his country and the United States. Claudia Joy walks into the room as he is speaking, a move that visibly shakes him up. When Paolo moves to shake Michael's hand, Michael does so only after receiving a nod of approval from Claudia Joy. He stalks away from Paolo before Paolo can finish his sentence and meets Claudia Joy at the back of the room. She shoots Paolo a look of disdain and walks out, hand in hand with Michael. The story line concludes with Michael knocking on Paolo's hotel-room door and, when Paolo answers it, punching him in the nose. Paulo falls backward onto the floor with blood on his face, and Michael, jaw set, stalks away down the hallway.

In this episode, Claudia Joy, especially, provides a perspective on rape and domestic violence that gestures weakly toward second-wave feminism with her emphasis to Michael that rape is a means of exercising power over people who have done nothing to warrant it. Questions about where that power comes from and why some men exercise it whereas most do not are never answered, let alone asked. The wives' porch conversation reveals that threats of violence are common among women and that abuse can come from friends and family members; this, too, is an important insight resulting from feminist activism. But more pointed feminist analyses of gender violence—that it is almost always used by men to "dominate, punish, or degrade" victims (Benedict 1992, 15)—is absent from Claudia Joy's explanation. The only solutions on offer here are for a survivor to pretend as if the attack did not bother her, to become skilled at self-defense, or to own a gun. Although this story line would have been ideal as a vehicle for calling out and challenging the patriarchal system underpinning gender violence, it fails to do so; it neither illuminates the ways in which sexual violence has been used historically as a form of patriarchal oppression (Benedict 1992; Cuklanz 2000; J. Katz 2006; Meyers 1997; Nettleton 2011) nor explores the military's role in perpetuating and enabling such violence within its own ranks. Making such a critique would probably lose support of the DoD, which has proved ineffective at solving or even significantly curbing the epidemic of sexual assault plaguing every one of the military's branches.

As I discuss in chapter 4, sexual violence against service women[13] has been widespread since 2001 but was only sporadically documented in news reports before the release of *The Invisible War* (see, for example, Amy Herdy and Miles Moffeit's *Betrayal in the Ranks* [2004] or Helen Benedict's *The Lonely Soldier* [2009]). In 2010, Congress member Jane Harman noted provocatively that "a female soldier in Iraq is more likely to be raped by a fellow soldier than killed by enemy fire" (Gibbs 2010), but despite these attempts to publicize the problem, it was cloaked by radio silence. Across the few media accounts documenting sexual assault by troops on other troops, a clear pattern emerged: when women reported their attacks using military channels, the commanders to whom they reported typically responded by protecting the accused and dismissing or downplaying victims' claims. Such stories have been so widespread—across all branches of the military and from the top to the bottom of the military hierarchy—that they suggest the DoD was either unprepared to deal with the wave of service women who were deployed after September 11, 2001, or criminally negligent in dealing with sexual assault of military personnel (perhaps both).

Despite clear evidence of a persistent sexual assault problem throughout the military, the soldiers depicted in *Army Wives* experience no such assaults or even threats of such assaults. For survivors, their families, and friends, such a story line arguably would have enhanced the program's authenticity and verisimilitude; its absence speaks volumes about the DoD's position on military sexual assault. Claudia Joy's vague explanation to Michael that rape is about power neither identifies rape as a symptom of structural patriarchy nor implicates the Pentagon in enabling the continuation of military sexual assault. Claudia Joy's decision not to push for an investigation of Paolo (although she tells Michael, "he's probably been getting away with it for years") could serve as a cautionary tale for other survivors of military sexual assault deciding whether to report their assailants: better that your husband defends your honor than demand that the Army change.

This qualifies as an *Army Wives* pattern in that it identifies sexual and domestic violence as problems but then refuses to analyze the system that causes such violence to persist. (Research by both Marian Meyers [1997] and Pamela Hill Nettleton [2011] shows that such a pattern is typical of media coverage around domestic violence.) During season 1, Denise and Frank Sherwood's son, Jeremy, is abusing his mother by hitting her, and when she learns that he is continuing to do it, "even after Michael [Holden] talked to him," Claudia Joy tells Denise, "I don't know what to tell you . . . except that I'm here for you" ("Art of Separation" 2008). Nothing is wrong with supporting friends who are the victims of gender violence; likewise, nothing is wrong with Denise learning self-defense techniques so that she can fight back against future attacks or Roxy learning to kickbox or Pamela carrying a gun (although evidence shows that Pamela is more likely to be victimized with the gun than to be able to use it against her stalker [Gerney and Parsons 2014]). Absent solutions that go after causes rather than treat symptoms, *Army Wives* proves to be inadequate before the task of stopping gender violence; instead, it illustrates how a postfeminist approach to such violence may actually aid in its proliferation.

Postracial Army

In addition to being infused with a military-friendly, postfeminist sensibility, *Army Wives* portrays military life as postracial: devoid either of scenarios in which race is a salient category of identity or of instances of racial discrimination. This is particularly odd considering that Fort Marshall is located in South Carolina, where the Confederate flag—symbol of loyalty to antebellum institutions, including slavery—flew over the statehouse throughout the years when *Army Wives* was filmed.[14] As Ono asserts, postracism such as that in *Army Wives* is the "perfect elixir to help society forget about the icky historical abomination known as racism"; it "beckons its unknowing subjects to embrace and live within a mental habitus of preracial consciousness. . . . Postracism disavows history, overlaying it with an upbeat discourse about how things were never really that bad, are not so bad now, and are only getting better" (2010, 227). In a pithy affirmation of postracism, the Indian American South Carolina governor Nikki Haley remarked during a gubernatorial debate in 2014, "I can honestly say I have not had one conversation with a single CEO about the Confederate flag. . . . We really kind of fixed all that when you elected the first Indian-American female governor. . . . When we appointed the first African-American U.S. senator, that sent a huge message" (Edwards 2014). Haley saw no problem with the Confederate flag because her CEO informants did not; she thus endowed *them*—privileged white men, most likely—with the right to determine whether South Carolina should continue to fly it. Haley likewise shrugged off any suggestion that racism persists in South Carolina because the executive office was led by a woman of color and an African American man represented the state in the Senate. Haley's statement parallels what Ono has noted about media coverage of Barack Obama's presidency: "That a Black man became the president of the United States implies that past racial barriers to occupying that office are now gone. Racism is passé. Today, anything—even tremendous political and international power—is possible" (2010, 228).

Army Wives, to its credit, had a racially diverse cast across its seven seasons, especially the last two. For example, cast members of color play characters Joan and Roland Burton, who are intelligent and competent, wise and professionally ambitious; the Latino Hector and the African American Quincy are good soldiers, loyal to the military, if not always to their spouses; the African American lesbian Charlie is a compassionate leader of the Fort Marshall community center's youth programs; and the extras appearing in every episode suggest that today's Army is racially diverse. Beyond this, however, the program's portrayal of people of color consistently lacks any indication that they encounter racial discrimination either within the Army or without. On the contrary, *Army Wives* portrays the Army as a color-blind meritocracy in which qualified officers such as Joan Burton lead battalions with nary a hint of racial resentment from the white soldiers who are subordinate to them or racial discrimination from higher-ranking white officers. Such color blindness is a hallmark of post-racial discourses and is prevalent in the white ranks of the Army as well: for example, Jason Dempsey and Robert Shapiro's (2009) examination of racial and ethnic discrimination in the Army reveals that Hispanic and African American soldiers report they experience a great deal of discrimination but that it goes unnoticed among the mostly white officer corps.

Postracial mysticism appears, for example, in the depiction of Joan Burton as a more talented warrior-strategist than is her white male rival, Evan O'Connor (later found to be both dishonest and incompetent). Evan taunts Joan as they prepare to lead opposing teams in the annual war-games exercise at Fort Marshall, telling her, "I guess we're finally going to find out who the better man is." Joan remarks, demeaningly, that unlike her, Evan is a "pencil pusher": "Let me remind you, I've commanded more than a desk in my career. I know what it takes to lead in combat, and believe me, you don't have it." She leans in toward him and asserts, menacingly, "I'm gonna kick . . . your . . . ass" ("Onward Christian Soldier" 2009). This scene, Joan's winning performance during the subsequent war-games exercise, and numerous other episodes that showcase her intelligence and heroism construct Joan as an ideal Army officer whose race is never a consideration in whether others will respect her authority—she is a perfect embodiment of the postracial meritocracy that the Army wants viewers to believe that it is.

An additional technique that *Army Wives* uses to render race relations unproblematic is to cast the Army as a benevolent paterfamilias. For example, the successive episodes "Duty to Inform" and "Need to Know Basis" show the white Trevor LeBlanc embodying such qualities as he works with Joan Burton to recruit a promising African American high-school girl. This narrative arc begins after Joan assigns Trevor to be a recruiter—a position he is dubious about after being awarded a Silver Star medal. Trevor starts his new duties by trying to talk to members of a high-school track team training in the town square; he scares them away, but the next day, the African American Vanessa Jones returns to the recruiting office to see Trevor. Trevor asks her, "Have you thought about what you want to do after high school?" "Work, I guess," she replies. Trevor pushes her to consider the Army: "This is your time, Vanessa. You gotta make decisions for yourself. . . . The Army can give you choices you never thought you'd have." He invites her to candidate physical training (PT) sessions the next morning, which she reluctantly agrees to attend ("Duty to Inform" 2010).

The story continues in "Need to Know Basis" (2010), when Vanessa fails to appear at a PT session, even after excelling in the first one. Although Trevor is disappointed with Vanessa, instead he sells the Army to Martinez: an overweight, out-of-shape Latino man. Trevor encourages Martinez to continue to train. "There's a warrior inside you," Trevor insists. "You're just setting him free." After the PT session has ended, Trevor visits Vanessa's dilapidated home, where a rusting car sits in the front yard, falling apart. Vanessa's sister answers the door, explaining that she is Vanessa's legal guardian after their mother abandoned them. Reluctantly she tells Trevor where Vanessa works but warns him, "She don't have time for the Army. She needs to work!" She slams the door in Trevor's face as he thanks her for her time.

Trevor visits Vanessa at the burger joint / bowling alley where she works behind the counter. Angry, she tells him, "I got no time for playin' soldier, okay?" Trevor tells her, "We can work around your schedule. . . . And as far as money goes, once you sign up, the Army'll pay for your college." "College?" she asks incredulously. "How 'bout next month's electric?" Trevor continues undeterred, telling Vanessa about the signing bonus and concluding with, "I'm talking about your life, Vanessa." "What you know about my life, LeBlanc?" Vanessa rebuffs Trevor, telling him, "I got customers." Unsettled, he tells her, "If that's how you feel, I'm gonna need my [Army-issued PT] T-shirt back. . . . Yeah, that's government property, and if you're not going to enlist, I need it washed and folded and back on my desk by 1500 hours. Tomorrow." He walks away, angry that he has lost a promising recruit.

A subsequent scene sees Vanessa walk into the recruiting office and drop her T-shirt on Trevor's desk. "Okay—we done?" she asks. Trevor looks away and rifles through some papers as Joan Burton walks through the door, prompting everyone in the office to stand up and salute her. "I'm looking for prospect Vanessa Jones," she announces. "Here," Vanessa answers weakly. "I'm Lieutenant Colonel Joan Burton. Sergeant LeBlanc suggested we talk. Let's take a walk, okay?" As they walk, Vanessa asks, "People always stand up for you like that?" Joan replies, "Oh, yeah. I'm a lieutenant colonel. I'm in charge of fourteen hundred soldiers." Incredulous, Vanessa asks, "For real? And they gotta listen to you?" Joan laughs, "For real. They have to take orders from me." Joan compliments Vanessa on her sprinting time and tells her,

> You know, track was my way out of the South Side. . . . South Side of Chicago. Grew up in the projects, and my parents split when I was six. Raised myself more or less. In high school, most my friends were on their way to getting pregnant or in jail. Me too, . . . except for one thing: I was fast. So my track coach told me about an ROTC scholarship where I could go to college for four years and then do anything I want. He opened a door that I didn't know existed. I always dreamt about going to college but thought it was out of reach. . . . I guess I fell in love with the Army. Been around the world a couple of times, got married, had a baby all while serving my country. It's a great feeling. ("Need to Know Basis" 2010)

Vanessa tells Joan, "I don't have the grades to go to college. I'm barely gonna graduate from high school next month." Turning to face Vanessa, Joan says, "Look, Vanessa, you don't have to be me. But you do have to be you. And you have to choose. There's a world of possibilities past the end of your block. But you're gonna have to make this happen. Sergeant LeBlanc says you have everything it takes to be an outstanding soldier. You could start a whole new life for you." Vanessa, appearing bewildered, asks, "He said that about me?" Joan replies with a decisive, "He did," and hands Vanessa her business card: "My email's on there. Let me know how you do." Joan then gets into a waiting car, door opened by her driver. Vanessa looks down at the card and up at Joan, waving as the car drives away, music swelling to end the scene. The story line ends with Trevor walking into Joan's office, where he tells her, "Prospect Jones is on board, ma'am. . . . I'm not sure what you said to her, but she brought her papers in right away." Joan looks at him admiringly: "So your first recruit. That's a big one. How does that feel?" Trevor replies, "It feels really good. I think I'm helping this girl to change her life." Joan affirms him: "Hmmm—that's pretty powerful stuff. . . . Now you have a responsibility, Sergeant. See her through" ("Need to Know Basis" 2010).

Although this one is far from the only narrative arc that showcases *Army Wives'* postracial politics, it is particularly illustrative of how easily postracialism can be woven into militainment. Throughout the scenes that this story line comprises are overt statements of the many benefits of the Army: health benefits for the enlistee and all dependents, college tuition coverage through the GI Bill, a path out of poverty, and so forth, all expressed through a paternalistic narrative of a white man shepherding a poor African American girl through the enlistment process. *Army Wives* recognizes no structural barriers to racial equality, for example, erasing any suggestion that Vanessa's or Joan's childhood poverty could have roots in racist housing and education policies or race-based wage discrimination. Instead, the poverty conditions of each are attributed to their respective parents' abandonment, thus allowing the Army to step in and act as paternal substitute. And what a generous parent it is, causing Joan to fall in love with it and presenting Vanessa with a means to live out the American Dream.

• • •

Lifetime has made *Army Wives* crucial to solidifying its brand and maintaining its profitable connection to the military-industrial complex. Extending Lifetime's brand with *Army Wives'* and *Coming Home's* feminized militainment also allows the Army (and perhaps other branches of the military) to make inroads with women, thus far a leery group of potential recruits. Whether as mothers or future recruits themselves, women and girls do not flock to the military the way men and boys have (Enloe 2000). Finessing the genres that make up this hybrid program, *Army Wives* opens up the relatively unknown world of military life to civilians and situates it within Lifetime's woman-attracting dramatic form—one proving to be financially successful almost since its inception. This wedding benefits both the Army and Lifetime, as each exploits women for its own purposes.

Robin Andersen notes in her analysis of gender in news coverage of the Iraq War that "gendered conventions used to tell the stories of war make war acceptable to the public while they reinforce a society based on gender inequality and the violence that promotes war" (2005, 370). Although she is referring specifically to news stories, the same can be said of *Army Wives* and its treatment of the (mostly) women who provide support for deployed soldiers and officers; it is thus an ideal vehicle for the diffusion of banal militarism through feminized militainment. The core cast of *Army Wives* never questions war or violence—even when ample opportunities, such as the death of a husband or son, arise to do so. And while *Army Wives* touches weekly on difficult subjects, such as injured soldiers' painkiller addictions and marital infidelity among spouses separated by war, it also makes the larger context for these problems glaringly absent.[15] Neither soldier nor spouse ever voices doubts about the military mission in Iraq or about the deprivation that the branches of the military—and their stateside families—experience. This is despite news coverage of these very subjects (see, for example, Dana Priest and Anne V. Hull's Pulitzer Prize–winning *Washington Post* series from 2007 on the horrific conditions experienced by wounded soldiers recovering in the Walter Reed Army Hospital) and of alternatives to war espoused by some military family groups, such as Military Families Speak Out. Noteworthy, I believe, is Amanda Holden (the high-school-age daughter of Fort Marshall's then second in command, Michael Holden), the one character on *Army Wives* who voices opposition to the war and even participates in a peace rally but who dies when a serviceman suicide bomber attacks a bar near Fort Marshall in order to kill his wife, at the end of the first season.

As I have presented in this chapter, numerous episodes of *Army Wives* feature characters mouthing the mantra that the Army's missions in Iraq and Afghanistan are "keeping us safe at home." Thus, anything the wives and Roland do must be considered in light of the sacrifices that their soldier-spouses make while deployed. Marital fidelity is one such crucible, and it is on that all judgments of fellow Army spouses are based. When Denise and Frank separate during season 2 and Denise has a romantic relationship with one of her former patients, it is not the professional breach of ethics that her friends are concerned with; it is her infidelity to Frank (or, as Roxy puts it, her "cheatin' on her husband"). According to Biank's book and the program, soldiers believe that a stateside spouse's infidelity is the worst possible affront to a deployed spouse. This message is conveyed repeatedly from Lifetime to

Army Wives viewers, too, perhaps to solidify additional support for its marriage to the military-industrial complex.

Lifetime's rendering of *Army Wives* is also a sales pitch, selling military life and endless war via soap opera to the wary public and marrying off Lifetime's "affluencers" to this complex. Although this arrangement confers numerous benefits to Lifetime's brand, its corporate partners, and Operation Homefront, for example, benefits accruing to military spouses are unclear at best. The idea that Army wives should quietly acquiesce to whatever the Army requires of their spouses and families is problematic at every level: although military personnel are expected to follow the orders of their superior officers, this is not required of civilians, nor should it be if robust discussions about the military are to be had.[16] As the Military Families Speak Out website reveals, military-family dissenters do exist, and they take issue with the wars in Iraq and Afghanistan and with being silenced. They also have a different idea of how to support the troops: pull them out of war zones and bring them home. Unfortunately, *Army Wives*' object lessons for military families, especially wives, encourage the continuation of this political suppression—even embedding it into the unwritten code of marriage. *Army Wives*, in its use of extratextual elements such as brick-and-mortar political figures, events, and settings, surely contributes to public understandings of military family life—particularly because treatments of this topic are virtually absent from other popular media.

Attempts such as this one to fix the meaning of media representations' objects illuminate the power inherent in the process. Stuart Hall reminds us that even regimes of representation that become dominant—such as that which assigned negative meaning to the military pre–*Army Wives*—can be intervened into and altered, if the intervention "locates itself *within* the complexities and ambivalences of representation itself, and tries to *contest it from within*" (2001, 342, italics in original). As I have shown, *Army Wives* works as just such a strategy for contesting negative views of the military with a serial drama that locates itself amid the "complexities and ambivalences" of military discourses, foregrounding the personal lives of military personnel and their families and resolving problems they encounter with a mixture of social support, military benefits, and instruction in self-care (particularly self-defense). Through *Army Wives*' dual marriages, the putatively prowoman Lifetime network encourages women's capitulation and fidelity to the Army and to the media-military-industrial complex: a union that gives new meaning to the term "shotgun wedding" and probably has President Eisenhower turning in his grave. Although *Army Wives* received its marching orders in 2013, by then it had done the work for which it had been tasked by Lifetime and the Department of Defense: personalize the military, portray the Army sympathetically, and do it all with love.

2

Counterintuitive Mothering in the Media-Military-Industrial Complex

> Don't burn bridges because you never know when you'll run into that annoying soccer mom again somewhere down the road.
> —Sheryl Garrett and Sue Hoppin,
> *A Family's Guide to the Military for Dummies* (2009)

Although not intended for the topic of this book, the tip for military mothers in the epigraph works as an allegory for the evolving meanings concerning mothers and war found in media culture, a continuation of a discursive project to militarize mothers by strengthening their articulation to the MMIC. In this context, peace-loving Soccer Moms are recast as supporters of war and Bush-era security measures. Just as *Army Wives'* representations of military marriage and family life were influenced by the Lifetime Network's strategic alliances with the Army and allied military organizations, news representations of mothers associated in one way or another with the military are not simple reflections. Rather, they too have been shaped by organizations invested in articulating particular meanings to martial motherhood. In concert with

PR discourses, newspaper, TV news, and NPR stories situate mothers in the military-industrial complex by constructing performances of motherhood that align with prowar, promilitary propaganda and, in the first decade of the twenty-first century, specifically with claims that patriotism equated to support of President Bush; that waging war in Afghanistan and Iraq would keep the United States safe from terrorism; that U.S. troops were winning the hearts and minds of Afghans and Iraqis by "doing good"; and that protesting the Bush administration's wars dishonored service-member children and was simply unpatriotic. These discursive performances in news media worked together, I argue, to produce a post-9/11 regime of truth around motherhood that effectively militarized mothers by featuring, to the virtual exclusion of others, mothers whose words and actions aligned with propaganda about war and the military circulating in public discourse throughout most of the early years—2004 to 2008—of this fifteen-year (and counting) period of war reporting.

The mothers in the news-media representations that I examine in this chapter are either those with an official connection to the military—military mothers, whose children are in the service—or those with an unofficial, but supportive, relationship to the military and to war, so-called Security Moms. Cynthia Enloe observes that "the more militarization transforms an individual or a society, the more that individual or society comes to imagine military needs and militaristic presumptions to be not only valuable but also normal" (2000, 3). Mothers who dominate this news coverage work to normalize such militarism by articulating specific Bush-era characteristics of it to maternal love and pride using the war- and military-rationalizing language emanating from the George W. Bush administration. Marshaling maternal support for war and the military has historically been a difficult task for governments attempting to garner the troops needed to wage war; this is especially so with the all-volunteer force. And wherever military conscription is absent, Enloe explains, a state "attempting to fill its military's ranks" must focus its "energy and resources in trying to shape . . . citizens' ideas about what constitutes an acceptable form of masculinity and an acceptable form of femininity" (2000, 236). A successful recruiting strategy thus requires the state to win over and maintain "at least the passive cooperation of women who are the mothers" of potential recruits. Thus, the "militarization of mothers—and the very idea of motherhood—has been crucial for any successful manpower [sic] formula" (237) for the military. After 9/11, U.S. civilian news media have played an important role in militarizing mothers as well as the "very idea of motherhood"—a continuation of a political and cultural project under way since the 1991 Persian Gulf War and part of an attempt at a (representational) regime change that transforms putatively peaceful Soccer Moms into militarized mothers. As I explained in chapter 1, the Pentagon mandates through its

ELOs that its supported media projects recruit as well as entertain. Although I work with news and not entertainment media in this chapter, my analysis suggests that the reporters and editors who create stories about mothering in this context operate with a similar mission to valorize militarized mothers and obscure or even discredit those who either challenge the military's recruitment of children or oppose war.

News and entertainment accounts of recent wars that the United States has waged—in the Persian Gulf (1991) and those in Afghanistan and Iraq—have included mothers who were vocally supportive of these wars and their aims. Such maternal enthusiasm for war represents a dramatic shift from the 1970s and '80s, when U.S. mothers and other women worked en masse as antinuclear activists, fighting to prevent nuclear war and the proliferation of nuclear weapons that marked the later decades of the Cold War (for examples, see Managhan 2012). The Cold War's end brought about major changes in both international and domestic politics, in part through optimistic rhetoric about the "peace dividend" and the transformation of swords into plowshares. But just as activists were pushing their governments to make a peaceful transition to a post–Cold War world, in the summer of 1990, the United States was leading a small coalition of countries to war with Iraq, whose troops threatened to invade Kuwait (the eventual invasion of Kuwait was described in various media outlets as "the rape of Kuwait"). In January 1991, U.S. bombing of Iraq began, and by the end of February, it had ended: Iraq had been pushed out of Kuwait, back into borders that were subsequently governed by a regime loaded down with U.S.-imposed economic sanctions.

Although the Gulf War was short-lived relative to the two U.S.-initiated wars that came after it, it was significant for many reasons; not the least of these was how news media played a willing role in circulating propaganda produced by PR firms to mobilize support for a war between countries on the other side of the world, whose value to the United States was not immediately apparent to many people. Numerous scholars have analyzed the campaign's components, including the "rape of Kuwait" slogan that served to justify defending a feminized Kuwait, along with the use of yellow ribbons tied to trees, lampposts, and other public spots, which was meant to show support for the troops (e.g., Jeffords 1991b; Kellner 1992). Roger Stahl's genealogy of the yellow ribbon reveals that since the Gulf War, its use in a martial context evokes its history as a feminine symbol of chastity—a marker for "feminized territory." Sporting yellow-beribboned landscapes, the United States during the Gulf War was thus clearly gendered "as docile, domesticated, and feminized." A public relations triumph of the image, the yellow ribbon campaign also accomplished another, more substantial goal: "Winning the home front battle in this sense means politically disarming and domesticating the citizen, which means defining the citizen's rightful place not in public life but rather in supportive role under a strict presidential father figure. The yellow ribbon is the totem of this transformation" (Stahl 2009, 545).

Following Stahl, Tina Managhan argues further that the yellow ribbon campaign's specific appeals to women that they festoon public spaces with the ribbons, teach grade-school students about the war using PR talking points endorsed by the DoD, and incorporate into their informal conversations these same talking points also refigured women's "distinctive perspective as mothers and caretakers . . . that tends to situate women at odds with the military state" (2012, 75). These actions, Managhan claims, "effectively collapsed the pre-war gender gap in women's support for the war" (75) and showed that women could effectively perpetuate the "myth of national community unified at a time of war" (77). Through these actions, women thus actively contributed to remilitarizing the United States and challenged a deeply rooted, historically enduring belief that women, and especially mothers, owing to their essential, peace-loving natures, universally oppose war and its ensuing violence.

Managhan concludes, therefore, that "unlike the antinuclear protesters who left their families and protested against the military state in an attempt to ensure their children's future and the safety of the world," during the Gulf War, "*reasonable* mothers could work with the military to further their own ends" (2012, 101, italics in original). This construction of a peacemaker turned reasonable, war-supporting mother was central to Gulf War propaganda, for, within its "predominant discursive frames," "the military arm of the sovereign American state was being employed in the service of biopolitical aims—in the service of life—and not just American life; it was being employed in the service of collective security as part of a move away from Cold War politics towards a new world order" (Managhan 2012, 101).

My reading accords with Managhan's but extends into the post-9/11 militaristic regime of representation that I examine throughout this book. I argue that through supporting activities that underwrite war and support the military, news representations of militarized motherhood further banalize militarism and instruct women on how to perform what one news anchor calls "counterintuitive" mothering (ABC 2007): a practice that entails negotiating the stark life-and-death contradictions that structure this martial context of life. After 9/11, discourses emanating from news media, DoD marketing programs, and public relations campaigns using Astroturf,[1] think tanks, and front groups together constitute the martial maternal subjectivity of Security Moms and military mothers by endowing these maternal subjects with bellicose, propaganda-reinforcing attributes to the virtual exclusion of other, more peaceful, qualities. The resulting regime of representation markets militarism to and through mothers by providing instruction on how they can navigate the paradoxes of biopower in a context in which maternal power over life meets the violence, injury, and even death incurred by militarism.

Because news and DoD discourses must acknowledge the negative aspects of warfare and the military, they include a few mothers who express war-related concerns for their children or themselves. At times, their voices are poignant, betraying sadness, fearfulness, and anguish; but even these are limited to a constrained range of affect. News stories include very few angry mothers, for example, and when they do appear, their fury is defused with counterpronouncements made by mothers whose feelings comport with historically specific conventions of war reporting—an indication that maternal anger equates to a lack of patriotism or disrespect for their service-member children. Even those accounts that treated the war critic Cindy Sheehan with a modicum of sympathy failed to critique the military or the Pentagon and instead focused on refuting Sheehan's criticism of the Bush administration's rationale for going to war with Iraq. Those few stories that included criticism of the military strategy in Iraq and Afghanistan failed to substantively challenge militarism or war making in these countries.

Discursive management of popular sentiment for the 1991 Persian Gulf War serves as a propaganda boilerplate starting in late 2001, when the second Bush administration began laying the groundwork for invading Iraq. Similar to Managhan's reading of Gulf War mothers' discursive constitution, my analysis shows that post-9/11 mothers participate in, reinforce, and legitimate the military's biopower by influencing the constitution of meanings around war and "security." When mothers—who have historically been entrusted with the reproduction and care of human life—can be literally and figuratively enlisted to undertake the activities that war entails, they provide moral cover for the violence, death, and destruction caused by war (Stabile 1994, 126). News representations of martial motherhood thus make a difference in how the public regards the military and the wars in Afghanistan and Iraq themselves, just as Managhan shows they did in the Persian Gulf War. Casting the military as paterfamilias (in this case, ruling over military families and security-minded mothers), the news representations that I examine reveal scattered ambivalence about both the Afghanistan and Iraq wars and what responsibility the military has for these martial mothers. Overall, however, these accounts constitute motherhood such that any mother can find a place in the MMIC.[2]

A combination of civilian news stories and military marketing and PR discourses constitutes two maternal subjects by emphasizing them in news coverage of mothers during this time, disciplining those whose behaviors exceed the discursive bounds constraining them (and therefore violating norms of cultural propriety governing martial motherhood), and situating them vis-à-vis the military and the wars in Iraq and Afghanistan. In so doing, these discourses ascribe to mothers a selective set of martial meanings.

Tracking discourses about mothers between September 11, 2001, and December 2015 reveals the moments when these mothers' stories are told and the formulae used to tell them. For example, news stories about military and soldier mothers tend to appear around Mother's Day, Veterans Day, and Memorial Day in accounts that superficially convey gratitude for the sacrifices they have made. There are exceptions, of course. Stories such as those about Cindy Sheehan—the mother of Army Specialist Casey Sheehan, killed in Iraq in 2004—publicly protesting the war are not holiday bound. But perhaps not surprisingly, quantity does not equate to quality of representations: in-depth coverage of the lives and feelings of military mothers is in short supply in this regime of representation. On the other hand, the concerns, feelings, and politics of another group of mothers—Security Moms—proliferated in news discourse between 2004 and 2008. As I explain in the following section, Security Moms serve a clear purpose in the MMIC: their creator think tank constructed and deployed them to influence voters, women in particular, to support the election of George W. Bush in 2004, conservative congressional candidates in the midterm elections in 2006, and Senator John McCain for president in 2008. Their constitution as antinomic to Soccer Moms works to make their maternity appear to be the reasonable choice for mothers facing what media present as unrelenting and frightening threats from terrorism.

Securing Mothers in a Post-9/11 World

Soon after the United States had begun its preemptive war on Iraq and then President Bush had declared "Mission Accomplished," and amid a massive pro-paganda campaign to convince the public of the involvement of Iraq's Saddam Hussein in the events of September 11, 2001 (McLaren and Martin 2004, 288), the Security Mom[3] debuted in news narratives covering women's electoral preferences. Much like the Soccer Moms of preceding campaigns, Security Moms emerged during a presidential campaign season—in this case during the 2004 contest between George W. Bush and John Kerry—ostensibly as a swing voting bloc (e.g., see Tumulty and Novak 2003). But unlike the more peaceful Soccer Moms, Security Moms functioned to legitimate both right-wing military policy and a patriarchal gender dynamic prevalent in public discourse after the September 11 attacks (Enloe 2007; Faludi 2007). News stories from this time constructed Security Moms as being desperate for protection, especially that offered by a strong patriarchal figure such as George W. Bush, whom Security Moms in these stories claimed to trust completely. In their performance of Bush administration propaganda about the War on Terror, Security Moms' discursive constitution encouraged adherence to a historically specific, post-9/11 security regime, their fearfulness providing a rationale for heightened state surveillance and the incorporation of surveillance and security technologies into their domestic lives (Grewal 2006; Hay 2006).

Media institutions in the United States continually produce labels such as "Security Mom" for human behaviors, compressing layers of complex and often-contradictory practices into catchphrases: think "Mean Girls" or "Generation X," for example. Instead of taking these labels at face value, I posit that the gendered life practices captured in these phrases and then circulated throughout the media in both news and entertainment are more significant than their lighthearted media treatment would suggest. As the Security Mom construction circulates through media windows, for example, its meanings become increasingly multilayered and valuable for political institutions, political parties, polling organizations, media corporations, and the public relations and marketing industries. Appearing after 9/11, Security Moms fit together with military mothers in a regime of representation that ascribed meaning to and offered instruction in performing a martial motherhood that aligned with Bush administration propaganda about both the wars in Iraq and Afghanistan and the necessity for increased security measures within the borders of the United States.

Following Lana Rakow, who argues for the value of analyzing identity, I too challenge "the notion of identity as a stable and unvarying natural category without political or material consequences" (2010, 139). She cites the "rising incidences of hatred and threatened violence in response to [Barack] Obama's election"—a stark illustration that the "politics of gender, race, and class are far from over." In this example alone, it is "possible to see the contested and arbitrary nature of identity categories, as well as what is at stake in the process to define and enforce them" (139). Along with military mothers, the discursive construction of Security Moms occurs as a result of converging efforts by powerful and resource-rich organizations that stand to gain when their constructions are perceived as *prescriptive* as well as *descriptive*. I concur with Fred Fejes, who observes that, "updating Foucault, it would seem that today the consumer-based media, and not the state, the church, or the scientific professions, are the far more effective creators and regulators of identities and desires" (2001, 207). When these media work in concert with the DoD and other military organizations, they create an even more effective system for producing and disciplining identities that advance the agendas of the MMIC's constituent industries.

Such identities that come in and out of vogue in mainstream news media tell important stories about both the media and the political interests that influence their content. Since the 1990s, U.S. news media have popularized groups of women and men whose identities supposedly cohere around particular practices: Soccer Moms and NASCAR Dads, for example. Patterns of representations that have constituted and politicized the meanings of Security Moms and military mothers encouraged gendered conduct that buttressed the specific military and foreign policy agendas of the Bush White House after September 11, 2001.

As a media-generated identity, the Security Mom is productive of a lifestyle used to sell a militaristic politics of motherhood in much the same way as consumer products are marketed. It thus aims to govern private as well as public conduct by appealing to women's desires to exercise political agency by choosing a politics that will best serve their family's interests. But the politics that Security Moms practice did not emerge organically from average women's everyday practices; instead these moms were produced as part of an Astroturf campaign attempting to militarize maternity, to advance the agenda of the Bush White House, and to remedy the gender gap plaguing Republican voters at that time.

Representations of the Security Mom lifestyle emerge from interactions between numerous institutions: news organizations, TV networks, advertisers and marketers, think tanks, and political parties, all of which contribute to a discursive exhortation that mothers choose the Republican Party and thus nurture both family and national security. Such appeals are not at all accidental; rather, as Nikolas Rose reveals, "it is the expertise of market research, of promotion and communication, underpinned by the knowledge and techniques of subjectivity, that provides the relays through which the aspirations of ministers, the ambitions of business, and the dreams of consumers achieve mutual translatability" (1996, 162). The Security Mom embodies one such relay, aligning neatly with the ministerial aspirations of the post-9/11 Bush White House, the Departments of Defense and Homeland Security, and the business ambitions of corporate news-media outlets perpetually in search of affluent demographic groups to which to pitch their narratives and, most importantly, their sponsors' wares (Bagdikian 2004; McChesney 2008). As I demonstrate later in this chapter, news media constitute Security Moms as subjects whose political affiliations wax and wane as domestic and geopolitical conditions change around them. During the peace-dividend years of Bill Clinton's presidency, news stories about Democratic, liberal Soccer Moms abounded. After 9/11, news reports shifted to referring to Security Moms, whom they cast as safety-obsessed Republicans (some newly so, having just abandoned the Democrats), voting to protect themselves and their families from terrorists. Even after the campaign to militarize mothers had subsided, vestiges of Security Moms remained in public discourse, embodied by Sarah Palin and her "Mama Grizzly" supporters such as the former GOP Congress member Michele Bachmann.

As a generic modifier, the term "security" denotes safety and comfort. Its use after September 11, 2001, however, references a construct that is discursively articulated to all of those practices falling under the sign of the Global War on Terror (GWOT) begun by the Bush administration (some continued under the Obama administration, while new ones are being added by Trump's administration): wiretapping, internet and other digital surveillance, no-fly lists, preemptive war, and a heightened militarization of society, among others (McLaren and Martin 2004; Grewal 2006). News media constitute Security Moms to legitimate these measures, and by referencing their former incarnation as liberal Soccer Moms, they instruct other concerned mothers on how and why they must recalibrate their politics, too. In so doing, news discourses justify patriarchal masculinity, sanctioning it as acceptable—even necessary— to make home and the homeland safe from external threats.

Time magazine's coverage offered Security Moms their most visible debut. "Goodbye, Soccer Mom. Hello, Security Mom," the June 2, 2003, cover headline trumpets, as the story inside claims that the Soccer Mom has "morphed into Security Mom" (Tumulty and Novak 2003). *Time*'s initial narrative sets the tone for subsequent treatments of Security Moms and hews to the same formula and style of expression: using passive voice, reporters disavow any responsibility they or other journalists have for constructing and propagating the identity, while they simultaneously endow it with specific traits, often relying on only the slimmest—or no—evidence to do so. "Swing voters have always been elusive creatures, changing shape from election to election. The profile and assumptions about them in one contest seldom apply to the next one. This axiom is proving true again with that most-talked-about slice of American political demography: the Soccer Mom. Since 9/11, polls suggest she has morphed into Security Mom—and that development is frightening to Democrats, who have come to count on women to win elections" (Tumulty and Novak 2003). Even while reporters Karen Tumulty and Viveca Novak claim no responsibility for the emergence of this new bloc, they personify it and ascribe political qualities to its members.

> She used to say she would never allow a gun in her house, but now she feels better if her airline pilot has one. She wanted a nuclear freeze in the 1980s and was a deficit hawk in the 1990s, but she now believes the Pentagon should have whatever it wants. Her civil liberties seem less important than they used to, especially compared with keeping her children safe. She's someone, in short, like Debbie Creighton, a 34-year-old Santee, Calif., mother of two who voted for Bill Clinton twice and used to choose the candidates who were most liberal on abortion and welfare. "Since 9/11," Creighton says, "all I want in a President is a person who is strong." (Tumulty and Novak 2003)

When media texts yoke "mom" to "security" during this tumultuous time in the United States, we should consider the historical and ideological uses of both terms. Here "mom" refers to a traditional, patriarchal mothering practice: one ceding responsibility for her safety and that of her family to a strong, male figure—President Bush—in the interest of domestic security (for a book-length analysis of the resurgence of intensely patriarchal protection narratives circulating since September 11, 2001, see Faludi 2007). In the context of these political news stories, "mom" naturalizes family and domestic caretaking responsibilities as those properly belonging to women, whose parental fears and concerns after the September 11 attacks are adroitly exploited in this discursive regime.

The conservative media commentator Michelle Malkin's inflammatory manifesto in *USA Today* several days before the Democratic Party's national convention in July 2004 fleshes out the Security Mom further: "I am what this year's election pollsters call a 'security mom.' I'm married with two young children. I own a gun. And I vote. Nothing matters more to me right now than the safety of my home and the survival of my homeland. I believe in the right to defend myself, and in America's right to defend itself against its enemies. I am a citizen of the United States, not the United Nations. . . . What I want is a commander in chief who will stop pandering to political correctness and *People* magazine editors, and start pandering to me" (2004, 11A). Reporters complied with Malkin's demand to seek out more Security Moms, who granted interviews to television programs, print media outlets, and radio news shows throughout the 2004 campaign season, their votes sought by Democrats and Republicans alike. Although Malkin's extreme-right political position was not the only one these Security Moms held, in television news stories it dominated and defined these mothers as more of them voiced that position than any other (Malkin is, by her own account, a Soccer Mom too [Grewal 2006, 32]). Together, Malkin's op-ed and reporters reproduced the common-sense view that, en masse, these women have moved rightward on the political spectrum after the 9/11 attacks disrupted their halcyon days as peace-loving Democrats who could simply enjoy their children's soccer games without fear.

Security Moms' nurturance was thoroughly steeped in militarism and prowar sentiment, despite the inconvenient fact that by 2004 U.S. voters were expressing increasing dissatisfaction with the Iraq War, particularly its apparent endlessness and ever-increasing casualty count (Harris and Muste 2004, A4). Security Moms were therefore useful for legitimating unpopular Bush administration war policies among mothers who had historically supported Democratic—or Republican—presidential candidates (since the 1980s, this gender gap has afflicted Republican candidates; the 2004 election was no different [Center for American Women and Politics 2004]). By fusing maternal nurturance with the public and private practices of the post-9/11 security apparatus in the United States, and clearly expressing the belief that only George W. Bush could keep them and their families safe, Security Moms accomplished a public relations feat by creating the impression of wide maternal support for the Bush administration.

My use of "public relations" here is meant to acknowledge the Astroturf campaign that produced Security Moms and thus created the illusion of popular support for policies that, at the time the construction emerged, had become deeply unpopular among the U.S. public. The media source-monitoring organization Center for Media and Democracy and the Institute for Policy Studies reveal that a group called Family Security Matters (FSM) created and then spun Security Moms through a variety of media windows. FSM is a front group for the Center for Security Policy, a "hawkish security policy and think tank and advocacy group" that advocates U.S. military interventions as a means of achieving stability in the Middle East (Source Watch 2008). Soon after it was formed, FSM "claimed to represent 'security moms'" and acted to "communicate to American women what we need to know" (Source Watch 2008). It is noteworthy that at this time the founder of FSM and its chief spokesperson, Carol Taber, was also on the board of the Independent Women's Forum, or IWF (Right Web 2012).[4] Another spokesperson for the group, Gay Bryant, describes FSM as a "non-profit, non-partisan communications initiative formed by a group of passionate women." Their role, she continues, is to "build grassroots efforts and resources for making the Security Moms voice heard in the White House and on Capitol Hill" (Source Watch 2008). Thus, whereas Security Mom's male counterpart, NASCAR Dad, was both ideological and commercial (see Vavrus 2007), Security Mom's identity became less a site for showcasing consumer commodities than a pitch for mothers to embrace Bush administration policies, politics, and propaganda—decidedly difficult to sell to voters who were otherwise disinclined to support military expenditures and militarization.

Embodied by Debbie Creighton, among others, Security Moms also modeled a feminist politics disarticulated from progressive second-wave goals of dismantling patriarchal laws and practices and rearticulated to a markedly patriarchal and militaristic ideology. Because Security Moms were liberal in their Soccer Mom incarnation, they lent credence to the notion that feminism and liberal positions on issues were impractical and even dangerous after September 11, 2001. Ironically, the programs that allowed girls and women to play soccer and other sports in public educational institutions came about, as Inderpal Grewal points out, only because of successful feminist agitating to pass Title IX; this resulted in "a huge influx of girls and women into recreational activities as well as increased school and college athletic opportunities for them" (2006, 33). Such an erasure of a movement's political roots is a classically postfeminist denial of the important of feminism in women's lives today, as is the accompanying expressed desire to be led by a "strong" and patriarchal male figure.

Not surprisingly given Security Moms' hawkish think-tank origins, they were referred to by news media as "target demographics," described as mainly white, mostly Republican, eighteen to forty-nine years old, fiercely protective mothers living in traditional, nuclear-family households. Although a few Democratic and undecided Security Moms appeared in news stories, they were far outnumbered by Republican women. In describing Security Moms, broadcast and cable news programs ascribed these qualities to them: "More than any single issue, security has defined that battle for women voters and has created a new swing group, the security mom" (NBC 2004a); "concern about terrorism and the safety of their young families has turned these soccer moms into security moms" (CNN 2004). Security Moms, moreover, understand that "during crises . . . mommy issues often take a backseat to security" (Fox News Channel 2003). "The women who are worried about the war in Iraq are worried about the safety of their own families. And they accept the idea that we are fighting over there to protect ourselves over here" (NBC 2004a). They are "voting this year not only for a president but for peace of mind" (NBC 2004d). On Fox News, FSM's Carol Taber defines Security Moms "both demographically and psychographically. Demographically she's a woman with children in the household. . . . Psychographically, when they go to the polls, they have the A-number-one concern, the safety and security of their children, and they're going to be voting on this issue" (Fox New Channel 2004). Terms that are most commonly found in marketing research, "demographic" and "psychographic" suggest that the Security Mom's greatest value lay in her ability to market a politics to both women and news-media outlets: one that reproduced and reinforced Bush administration claims about war and homeland security and recapitulated planks in the 2004 Republican platform.[5]

On this same program, Taber reported that her organization's focus groups with undecided female voters revealed that the security of their families was their "A-number-one concern." Further, "President Bush scores very well here because they really do see him as a strong and resolute leader. But they don't see the same thing in John Kerry. . . . Some women said about Mr. Kerry, 'I don't trust him.' Some said, 'I don't know what it is about him; I just don't like him.' Some women said he looked sneaky. . . . Some women said he's too rich to be president. . . . They saw President Bush . . . as very strong, very consistent, and a defender of America and American families" (Fox News Channel 2004). Throughout news coverage of Security Moms, commentators claimed that President Bush was the most trust-inspiring presidential candidate and stood in stark contrast to John Kerry, whom they cast under a cloud of suspicion. President Bush's benevolent patriarchy thus comes to appear both inevitable and desirable for women to embrace. One Security Mom with a military husband, for example, told CNN that she believed President Bush was the candidate who would do the right thing for the armed forces. "In my heart, I know that President Bush is looking out for these guys. I mean, in his heart he's doing what he thinks is best," she told CNN (2004). Although not referring specifically to Security Moms, Enloe aptly explains the phenomenon voiced by these women: "It is much easier to claim the authority to speak for others if one can claim to be The Protector; it is much easier to be silenced and to accept that silencing if one absorbs the self-identity of The Protected" (2007, 60). Although these Security Moms were not literally silent, they ceded their right to vocalize criticism when they capitulated to the paternalism of President Bush, who by then had accumulated a long record of intolerance to criticism of his administration (McLaren and Martin 2004).

Security Mom discourses constructed George W. Bush as The Protector and Good Father, the preferred alternative to John Kerry's effete elitism. But by also mixing incestuous metaphors and using language such as "wooing" and "courting," the same discourses presented both Bush *and* Kerry as suitors pursuing Security Moms as if they were potential romantic partners. For example, one Fox correspondent exclaimed, "The courtship is on!" (Fox News Channel 2003). And on *The Early Show*, a correspondent opined that both candidates' appearances with their wives in televised interviews with Dr. Phil were attempts by President Bush to "win more women over" and by Senator Kerry to "try to win them back" (CBS 2004). The gendered dimension of this coverage played into traditional expectations about male protectiveness and female vulnerability that Susan Faludi (2007) and Enloe (2007) argue have prevailed in public discourse since September 11, 2001. The attacks of that day and subsequent responses to them reactivated and intensified a narrative in which Security Moms play the part of women seeking protection from terrorists for themselves, their children, and their country. And across these Security Mom discourses, commentators and guests alike encouraged Security Moms to accede to Bush's benevolent patriarchy.

In numerous examples, Enloe (2000) illustrates that militarized mothers such as these aid in the process of recruiting bodies to fight wars because, despite military service being associated with masculinized patriotism and nationalism, recruitment is still a difficult business. This is particularly so with all-volunteer forces attempting to win simultaneous wars in Afghanistan and Iraq (during the time Security Moms were prevalent, most branches of the military were having trouble meeting their recruitment goals—see Cooper and Jaffe [2004] and Moniz [2005]). Enloe argues that, historically, this situation invites "recruit-hungry government officials" to "wield more than the idea of masculinized, militarized citizenship. They have needed to craft and deploy a specially honed concept of motherhood. Designing militarized motherhood, however, also requires marginalizing or suppressing alternative notions of motherhood" (2000, 247). Indeed, the 2004 Security Moms displaced in news stories the once-ubiquitous (and liberal) Soccer Moms in an attempt to secure U.S. mothers' allegiance both to the GOP and to the War on Terror. Security Moms performed as exemplary militarized mothers by exhibiting obedience to what the commander in chief asked of them and trusting that he was doing what was best for them, their loved ones, and their country. Instead of being asked to relinquish their children to the war effort, these contemporary militarized mothers were pushed by individuals and groups ancillary to the military to capitulate to the rationale underpinning the GWOT, including the wars in Iraq and Afghanistan. It is worth noting that in these news stories not one Security Mom questioned the wars or national security policy, despite the public's increasing skepticism about both during this time.

As well as lining up behind the objectives of the GWOT, Security Moms expressed neurotic fearfulness for their children's safety, concerns they voiced to further justify their political position. One fretted, for example, "I watch my kids go to school, and I hope they come back" (NBC 2004c). Another echoed her paranoia: "I don't let my kids go anyplace. I'm—you know, we're talking about going on vacation. Where can we go? How do we get through the airport? How do—where is a safe place?" (CBS 2004). Michelle Malkin's manifesto included the following confession, thus showcasing not only her neurosis but also her ability to echo a Bush administration talking point connecting two figures—Osama bin Laden and Saddam Hussein—whose alleged collusion justified waging war on Iraq: "I make my husband take his cell phone with him everywhere—even on a quick milk run or on a walk to the community pool. We have educated our 4-year-old daughter about Osama bin Laden and Saddam Hussein. She knows that there are bad men in the world trying to kill Americans everywhere.... And at night we ask God to bless our troops as they risk their lives trying to kill the bad men before they kill us" (2004, 11A). These Security Moms' words rationalize a society in which They (the "bad men") are separated from Us (Americans and "our troops"), as a means of minimizing the threat They pose to Us (Low 2003, 139). Moreover, they express justification for *good* mothers to deploy those surveillance technologies that are marketed to quell the fears of anxious parents. Cindi Katz refers to this as the "child protection industry": "part of the $1.1 billion home surveillance industry brought about by the migration of spy technologies and logics across the domestic frontier. Its products enable parents to monitor from afar their children, childcare workers, and others interacting with their kids" (2001, 48).

Security Moms expressed fears that because even home is not a safe enough refuge from terrorists, mothers must fully commit to taking every protective measure possible, perhaps even moving to a gated community or installing security technologies such as GPS devices in their children's clothing (Goodman 2007) or nanny cams (Rodino 2005). News reports instruct mothers that to subdue their anxieties and optimize their ability to protect their families, they must employ security technologies that increase their surveillance capabilities. This news coverage thus has a dual propaganda function: to sell the

GWOT and to rationalize the defensive actions, services, and products that metaphorically transform home into a fortress from which to guard against terrorists—a twenty-first-century update to home-front support activities such as planting victory gardens or buying war bonds.

News media expanded beyond the home front as well in their constitution of Security Moms as a synecdoche for how "everything changed" for the United States after 9/11. As such, these Moms' actions served to legitimate GWOT tactics, including the invasion of Iraq and everything else falling under the sign of "security" at this historical moment. One reporter, for example, used an image evocative of the security checkpoints at airports to claim that Security Moms are on one side of a "security threshold" that Democrats will have to "pass" before they can expect Security Moms' support (PBS 2003). During the 2006 congressional election season, another Security Mom, this one a former codirector of the group Security Moms for Bush, offered mothers a stark choice for the upcoming midterm election: "Moms have a choice this November when they go into the voting booth. They can choose to vote for officials who have supported programs such as the NSA surveillance program, CIA detainee program or the PATRIOT Act—the programs which have made this country safe and not have an attack in five years—or they can vote for those who have sought to undermine or even rejoice when they killed those programs" (Fox News Channel 2006).

The figure of the Security Mom thus embodied attributes and beliefs that made controversial policies seem practical, rational, and sensible for women to embrace. Connecting a policy—or even a war—to maternal love, as these news stories did, justifies it, enhances its attractiveness, and deflects consideration of its controversial aspects. In the case of the Iraq War, contested policies included the rationale for conducting a preemptive war, the use of torture in prisoner interrogations, and the Bush administration's numerous attempts to quash dissenting views on the war. Because of Security Moms' ability to obscure these controversies or make them palatable to voters, in 2004 they became part of the Right's strategy to eke out enough public support for an increasingly unpopular war and to push President Bush to a second term. After the 2004 election, their reemergence in 2006, 2008, and again as Mama Grizzlies suggests a continuing need to buttress neoconservatism and cast in a positive light those Bush administration policies being subjected to public scrutiny and protest (e.g., the NSA's wiretap program, to which the Security Mom quoted earlier refers, was made public in December 2005 by James Risen and Eric Lichtblau of the *New York Times*—to widespread public dismay and White House chagrin).

Exemplifying this effort, a *CBS Evening News* segment on the 2006 Security Moms introduces Julee Floyd with, "Since September 11, there has been a serious side to almost every decision mom Julee makes." Floyd elaborates:

"I would say after 9/11, you know, there are all sorts of issues that you start thinking about. What if I was on that plane? What if I was on that building? What if my child ended up being in that building?" (CBS 2006). On Fox News, a Security Mom for Bush cocaptain ends her entreaty to voting mothers by reiterating her belief about mothers' electoral options: "Look, moms have a choice: When they go to the voting booth, they can choose to wake up in a country where they get up in the morning and worry about whether or not they are going to get their kids to school on time or wake up in a country like Israel, where it is a leap of faith to put their kids on the school bus every morning or take them to the pizza parlor or the mall" (Fox News Channel 2006). This Security Mom's sentiment offers no real choice: mothers must support the candidate and party promising to best protect their families or risk the United States turning into a "country like Israel" (whatever that means). Michelle Rodino argues that such *maters bellicosa* have historically operated with this sort of binary logic: in their incarnation as Security Moms, they also exhibit "the durability of maternal constructions that advocate destruction in the name of preservation" (2005, 383). Such is the paradox of the Security Mom: as she accepts war and the trappings of a security state to ensure that her children will live safely, she consigns Iraqi and Afghan children (and adults) to living in a war zone, surrounded by chaos and violence.

The story of the Security Mom offers a cautionary tale for news consumers, feminists, and anyone else concerned about achieving gender justice, for it plays a role in reproducing the (masculine) protector / (feminine) protected dichotomy that Enloe identifies. Such a dichotomy is fraught with problems, not the least of which is that the "protected's natural habitat is the domestic sphere—that is, the sphere of life where caring matters more than strategizing. Consequently, the protected is feminized insofar as the protected needs somebody who can think strategically and act in her (the protected's) best interests" (2007, 61). This binary also vests protectors with exclusive rights to understanding national security matters and therefore sole province over and responsibility for protecting mothers and their children from terrorism.

The Security Mom construction reproduces and rationalizes patriarchal "family values," prowar propaganda, and maternal fearfulness, all of which gave credence to Bush administration policies and politics. Corporate news media credulously accepted claims about Security Moms, never disclosing (and perhaps not knowing) that the source for this construction was a front group for a right-wing think tank, one that existed solely to promote Bush administration policies. The Security Mom is not the first example of a media construction being deployed to govern maternal conduct (for many other examples, see Douglas and Michaels 2004); nor is it the only example of an attempt to militarize mothers, as Enloe (2000) Managhan (2012), and Stabile (1994), among others, have shown. However, Security Moms' politics are taken up in news reports with such ready credulity that they stand as a reminder to regard news constructions of mothers in the context of war with great skepticism.

More optimistically, this case also suggests that voting mothers are dubious about enlisting as Security Moms, despite Family Security Matters' best efforts to influence their hearts and minds. That is, although *news outlets* uncritically adopt the Security Mom construction and promote its politics, the women for whom this campaign was intended appear much less receptive to its claims and premises. This campaign, in other words, could be considered at least a partial failure. To reiterate Elder and Greene's conclusion about the 2004 election, "Mothers, like women overall, were distinctive in being less supportive than men on most defense and war-related issues in 2004" (2007, 11). Their data show that the gender gap that this campaign attempted to redress resists think-tank machinations and instead remained about the same size in 2004 as it had been in prior election years. This is but one example from this time period that illustrates a stark difference between what the news media and the general public are willing to accept about grounds for war and increasing security measures. For example, while U.S. news media beat the drums of war loudly and persistently in late 2002 and early 2003 (something that many reporters and even then secretary of state Colin Powell have issued post hoc regrets about having supported [see *Buying the War* 2007]), protests against the United States going to war in Iraq erupted globally. After a weekend in February 2003 that saw hundreds of thousands of people in the streets opposing the upcoming war, President Bush responded with the following: "Size of protest—it's like deciding, well, I'm going to decide policy based upon a focus group" (Purdum 2003).

Dismissing enormous and widespread opposition to war as a "focus group" pithily captures the antidemocratic sentiments characterizing President Bush's policies and actions during his two terms in office. But it also points to a perhaps unconscious gesture toward the important role that marketing and branding played in the Bush administration's attempts to sell the Iraq War as a product (Solomon 2005 and Stahl 2010 document this in great detail). Security Moms fit well with the larger Bush propaganda-marketing campaign and further articulated consumerist notions of "freedom" and "choice" to war policy in an attempt to win public consent for a war that large segments of the public opposed. I suspect that we will see more constructions like them in future propaganda campaigns, though they may appear alongside militarized mothers such as those who are the subject of the next section.

Militarizing Mothers

Whereas Security Moms proliferated across civilian media outlets during their reign, military mothers kept a relatively low profile. However, although representations of the latter were fewer and mainly less spectacular, they cohere ideologically with Security Moms. With few exceptions, representations of military mothers in the news stories I have reviewed exhibit both pro-Bush and resigned-to-war sentiments and are marked by emotional expressions: of patriotic pride, fearfulness about their soldier children's fates, and in some cases, grief. News representations of military mothers coalesce around two types of activities: all those involved with mothers making connections with one another for mutual support—often through their work with sanctioned groups such as Blue Star Mothers—and those around self-professed "Peace Mom" Cindy Sheehan's protests of the Iraq War. Military mothers I discuss in this section are constructed from a combination of news, military marketing, and PR discourses, and although these mothers are fewer in number and, apart from the coverage of Sheehan, not as visibly linked to a PR campaign, they reflect and amplify ambivalences that have surrounded them historically, both within the public and among the military's branches.

Historically and currently, mothers have been the family members most resistant to children's military enlistment (Bailey 2009; Turse 2008). To overcome or defuse their resistance and therefore maintain the AVF, the Pentagon employs a marketing program intended for potential recruits, known as Joint Advertising, Market Research & Studies (JAMRS), one part of which specifically targets their parents. Laying out JAMRS's strategy in the American Marketing Association's *Marketing News* magazine, the author Christine Birkner (2013) explains that although the U.S. military is a brand "unlike any other," it must market itself similarly to recruit effectively. JAMRS marketing must thus account for the fact that military recruitment is typically hobbled by parents—"by mothers, in particular." In this same piece, the military historian Beth Bailey notes that, in order to overcome such maternal resistance and also to recruit for the Iraq War, JAMRS devised a recruitment campaign that associated the war in Iraq with "World War II, the 'good war,' heroic service and defending the nation. The [campaign's] ads showed the ways the military was good for young people, that parents didn't have to worry about it." Recognizing social media and the internet as "major tools in marketing to parents," branches of the military have set up support sites for parents—and especially mothers. The "Navy for Moms" site, for example, is based on the idea that a "mom's instinct is to protect her child and she can start having her questions answered, not by the Navy . . . but by other moms who have been through this," according to the Campbell Ewald advertising agency's managing director (quoted in Birkner 2013, 30).

JAMRS's own materials explain that it sustains the AVF by exploring the "perceptions, beliefs, and attitudes of American youth as they relate to joining the Military" and helps to "ensure recruiting efforts are directed in the most efficient and beneficial manner" (JAMRS, n.d.). Although this may seem innocuous, Nick Turse has revealed that JAMRS feeds information to military recruiters from a database that comprises detailed personal information—including the Social Security number, grade point average, and ethnicity—of close to 90 percent of high-school students in the United States (2008, 152). Working hand in glove with JAMRS's teen targeting is mom marketing, which relies on similar data-mining techniques to "influence the mothers of teens to send their sons and daughters off to war" (Turse 2008, 159). Recognizing that mothers' objections vary, JAMRS identifies and then employs messages intended to elicit positive responses from a variety of maternal "types." In addition to mothers, this targeted recruitment rhetoric is sent to people who are influential in children's lives, such as "guidance counselors, teachers, and coaches," who may simultaneously work on mothers and therefore "make far greater recruitment inroads" (Turse 2008, 159). Turse probably uses "influence" deliberately to match the language found in JAMRS's own reports (which is, in turn, based on "affluencers" to whom marketing and advertising campaigns are directed—see chapter 1). One 2008 JAMRS report polled teens to identify the "influencers" in their lives and determine what the influencers were saying to them. The report acknowledges that media coverage of the Afghanistan and Iraq wars has hurt military recruitment goals by making influencers—parents, relatives (especially grandparents), educators, and others—less likely to recommend military service to the "youths" in their lives. Along with illuminating the material realities of the protracted Iraq War, media coverage, according to JAMRS, has made influencers fearful that young people will "face hardship, danger, and an unattractive lifestyle if they enlist" (JAMRS 2008, 8). Of all the influencers in a child's life, the report notes, parents—particularly mothers—are the least likely to recommend military service to children, with their resistance showing up across all three of the racial/ethnic categories studied: black, Hispanic, and white (14).

Beth Bailey's history of the Army after the end of conscription shows that for decades the DoD has recognized mothers as children's most important influencers. To overcome the obstacles that mothers pose to recruitment and to enhance recruiting prospects generally, the Army (as well as the other branches of the military) employs civilian advertising firms to brand it as responsive to the needs of populations from which it draws recruits (referred to as "markets"). Over the course of the twenty-year life of the Army's "Be All You Can Be" campaign (created and maintained by the N. W. Ayer agency), for instance, the campaign shifted the "focus from service toward opportunity, from obligation to benefit" (Bailey 2009, 195). To appeal to mothers, what recruiters emphasized most in the context of this campaign were college benefits from the GI Bill. "College benefits were a way to rebrand the army" both to appeal to mothers and to associate the Army with achieving a college education, according to Bailey (2009, 195). Although "Be All You Can Be" was replaced by other campaigns such as the successful "Army Strong," JAMRS continues its appeals to mothers and other influencers on the grounds that military service provides educational benefits and opportunities, as its own report reveals.

Through JAMRS, today the DoD has multiple platforms for influencing parents and their children: social media sites Instagram, Facebook, YouTube, and Twitter; websites that feature numerous downloadable documents such as "Joining the Military: What to Expect"; short videos of multiracial and multiethnic military parents expressing concerns about and pride for their service-member children; and *Futures*, a recruiting magazine sent to high-school guidance counselors that focuses on military career options rather than war and deployment. Using "engaging and informative articles to assist high school juniors and seniors in making career decisions," JAMRS promotes *Futures* as "an educational and personal glimpse into military life and the many employment opportunities available across all of the Armed Forces" (JAMRS Marketing Communications, n.d.). A related website, Today's Military, also links to support organizations such as Blue Star Mothers, Operation Mom, Air Force WingMoms, and Army Mom Strong. These sites encourage military parents to meet and support one another and inform themselves about military parenting by reading blog posts that cover topics including service, deployment, and challenges. Army Mom Strong even features a poem titled "A Soldier's Mom," by Anita Hoy. Among its lines explaining one mother's pride for her son's choice of military service are these:

> I gave life to my son in a place of peace and freedom. He committed that life to insure I will grow old in a state of security and Liberty.
> I raised and protected my son from birth to manhood. He raised his hand and vowed to protect us all to the death. (Hoy 2016)

Sentiments expressed in "proud Army mom" Hoy's poem echo JAMRS's messaging, which in turn infuses civilian news stories about military mothers: the pride they feel about their children's service, their gratitude for the discipline their children receive from the military, and the persistent belief that their children's military service works to keep the United States safe and free. These themes emerge in news coverage in three discernible patterns: first, stories about military mothers appear on or around Mother's Day each year (and, to a lesser extent, on Veterans Day and Memorial Day) and focus on sacrifices both they and their children are making; second, news stories feature scenes of military mothers socializing with and supporting one another, usually through events organized by members of sanctioned support groups such as Blue Star Mothers; and third, during the time the self-described "Peace Mom" Cindy Sheehan was protesting the war in Iraq (mainly 2005), news stories trained their lenses on her activities as well as prowar rallies intended to challenge Sheehan's message. Sheehan's situation clearly posed a test to news outlets and their conventions for reporting war. Because she publicized her protest by camping near President Bush's ranch in Crawford, Texas, in order to gain an audience with him, news organizations could not avoid attending to Sheehan—despite her vigorous challenges to a war that the mainstream press corps had been loath to question or criticize (for in-depth analyses of how corporate news organizations helped to promote the war in Iraq, see *Buying the War* 2007; and Solomon 2005).

To minimize Sheehan's criticism and discourage other military mothers from joining her protest, TV news, in particular, attempted to marginalize her by including and glorifying prowar military mothers in their reports, thus casting Sheehan's as the least preferable maternal performance available to them. Once Sheehan's media moment was over and other military mothers appeared in her place to criticize the war in Iraq and President Bush, news organizations countered their criticisms, too, with statements by military mothers who were not critical of either. Such a turn to promilitary mothers (and fathers) parallels content found in JAMRS videos for parents. For example, one clip from Today's Military, titled "Service," features multiracial, multiethnic military parents explaining what they believe are the benefits of military service for their children and for the country. One parent, a father, delivers a forceful monologue expressing his belief that the United States is the best country in the world for the numerous freedoms it offers. A head-shot delivery is followed by photos of him standing next to his soldier son and then the whole family—son wearing fatigues, dad sporting a white T-shirt with "My Son Defends Freedom" in large black letters—while his voice-over touts military service as the best way to preserve these freedoms. Following the photo montage, the camera returns to the father, brow furrowed and issuing a veiled threat: "If anyone approached me with any negativity about my kid serving in the military, . . . uh . . . I'll stand up for my kids. No problem. There's just no better place to live. And they're defending it. I'm proud of that. Very proud" (Today's Military, n.d.).

Taken together, these media discourses provide military mothers and other civilian media audiences with a model of proper martial motherhood, which includes instruction in how to navigate criticism of the war in Iraq that they may harbor themselves or encounter in other quarters. Along with JAMRS discourses, formulaic news stories produced a discursive regime of truth about military maternity that worked in tandem with Security Moms to fix meaning around mothers such that they would support President Bush's war efforts, even if it meant that they sacrificed their children's lives to see them to fruition. The combination is a prescription for how all of us, and particularly mothers, should bolster the home front by broaching no criticism of war.

Holiday Honorifics and Maternal Connections

Mother's Day, Memorial Day, and Veterans Day all present opportunities for news outlets to pay at least brief homage to military mothers through either formulaic recitations of difficulties that military mothers face as they wait for their children or, in unfortunate cases in which their children have been injured or killed, explanations of how they cope with grief. Typical of these holiday honorifics is a clip appearing on a Hagerstown, Maryland, TV station on Veterans Day 2006: a voice-over reports that it is a "time of poignancy—at a time of war—for military mothers like Jean Duane, whose son Andrew is in the Air Force reserves." The camera cuts to Duane asserting, "There's a lot of gratitude and thanks for [Andrew] and for his comrades because we wouldn't be here if it wasn't for them" (Comcast Cable News 2006).[6]

Mother's Day reporting rituals include teas that Michelle Obama and Jill Biden's group, Joining Forces, hosted for military spouses across the country. (One mother of four service members who had met Obama and Biden at one of these teas, Elaine Brye, introduced the First Lady to the audience at the 2012 Democratic National Convention, where President Obama was nominated to run for a second term.) The annual celebration of mothers also drives stories about different support groups, such as the following one that helps military moms communicate with their deployed children. Interviewing members of a Missouri mothers' group, the reporter Martha Teichner proclaims, "For mothers of soldiers away at war, Mother's Day is the longest day in the longest, most agonizing wait of all" (CBS 2005c). To fight these Mother's Day blues, the group assembles care packages that include twenty webcams that they "managed to get to Iraq in time for Mother's Day." As the camera cuts to one of the mothers, Tracy Della Vecchia, conversing via webcam with her deployed son, Teichner intones, "To her, it's a miracle, the sight of her son, Marine Corporal Derrick Jensen, all the way from Baghdad. . . . And for however long she can keep him there, this mother knows her son is safe" (CBS 2005c). Two noteworthy features in these holiday honorific stories are their formulaic recognition of these military mothers' belief in the benefits of their children's service—exemplified by Jean Duane's statement implying that her son's service protects the home front—and the virtual absence of antiwar sentiments.

Holiday honorifics and those stories that feature military mothers connecting with one another provide local angles for news coverage especially, so my sample of news stories includes those appearing in local papers and broadcast-TV affiliate stations. Locally focused pieces encourage readers and viewers to get involved with troop-supporting community activities, illuminating one set of endeavors while obscuring others. For example, numerous military mothers express gratitude for the connections they make with other such mothers as they undertake troop-support projects. The following excerpt from the *San Jose Mercury News* typifies such a discursive construction.

> "The first time I walked into a meeting, I didn't have to say anything," said Debbie Parks, co-president who was comforted by hearing the stories of others when she joined [Blue Star Mothers] in 2008. "There is always somebody one step ahead of you on the military journey," said Parks, who lives in Campbell. Some will say that it is the advice of fellow mothers that makes the greatest impact. Mothers share helpful hints on how to contact those in the military using modern technology and web sites like Facebook and Myspace. Longtime military mothers stand by the adage that "no news is good news" and that just having a mom to talk to can relieve enough stress, worry and tension to get through the week. "You might meet someone in the store and not know that they haven't heard from their son in three weeks and they are serving in Afghanistan," Bayer said, but among group members, there is a common ground. "Things that other people cannot understand, they understand immediately, know how to comfort you, know how to encourage you, know how to support you," she added. Projects, fundraisers and activities also keep the mothers busy and their worries at bay. (Carney 2009)

Another California newspaper article features the Marine mother Dotty Selmeczki emphasizing the common experiences of military mothers. "She said she sees herself reflected in the freshly frazzled faces that now show up at 'Operation: Mom' support meetings in a veterans hall in Hayward. Previously, only about a dozen mostly Marine Corps mothers would gather in her Castro Valley living room for tea, sympathy and care-packaging. 'Last time we had three new moms, and sitting there reminded me so much of where we began. The same fears, same worries, same anxiety. . . . The reality of it all hasn't changed. A mom's heart never changes'" (Simerman 2009). This account is an especially direct attempt to fix meaning around military motherhood. "A mom's heart never changes" suggests that mothering is a static, essentialist state of being lived outside of politics and discourse. The ideological work that this assertion accomplishes discourages a critical perspective on the circumstances that cast these moms as military mothers in the first place—the *politics* of military motherhood.

This style of representing military mothers reprises in post-9/11 war reporting the therapeutic rhetoric that news outlets used to construct military families during the 1991 Persian Gulf War. In an analysis of TV news stories aired during that time, Dana L. Cloud argues that these narratives "played a key role in domesticating dissent by rearticulating political outrage as personal anxiety and reconfiguring the will to resist as the need to 'support our troops'" (1994, 155). Using gendered appeals to women in particular, news programs emphasized the "coping," "waiting," and "healing" of military family members (especially mothers) as a means of channeling families' antiwar sentiments into "themes of therapy." Such themes, Cloud shows, worked to personalize the political problems inherent in that war and moderated "the antiwar edge of 'harder' coverage (of danger, prisoners, protests, and the like)" (157). Like Persian Gulf War news discourses, military-mother stories after 9/11 permit some criticism of the Afghanistan and Iraq wars but tend to follow it with rhetoric that resituates antiwar comments into a support-the-troops frame.

As the wars wore on and these stories became particularly poignant, for example, a few mothers expressed dismay and frustration over both their children's multiple deployments and the uncertain end dates for wars. On those rare occasions when their aggravation morphed into criticism, it was likely to get the yellow ribbon treatment, something that occurs in this exchange between CNN's John King and the Blue Star Mother Lynn Stamm, "an Ohio mom who has had enough."

STAMM: When he told me he was going to be deployed for a third time, you just feel like you've been hit. It just takes the wind out of you. Because he's gone there, and he's come back twice. He wasn't hurt. And it's like you're so grateful that he came home. And then when he has to go back a third time, it's like, OK, how many times can we cheat death? How many times can we cheat him being wounded over there?

KING: Jordan's mom, Lynn Stamm, believes the president deceived the nation about the Iraqi threat to begin with and worries now her son is part of a mission that has failed and lacks a clear exit strategy.

STAMM: Well, it seems kind of ironic to me that you would have to keep people over there to validate the deaths that have already occurred and take chances that more people are going to die.

KING: The yellow ribbon out front says, "support the troops," but the sign in the car says, "bring them home." Stamm, among the military moms taking a more vocal role in the Iraq political debate, with her son's permission. (CNN 2005d)

Instead of challenging the wars and the politicians who start them (with or without their children's permission), by far the majority of military mothers in these discourses channel their negative emotions into supporting one another and their service-member children through activities such as assembling care packages for troops, welcoming returning service members, and voicing support for the military's work in Afghanistan and Iraq. The following story about two Nevada military mothers with sons on the front lines in Afghanistan illustrates this. Asked whether they would like their sons to be among those being brought back to the United States as part of the 2011 troop drawdown announced by President Obama, mother Michelle Nelson replies, "I do hope that if there's still work to finish, they let them finish. They have important work to do there." A voice-over follows, explaining that Nelson "feels that her son is helping to educate the people of Afghanistan what freedom is and how to establish it in their country." To aid them in this effort, Nelson's Blue Star Mothers group arranged for all of the 7-11 convenience stores in the area to accept food and toiletry donations that the group sent in care packages to Iraq and Afghanistan (CBS 2011). In this context, even the most mundane of activities can be turned into opportunities for mothers to voice prowar talking points and engage in another means of banalizing militarism.

A special class among military mothers, the Gold Star Mothers[7] who have appeared in news stories almost always expressed their belief in the Bush administration's war policies—a technique that made their commentary particularly potent. For example, a short segment about four Nashville mothers who started a Middle Tennessee chapter of Gold Star Mothers explains that a mother receives the gold star at her child's military funeral but thereafter is left on her own to grieve. The women in this report respond by opening a Gold Star Mothers chapter to provide a space for these mothers to grieve together: "a support network of women who understand what they're going through." With a subtle rebuke of Cindy Sheehan and so that the mothers' efforts are not misconstrued, one mother asserts, "There's nobody here that has anger against our country or the president; it's not about that. It's about our kids and that we're so proud of them, but we grieve them" (CBS 2007). Likewise, a story from the *Contra Costa Times* (near Cindy Sheehan's home in the San Francisco Bay Area) situates a Blue Star Mothers chapter as a bulwark against the prevailing antiwar sentiment there: "The chapter, now with about 100 active members, has funded thousands of care packages, supported wounded veterans returning home, comforted families of the war dead and helped new branches sprout across the state. . . . Together, the two East Bay groups have made the region a hub for unabashed troop support efforts, despite—or perhaps arising from—the region's thick anti-war strain" (Simerman 2009).

Stories such as these that featured local mothers expressing both certainty about the good being done by their service-member children and strong, "unabashed" support for the troops typify how women perform military motherhood in newspaper and TV news discourses. These accounts dovetailed with those produced by JAMRS for parents of service members and together produced prescriptive representations of martial mothering by using military-sanctioned channels for expressing fear and concern and easing anxiety: they voiced support for the troops and President Bush, as they provided material support in the form of care packages. From JAMRS's Today's Military site, for example, one can link to a support group called Operation Mom (five of the six support groups for military parents are specifically for mothers). Operation Mom describes itself this way:

> Our mission is to help military moms find the resources they need. . . . We understand that it's very easy to feel alienated. It's very easy to feel that you'll just fall between the cracks because other people cannot understand what it's like to lose a military veteran or to have a child come back fundamentally changed by war. We know. We understand. And that's why we welcome you with open, warm embraces. . . . You may not have the same points of views and opinions as everybody else here, but that's okay. That's what makes this space so valuable because we welcome differences of opinion. What we all agree on is that we are going to support each other, we're going to help each other cope, we're going to give each other strength as we put one foot in front of the other to be strong for our children; to be there to keep on giving and giving and giving despite the pressure, the frustration and the uncertainty. (Operation Mom, n.d.)

Operation Mom's therapeutic sentiments align with those in the bulk of news coverage about military mothers, including infrequent and reluctant appearances by vocally political, antiwar mothers. Like *Army Wives*, these news representations also do important work to fix meanings around military mothers as they prescribe and proscribe political positions vis-à-vis war.

Discursive Discipline and Cindy Sheehan

Of course, not every military mother reflexively accepted the wars in Afghanistan and Iraq, as the story about Lynn Stamm (in the preceding section) illustrates. In addition to Stamm, a few Gold Star Mothers' expressions of grief included taking jabs at the Bush administration's war policy. Such statements, however, were fleeting and aimed at just one aspect of policy at a time—multiple deployments, for example—rather than offering broader criticism of the rationale for war with Iraq. Albeit temporarily, all of this changed when Cindy Sheehan emerged in 2005 and reporters shifted focus to cover her anguished Iraq War protest and accusation that President Bush's rationale for war was a sham. Sheehan thus became the face of the antiwar movement in the United States as she repeatedly used her media appearances to push for a meeting with President Bush to discuss the human toll of the war on Iraq. My aim in this section is not to explicate Sheehan's story; other scholars have focused their research lenses on her—particularly Amy Pason (2010) in her examination of Sheehan's rhetoric in the context of the U.S. peace movement and Tina Managhan's (2012) research on the discourses of loss and support for the troops that constitute Sheehan as a Peace Mom. Although my understanding of Sheehan has been informed substantially by both Pason's and Managhan's work, my project consists of examining Sheehan's role in the news discourses that construct military mothers from September 11 onward.[8]

Whereas the other stories I examine in this chapter offered prescriptions for practicing martial motherhood, media reports about Sheehan offered the converse: an object lesson in how *not* to be a military mother, with instructions supplied by reporters and other military mothers who disciplined and attempted to neutralize this unruly military mother. Sheehan initiated contact with President Bush with a raw and emotional "open letter" just after he began his second term in 2004. Challenging him to see the Iraq War through her eyes, Sheehan wrote, "George, it has been seven months since your reckless and wanton foreign policies killed my son, my big boy, my hero, my best friend: Casey. It has been seven months since your ignorant and arrogant lack of planning for the peace murdered my oldest child" (2005, 3). Despite attempts to circulate the letter, news organizations did not pick up on Sheehan's protest until early August 2005, when she and other peace activists set up a protest encampment—Camp Casey—near Bush's ranch in Crawford, Texas, where he had been vacationing for five weeks. These early-August stories were reportorial in tone, providing basic information about Sheehan, her son Casey, and her demand that Bush meet with her (something he repeatedly declined). Some declared that a following was emerging around her, as in this report from the CBS affiliate station KLAS:

> The military mother who staged a protest outside of the president's Texas ranch is now getting support from people all across the nation. Cindy Sheehan's son was killed in Iraq. She is demanding a meeting with President Bush and is camped outside his Texas ranch. Dozens from across the country have now joined her. One calls her "the Rosa Parks of the anti-war movement. . . ." The White House says President Bush met Sheehan at a military base some time ago, but the forty-eight-year-old woman says she wants an actual talk with him, so she can tell him to bring the troops home. (CBS 2005d)

When it became clear that a large swath of the public sympathized with Sheehan, that she attracted hundreds of supporters a day (celebrities and politicians among them) to Camp Casey and inspired antiwar events across the United States, only then did news coverage broaden to include military mothers opposing Sheehan's antiwar politics. It is difficult to see this as anything other than an attempt to discipline Sheehan and subdue antiwar protests by groups such as Code Pink and Gold Star Families for Peace, which by that time were widespread and driving Bush's approval ratings down to the lowest level of his presidency. Implicitly and explicitly, these news discourses attempted to discredit Sheehan and other antiwar activists by repeatedly suggesting that Sheehan's position was tantamount to not supporting the troops—at this historical moment, an accusation that equated to accusing her and her fellow peace activists of being unpatriotic. Following the support-the-troops formula found in *Army Wives* (see chapter 1) and employing other cultural artifacts that Stahl (2009, 2010) has detailed, news coverage of Sheehan thus reinforced and amplified media outlets' efforts to manufacture support for U.S. troops, in part by suggesting that any criticism of war equated to a withdrawal of support for deployed service members. Tina Managhan notes that Sheehan and her followers, mindful of how their politics were being twisted in this way, thus modified their slogans to "support the troops, not the war" and "bring the troops home now," repeating them so often that "they could fairly be described as the rallying cries of the mainstream American antiwar movement" (2012, 107).

At first, the challenges to Sheehan and her politics were fairly mild and apparently organic rather than being obvious products of an organized campaign like that behind Security Moms.[9] One subtle, if rambling, rebuke for Sheehan came in a CNN morning news rundown that left viewers with little doubt that gossipy *People* magazine was CNN's sibling media outlet. After a voice-over announces that Sheehan's husband has filed for divorce, correspondents Carol Costello, Soledad O'Brien, and Kelly Wallace have the following exchange:

COSTELLO: Wow!

WALLACE: So some tough news for her. I believe they were separated since June, is that right?

COSTELLO: They were. They were separated, and it was because he kind of, like, retreated and she, like, wanted to immerse herself in all things her son.

WALLACE: I think there's a disagreement, too, in exactly how they're handling this.

COSTELLO: Yes.

WALLACE: And politically I think . . .

O'BRIEN: Yes, it's actually pretty common when someone loses a child that the families end up—a high number of families get divorced. That's sad news for that family.

WALLACE: Very sad, sure.

O'BRIEN: Especially after the obviously other sad news they've had. (CNN 2005e)

Wallace's "and politically, I think" interjection establishes Sheehan as an outlier even among her family members and suggests that responsibility for the couple's marital problems lies with Cindy's politics. Other correspondents' criticism expanded to extrafamilial territory soon thereafter. Appearing in a story about troops returning to Tuscaloosa, Alabama, from Iraq, Sgt. Jeremy Owens is asked by a reporter to comment on Cindy Sheehan's protest. After expressing sympathy to Sheehan for the death of her son, he avers, "This is what we do [for] our country. We can't pull out. We don't pull away from terrorists for one, and two, if we pull out, they'll come over here and fight us on our own land" (WVTM 2005). Owens's words do double duty in reproaching Sheehan and subtly expressing a discredited Bush administration talking point linking the war on Iraq with the terrorist attacks of September 11, 2001. According to Norman Solomon, during 2002 and 2003 the Pentagon "put out a profuse supply of bogus stories based on 'intelligence'—about Iraq's weapons of mass destruction and purported links to Al Qaeda—with the goal of promoting an invasion of Iraq" (2005, 56). Although this information was later disproved by a Senate Intelligence Committee report that harshly criticized Bush administration officials for misleading the public in their case for going to war with Iraq (Mazzetti and Shane 2008; CNN.com 2008), numerous individuals with both formal and informal Bush administration associations nevertheless persisted in making this link from 2002 and beyond as justification for the United States to fight on in Iraq. This articulation took on commonsense status to such an extent that it became part of the vernacular used by military personnel and civilians alike in their media appearances.

Although the veteran Owens has martial credibility that Sheehan does not, neither his nor any other veteran's authority can match that of a mother when she challenges dissenters from the party line on war. A few days into covering Sheehan's protest, news outlets started to feature military mothers who disagreed with her—a strategy they kept up until Sheehan left Crawford, Texas. Knitting together a reliance on women who support President Bush and admonitions to mothers critical of his war policy, this coverage mirrors that of Security Moms. CNN's Soledad O'Brien begins one such segment this way: "In Crawford, Texas, Cindy Sheehan continues her protest outside President Bush's ranch. She's been there since August 6, and she vows to stay there until the president meets with her. Her son was killed in Iraq. She wants to talk to the president about pulling U.S. troops out of the region. Do other military mothers agree with her? Jan Johnson lost her son, Justin, in the war. She's at the CNN Center in Atlanta" (CNN 2005a). Johnson is an ideal spokesperson for the Sheehan opposition; not only has her son been killed in Iraq, but he served with Casey Sheehan. O'Brien asks Johnson, "Tell me how you feel when you see the videotape of Cindy Sheehan and the protest she now has in Crawford, Texas." "I'm not for the protest," Johnson replies and then elaborates: "I believe that we should stay the course. We need to be there. To me, in a way, she's disgracing Casey, because Casey was over there trying to serve his country and help the Iraqi people. And by what she's doing, it's kind of taken away from the meaning of his death, I believe" (CNN 2005a). Rosemary Palmer, another military mother whose son had been killed in Iraq, follows Johnson. Unlike Johnson, Palmer enthusiastically supports Sheehan and adds that she will attend a pro-Sheehan vigil the next day in Cleveland—contra O'Brien's repeated prompts to disavow Sheehan. To mitigate Palmer's affinity for Shee-han, O'Brien ends the segment by turning again to Johnson and asking for her thoughts on Palmer's assertion that the United States needs to "fight it right or get out." Not surprisingly, Johnson explains, "I think it does need to be fought right, but to do that, we've got to stay there. People say, let's bring the guys home. Well, we bring the guys home, and then the terrorists are going to come see us here, is the way I firmly believe. And because of that, my husband leaves next week to go to Iraq to join the Georgia Guard, where his guys are at right now" (CNN 2005a). This exchange between mothers attempts to weaken sup-port for Sheehan's protest. By giving the prowar, anti-Sheehan Jan Johnson the first and last words in the segment, CNN privileges her position and alerts viewers to the opposition to Sheehan's protest that is brewing among military mothers—Johnson going so far as to cast Sheehan's activism as dishonorable to Casey. Because this is a CNN segment, it appears multiple times on differ-ent shows throughout the day, giving it even greater circulation to thousands more viewers as it moves through CNN's programming windows. (This is true of most of the CNN segments in my sample of military-mother coverage: like other CNN segments, they are recycled many times across its twenty-four-hour news day and often spill over into other days as well.)

On August 17, NPR gets into the act, airing a Sheehan-discrediting story that includes only mothers opposed to her protest. When the reporter Mike Pesca asks the Gold Star Mother Sherri Busch about Sheehan's activism, Busch opines that although "moms can be against the war," Sheehan appears to be "against our government, and that's very dishonoring." Following up, Pesca asks, "Do you think she's being used?" Busch replies in the affirmative and claims that she, too, might have been manipulated as she believes Sheehan has been, but she will not allow it because she is focusing on her son's beliefs and "what he was trying to do." Pesca segues from Busch with these words:

> Cindy Sheehan, so powerful a symbol because of her circumstances, is right there contradicted by a woman sharing her precise status. Sherri Busch isn't holding any press conferences, but now we know her opinion. So is the tally even? Is the fulcrum of moral authority now in balance? And the next mom we ask, will she tip the scales? If we are to afford Sheehan a status as someone with potency because she is grieving, maybe we should add up all eighteen hundred or so grieving moms or all ten or twenty thousand grieving dads, siblings, spouses, and kids, get their opinion, and say this is the most pertinent poll on the war we've taken yet. What would they all say? (NPR 2005)

Pesca's remarkable words blatantly attempt to undermine Sheehan and any "moral authority" that her protest possesses. And lest listeners are swayed to believe that Sheehan's criticism is legitimate, Pesca brings on a second guest—

Tracy Della Vecchia, founder of the MarineParents.com community—to discourage them. Della Vecchia guesses that "probably 80 to 90 percent of the folks that are in the [MarineParents.com] message board community as active members probably feel some regret for the kind of publicity that Cindy Sheehan is bringing upon the troops." Moreover, Della Vecchia adds of Sheehan's decision to publicly express her grief, "[It] is something that . . . I feel that at some point in time down the line, my gut and my heart tell me that she'll be regretful of some of the things that she's done and said." Getting the last word in the broadcast, Sherri Busch reappears to sympathize with Sheehan—but for performing her grief improperly and not for the loss of her son: "I feel sorry for her now. I'm not angry with her at all, but I feel very sorry for her because she's just lengthened her stay in this horrible grief that we all have to go through" (NPR 2005). NPR's treatment works alongside segments from other outlets to discipline the unruly Sheehan by producing a sympathetic—even empathetic—response to her grief, as they criticize the form of its expression. Each of these reports emphasizes that Sheehan is not a spokesperson for military families, and some symbolically expel her from the military-family community altogether with suggestions that she is a bit of a crank who dishonors both her dead son and the U.S. government with antiwar activism and criticism of President Bush.

News stories such as these were but one part of the plan to discredit Sheehan. Pro-Bush, prowar forces that successfully created and deployed front groups and Security Moms to manufacture consent for their policies reappeared to malign Sheehan. Like Security Moms, many prowar military mothers in these stories appeared as part of an Astroturf campaign—one that reporters failed to disclose to viewers. To challenge the sympathetic Sheehan, prowar forces organized a PR campaign through the front group Move America Forward (MAF). Hatched in 2004 by the PR firm Russo March & Rogers, MAF has "strong ties to the Republican Party," according to PR Watch's John Stauber. In addition to managing the 2005 "You Don't Speak for Me, Cindy" caravan tour and supplying anti-Sheehan spokespersons to news outlets, MAF caravanned across the United States during September 2007 to promote the troop surge to Iraq occurring at that time (Stauber 2007). "You Don't Speak for Me, Cindy" started in California and stopped in various cities along the way, with Crawford, Texas, as its ultimate destination. Reporters followed the tour, faithfully transcribing its members' messages as they spoke at conservative Christian churches and town squares. In a quote repeated across several different stations' broadcasts, one member of the tour claims that Sheehan is in the minority: "She's not the majority. We are supportive of what our president's doing. I don't agree with everything George Bush does, but he's my brother in the Lord. He's our president, and he's our commander in chief, and we must support him. . . . To deny support to him is to say to the troops, even

Cindy's son, 'it was for naught'" (CBS 2005b). This quote captures the rhetorical work that the tour accomplished. By equating criticism of President Bush to dishonoring those troops killed in service, members of this anti-Sheehan tour set out clear political stakes for Sheehan's supporters: if you fail to support the Iraq War, you effectively convey to the troops that their labor, injuries, and deaths were meaningless. For mothers mourning children killed or injured in Iraq, this may be a bridge too far—which is, of course, the desired outcome of MAF's campaign.

Other mothers who were not officially associated with the tour but who were no less a part of the anti-Sheehan PR campaign also pop up in these discourses. The Idaho military mother Tammy Pruett, for example, appeared with President Bush at a prowar rally in Idaho in late August to condemn Sheehan. Covered by CNN, Pruett proclaims to the invitation-only crowd of nine thousand plus about the way Sheehan has "chosen to mourn," "It wouldn't be the way that we would do it. But we respect her right." President Bush follows Pruett with the vigorous assurance, "So long as I'm the president, we will stay, we will fight, and we will win the war on terror." After the rally, Bush met with the families of nineteen troops killed in Afghanistan and Iraq. One grieving mother among them was Dawn Row: "a Bush supporter. . . . This was [Row's] second meeting with him, something denied Cindy Sheehan," correspondent Dana Bash adds. Shifting attention to Sheehan and her supporters at Camp Casey and using passive voice, correspondent Ed Lavendera reminds viewers that "Sheehan's motives have been questioned, and she's accused of pushing the political agenda of left-wing organizations." Remarkably the segment then turns to MAF cofounder Melanie Morgan, with no disclosure of her group's right-wing political agenda. Angrily, Morgan declares, "Our patience has snapped. We can't stand it a moment longer, listening to the anti-American message that is coming from Crawford, Texas, from Camp Casey" (CNN 2005c). Pruett, Morgan, and others act on behalf of the Bush administration to amplify its accusation that criticizing the war equates to being "anti-American," a tactic that Solomon notes Bush proxies used prolifically throughout these early years of the Iraq War to marshal support for the war and for the administration (2005, 159). In this case, it served to further reinforce boundaries around this discursive field of military mothers and enumerate those activities that could earn women the anti-American label.

CNN stoked the spectacle the following day with a segment headlined "Military Moms Battle," introduced by Carol Costello: "The war of words over Iraq escalates on the home front. Cindy Sheehan made an emotional return to Crawford, Texas, on Wednesday to resume her protest at Camp Casey. President Bush also sent out a message Wednesday, meeting with military families in Idaho and enlisting the support of a military mother of his own. Are we seeing a new battle emerge, that of military moms?" (CNN 2005b). As with so many Security Mom stories, reporters refuse responsibility for framing this story as if it were a pitched battle or for fomenting discord, which they claim to simply report. CNN audiences, in particular, are privy to multiple, recycled scenes from this "battle," one side of which is manufactured (but undisclosed as such) by a PR firm run by Bush loyalists, while the other is represented by an apparently outgunned progressive PR firm. In these iterative segments, Cindy Sheehan's protest is disparaged by several, mutually reinforcing, actors: other mothers whose sons had been killed in Iraq; Tammy Pruett, whose prowar position gains credibility by being voiced by a mother of five soldiers and wife of one—all serving in Iraq; and military mothers on the "You Don't Speak for Me, Cindy" tour. All appear in a context of an information-management operation that granted Bush administration war policies uncritical news coverage throughout these early years of the Afghanistan and Iraq wars (DiMaggio 2009; McLaren and Martin 2004; Mirrlees 2016; Solomon 2005).

In many of these accounts, reporters simply repeat Bush administration talking points, devoid of the scrutiny and skepticism they direct at Sheehan. In this same CNN segment, the *Washington Post* reporter Mike Allen repeatedly and without any analysis echoes what President Bush and representatives of his administration have claimed about the war, explaining for example, that the president is "trying to remind the American people that the 9/11 Commission said that every time Al-Qaeda wins, that every time that a free nation shows a weakness, that that emboldens them. He's trying to . . . take a very complicated and difficult situation and point it in stark terms that to withdraw is to concede. We're going back to the election, where the idea is you're with us or you're with the terrorists" (CNN 2005b). Contributing to the network's pattern of promoting Bush administration perspectives as neutral or commonsensical while casting those of antiwar groups and Sheehan as unpatriotic and dishonorable, CNN's John King makes the following claim about Sheehan in *Voices from the Homefront*, a lengthy segment airing in October 2005: "While she bristles at the suggestion, marching in the willing embrace of liberal politicians and groups makes it easier for critics to say that Cindy Sheehan is, without a doubt, the voice of a grieving mother; [but] it is also the voice of an anti-Bush partisan." Following this and without any evident irony, King narrates a long tale about Bush-endorsed Tammy Pruett and her family of five sons and husband, all of whom had served in Iraq with nary a criticism of that war (CNN 2005d). Pruett's hidden affiliations with a right-wing front group and the Bush administration spare her from the rhetorical attacks that CNN—a network whose CEO mandated pro–Iraq War coverage (*Buying the War* 2007)—makes on Sheehan.

Covering Cindy Sheehan offered news outlets instruction in neutralizing criticism by presenting alternatives to war-protesting military mothers. By the time the 2007 troop surge was in force, protesting mothers saw their criticism countered by mothers who supported this last-ditch effort to win the war in Iraq. A January 2007 ABC News *Top Priority* segment that aired nationally and brought together two politically disparate mothers—Anne Roesler, a mother of a son experiencing PTSD and member of the antiwar group Military Families Speak Out, and Carla Lois—exemplifies this strategy. Roesler establishes her antiwar credentials immediately, exclaiming to the interviewer Juju Chang, "It's time to end this war, to defund the war, to make sure that the troops are supported so that they can get home safely, and then to make darn sure that they're taken care of once they get here, because we're now looking at tens of thousands of American troops who are suffering from injuries that we can't even see, things like posttraumatic stress disorder." When Chang presses her for her thoughts on the troop surge, Roesler does not equivocate: "You know, this is the fourth time we've seen a surge. My son was—has been part of the surges in the past. And they made absolutely no difference other than to increase the deaths on the part of both innocent Iraqi civilians and our own troops." A rattled Chang turns to Carla Lois for her "slightly different take on the surge." Lois explains that her "son served in both Baquba and Ramadi": "And he always said to me in his phone calls, in his emails, you know, that they were there—they felt that they were making a difference. That wasn't the case every day, but . . . but they did feel it. They were making a difference, and he feels that what we're doing in Iraq is right." Chang's follow-up, albeit brief, is rhetorically significant for how it equates support for the troops to support for staying the course in Iraq: "And has your opinion of the war changed at all from the beginning? I know you very much support the troops who are there." Lois avers, "I do support the troops, you know. I—I tell people that there's no one who was more antiwar than the families of those who have children in harm's way or family members in harm's way. . . . But, you know, we're there now, and I think that we really do need to give this new proposal that the president and his advisers have put forth . . . that one last chance. I think we owe it to the Iraqis and we owe it to the Americans." Countering with a pointed critique of both the surge and the Iraq War, Roesler concludes, "What we owe to the Iraqi people is restitution. We definitely have taken a sovereign nation and absolutely destroyed it. And we have a moral responsibility to rebuild that country, but it's not with our military." Rather than elaborate on Roesler's position, Chang instead attempts to mitigate Lois and Roesler's conflict by underscoring what they have in common: children serving in combat and the "counterintuitive" mothering necessitated by their being in mortal danger throughout their deployments (ABC 2007).

Although Cindy Sheehan, her many supporters in the peace movement, and antiwar military mothers all offered U.S. media numerous grounds to investigate claims about the Bush administration's duplicity around invading Iraq (claims that have since been confirmed by multiple investigations), few news organizations and journalists did so. Instead, they followed a pattern that began in the run-up to the war in Iraq (and continues to this day), documented by Fairness and Accuracy in Reporting (FAIR): in stories about the impending war between January 30 and February 12, 2003, ABC, CBS, NBC, and PBS allowed only 17 percent of their stories to express "skeptical or critical positions on the U.S.'s war policy." And "only one U.S. source, Catherine Thomason of Physicians for Social Responsibility, represented an anti-war organization. Of all 393 sources, only three (less than 1 percent) were identified with organized protests or anti-war groups" (FAIR 2003). According to Scott Bonn (2010) and Anthony DiMaggio (2009), news outlets maintained such an imbalance throughout most of Bush's two terms in office. I would add that news organizations obscured their reportorial dereliction of duty with uncritical incorporation of military marketing and PR discourses that, together with their news stories, constructed a model of proper military motherhood—one that reinforced JAMRS-endorsed activities such as care-package assembly and membership in officially sanctioned groups such as Blue Star Mothers as it disciplined unruly military mothers, Cindy Sheehan chief among them.

• • •

In this chapter, I have argued that discourses emanating from military marketing campaigns, news organizations, and public relations firms mutually, but asymmetrically, constitute maternal subjectivities aligning with a post-9/11 martial rationality that was promoted mainly by the Bush administration. Foucault's remarks about states and their ability to wage war are relevant here. He argues that a state's "power to expose a whole population to death is the underside of the power to guarantee an individual's continued existence. The principle underlying the tactics of battle—that one has to be capable of killing in order to go on living—has become the principle that defines the strategy of states" (1978, 137). Foucault locates the beginning of the "era of 'bio-power,' " or power over life, in eighteenth-century Europe with the creation of the army—one of the most significant disciplinary institutions, developed to bring about "the subjugation of bodies and the control of populations" (1978, 140). Although the U.S. military's technologies and strategies have changed greatly in the intervening centuries, its goals have not; today it works with other institutions such as legacy and social media to manage populations both abroad and at home. Such a Foucauldian perspective understands that power is not wielded with armaments exclusively from the top or by political elites but is "expressed through everyday discursive frameworks in which we are all implicated" (Hardin and Whiteside 2013, 131). The maternal subjectivities that these news discourses construct are not, therefore, imposed on women; rather, they hail mothers to inhabit them as a means of managing the fraught conditions of the post-9/11 moment. Military mothers who appear in news stories and JAMRS materials participate in activities suggested for them, make statements in support of the wars and about the benefits their children experience from military service, and, with few exceptions, stay out of the fray of war protesting.

As I have shown in this chapter, the subjectivities produced through martial motherhood discourses are constrained, their limits becoming apparent when a figure such as Peace Mom Cindy Sheehan appears and poses ideological challenges to the prevailing maternal narratives. To construct Security Moms, PR tactics and groups working through news organizations retool the liberal politics of Soccer Moms in order for their maternal practices to fit in a post-9/11, GWOT context. As part of this process, news discourses cast Soccer Moms as naïve and ineffective at the job of keeping their families and children safe from "bad guys,"[10] as head Security Mom Michelle Malkin calls them. Likewise, news treatments of Cindy Sheehan and the handful of other war-protesting military mothers serve both to discipline them and to set the bounds of acceptable criticism of wars that in some cases had killed or injured their children. In this case, we can see Foucault's notion of states exercising power over the life of a population emerging in discursive constructions of Security Moms and military mothers who give life to both the troops fighting these wars and to the meanings that articulate to wartime mothering.

An additional and significant means by which maternal practice is constrained in this dimension of the militaristic regime of representation is in the absence of mothers (or anyone else, for that matter) residing in Iraq and Afghanistan, who, with their unchanging "mom's heart," certainly suffer just as much as their U.S. counterparts. One news story ends with the Gold Star Mother Diane Layfield explaining that she is comforted by support she receives from other military mothers and their service-member children: "They are all our sons and daughters. . . . Who knows where we get the strength? I guess from each other" (Carney 2009). The context of this article clarifies that "all" the sons and daughters whom Layfield references here are U.S. service members, not Iraqi or Afghan sons and daughters whose mothers are surely just as grief filled about losing their children in attacks by U.S. forces. News discourses about mothers thus act as trajectories that guide us to identify with the maternal affects of U.S. mothers only—their fear, sadness, and grief—as they obscure the affects and even the very existence of populations of mothers living in lands targeted and occupied by U.S. military forces. These persistently absent figures signal that they lack both recognizability and grievability, in Judith Butler's terms. Mothers featured in news discourses express no empathy for the agony that mothers in Iraq and Afghanistan experience when their children are killed by U.S. drone strikes or other bombings and attacks.

The exception to such nationalistic maternity appeared in the *Washington Post*, just days before the war on Iraq began. The columnist Donna Britt told readers that as she evaluated the reasons for going to war proffered by the Bush administration, she could not silence the voice of her identity as an African American woman:

> [It] whispers that at this moment—in barracks, distant cities and far-flung deserts—other people's sons and daughters are eating, laughing, studying, hanging out as sons and daughters do. That weeks from now, they could be gone. Irrevocably. Not by car accidents or drugs or disease. Gone by virtue of a war not yet begun. . . .
>
> I see war primarily as a parent. I see it as a thief of sons and daughters whose loss is unfathomable. . . . Few talk about the calculations we inwardly make for war. No politician says, "Bombing Saddam Hussein—and unfortunately killing dozens, hundreds—who knows how many?—children will make our kids safer." No mother wonders aloud, "How many at-risk Iraqi youngsters—or Afghan, Palestinian or Israeli youngsters—are worth risking mine?" (Britt 2003)

That Britt felt compelled to whisper her misgivings about the morbid calculation that sacrifices some mothers' children to save our own reveals much about the meanings of martial motherhood constituted in this regime of representation. Perhaps most importantly, these maternal representations articulate to a bellicose and patriarchal right-wing ideology that is sold as the essential nature of mothers everywhere and therefore off-limits to scrutiny.

Such counterintuitive mothering that requires women to sacrifice their children and remain silent about the war making that destroys them is a politics that masquerades as a stance beyond politics—outside of discourse and therefore beyond the realm of public contestation. Protesting war on behalf of one's child and therefore challenging the prevailing meaning of martial motherhood, as Cindy Sheehan does, is behavior that these discourses treat with nationalistic opprobrium. The process of naturalizing *maters bellicosa* that unfolds in this chapter works discursively to simultaneously universalize and mask both war *and* its identity politics. With a single exception, the mothers whose images appeared in news and PR discourses were white, and most hewed to the neoconservative ideology that Bush administration officials held and promoted in their justifications for bombing and then occupying Iraq and Afghanistan. Yet in this part of the representational regime, they come to stand in for all mothers, regardless of racial, national, or class identity.

Media representations such as these are neither accidental nor inevitable: they emerge from the coordinated efforts of various actors and organizations with a stake in the outcome of war. In this case, news outlets partner either knowingly or not with groups whose mission is to garner and maintain support for wars and neoconservative foreign policy. As I discuss in the introduction to this book, U.S. media corporations have ties to the military-industrial complex through such defense contractors as General Electric and DynCorp, and these relationships influence war reporting—something documented extensively by numerous media researchers. The uncritical incorporation of PR messaging into news coverage, such as that constructing Security Moms and military mothers, can also be traced to the commercial imperative that even news divisions be profitable. To accomplish this, over the past several decades news organizations have laid off thousands of reporters and editors, newspapers have gone out of business, and both domestic and international news-gathering operations found in most media organizations work with only a skeleton crew (for more on how these trends are shaping the future of news, see Nadler and Vavrus 2015). Thus, these days press releases and VNRs issuing from front groups such as Move America Forward and special-interest PR campaigns easily find their way into news stories produced by harried, overworked reporters who may also share an ideological affinity with these groups' nationalistic messaging.[11]

For mothers after 9/11, these media signifying practices have worked to naturalize and depoliticize martial subjectivities as a means of bolstering military recruitment and public support for unpopular wars. Whereas these representations and those I interrogate in chapter 1 deal mainly with women who are not in military service, chapter 3 is an examination of constructions of military women in the context of combat operations.

3

"No Longer Women, but Soldiers"

The Warrior Women of
Television News

> This has to be Osama bin Laden's worst
> nightmare!
> —Catherine Callaway, CNN, November
> 2001

Before dementia claimed his speech, my normally talkative father, a veteran of World War II, would chat endlessly about his war experiences, at times breaking into song; in his repertoire was one with this refrain: "If WACs and WAVES can win this war, then what the hell are *we* fighting for?" As Dad remembered it, he and the other men in his outfit sang this ditty to express the frustration and discouragement that arose from fighting far from home in a war that did not always seem winnable. He and his compatriots would have welcomed any assistance in their efforts, he maintained, even if it came from WACs and WAVES[1]—women whose abilities and patriotism, they believed, were as strong as theirs. Perhaps his reminiscence became more WAC friendly as time went on, or perhaps his Army unit really was welcoming to these military women (the song's jettisoning of the feminine from its masculinized "we" suggests otherwise). Regardless, the song's suggestion that military women could "win this war" is one that permeates news stories exploring the issue of women serving in combat after September 11, 2001. And, like the song, these stories work to discursively constitute meaning around military women by affirming women as martially competent.

In the intervening sixty-plus years since that song's World War II debut, the question of whether women are suitable for combat has been debated repeatedly in military settings and media discourses of all kinds. By 2005, it seemed the debate had been all but settled when Joshua Goldstein, author of the book *War and Gender*, declared on an episode of *Nightline*, "I think the debate over women in the US military is over, in the sense that . . . it should be an all-male institution. That debate is over. The debate about where exactly the line should be drawn, about combat versus non-combat, that goes on. But it's getting narrower" (ABC 2005a). Eight years after Goldstein's pronouncement, Secretary of Defense Leon Panetta announced that the Pentagon had eliminated the combat-exclusion policy for women, giving the branches of the military and the Special Operations Command three years to open 250,000 or so jobs that had previously been closed to women (Bumiller and Shanker 2013). This decision was military driven, recommended by the Joint Chiefs of Staff to Panetta, who quickly acted on it (Eager 2014, 178). Paige Eager recounts that both Secretary of Defense Panetta and chair of the Joint Chiefs General Martin Dempsey had observed service women at work in Afghanistan and Iraq, which convinced them that the combat-exclusion policy was unfair. During a trip to Baghdad in 2003, General Dempsey boarded a Humvee, "slapped the turret gunner on the leg and asked, 'and who are you?' The reply was, 'I am Amanda.'" Dempsey realized then that a "female soldier was protecting a division commander in a combat zone," a situation that illuminated battlefield changes that he had not been fully aware of; he subsequently resolved to change the policy to "reflect those realities" (Eager 2014, 179).

In this chapter, I examine those realities as they are constructed in TV news coverage of women serving in combat arms in the U.S. military. Because the long-standing combat prohibition for women was lifted during this period, these representations offer a vantage point from which to observe news-media perspectives on women's suitability for combat before and after the ban's elimination. Between 2001 and 2013, when Panetta announced the end of the combat ban, service women deployed to Iraq and Afghanistan had been fired on, injured, and killed, occurrences that necessitated military and public discussions of the ban and especially whether tactics of contemporary warfare made it obsolete. In the TV news segments that aired after September 11, 2001, ninety-three different ones in all, I observed coverage spikes after service women were injured or killed or when gender-related military policy was under review at the Pentagon and in Congress. Incidents such as the 2003 attack in Nasiriyah, Iraq, that brought Army Private Jessica Lynch to fame, for example, spurred discussions over myriad issues surrounding women's suitability for combat.

But the pattern I expected to see—that prior to the combat ban's elimination news media would not favor women's inclusion but afterward they would—did not emerge among these representations. Instead, news accounts throughout this period were overwhelmingly favorable toward women in combat roles and together constituted an affirmative perspective on this issue—one that significantly departs from news coverage of women in other wars and conflicts, such as that documented by Tina Managhan (2012), Carol Stabile (1994), and Yvonne Tasker (2011), for example. This piece of the regime, which I have labeled Warrior Women,[2] is constructed from three overlapping discursive strategies. The first strategy emphasizes that in modern warfare, soldiers are always already in combat and should be trained for such conditions. The second equates service women to men by establishing that they are equally capable, that warfare is gender neutral, and that women warriors deserve equality of opportunity to break through the "brass ceiling." The third follows the second strategy closely, by minimizing those gender differences that have historically stood in the way of combat duty. Of course, there is not 100 percent agreement among these mainstream news outlets, which also proffer reasons for why women should not serve in combat arms: physical strength differences and motherhood are the two obstacles cited most often. But despite offering occasional challenges to women's warrior capabilities, TV news discourses mainly legitimate, normalize, and affirm women as warriors, constituting the meanings associated with them throughout this period.

Affirmation such as this should not surprise anyone who has had an eye on popular culture for the past fifteen years; there, a niche has emerged of warrior-approving accounts by and about women serving in the post-9/11 military. Books such as Kristen Holmstedt's *Band of Sisters: American Women at War in Iraq* (2007), Jane Blair's *Hesitation Kills: A Female Marine Officer's Combat Experience in Iraq* (2011), and Helen Thorpe's *Soldier Girls: The Battles of Three Women at Home and at War* (2014) reside with numerous film and TV documentary treatments of the same topic. In an anthology chapter titled "The Challenge of Warrior Women: Gender, Race, and Militarism in Media," I have analyzed six film and TV documentaries in this oeuvre (Vavrus 2017).[3] These representations are strikingly similar to the TV news stories in my sample, although news treatments are much briefer and more superficial than the documentaries. Here in chapter 3, I extend the analysis and argue that TV news stories play an important public role in constituting women as warriors, affirming them in that capacity with the discursive strategies I enumerate earlier, while also situating them as postfeminist, postracial martial subjects. Before illustrating these patterns, I offer a brief discussion of women warriors in military history and media.

Historicizing Women Warriors

Coverage of women in combat during this fifteen-year period parallels that of the feminist movement during the 1970s, according to Caryl Rivers, who refers to this as the "'front page' phase" of coverage. At a time when feminists were making enough social and political gains that reporters were forced to pay attention, news media started to regularly feature "'first' [woman] stories: first astronaut, first firefighter, first heart surgeon, and so on" (Rivers 1996, 105). Much combat coverage is of this variety and includes stories about the first women to graduate from Army Ranger school, awe-struck accounts of women in Marines infantry training camp, and memorials to the first U.S. service women to die while serving in Iraq and Afghanistan. A more recent news item showcased the first woman appointed by West Point to occupy the highest position in the cadet chain of command to lead its forty-four-hundred-member Corps of Cadets. It is worth noting that the highly regarded First Captain Simone Askew is African American (U.S. Military Academy 2017).

August 2015 saw news outlets reporting on the first women to graduate from Army Ranger school—a grueling course of training that only 40 percent of men complete each year. In an NPR interview, West Point graduates First Lieutenant Shaye Haver and Captain Kristen Griest both confirm that the difficulty of the training course had led them to at least briefly consider quitting. But for Haver, "the ability to look around to my peers and to see they were sucking just as bad as I was, kept me going." Just as Haver compares her performance to that of the men around her, Army spokespersons do the same with Haver and Griest. For example, the guest speaker at the Rangers graduation ceremony, Major General Scott Miller, assures the audience that the standards Haver and Griest met were identical to those of their male counterparts (Neuman 2015). And on *Good Morning America*, Ranger training brigade commander Colonel David Fivecoat emphasizes to Martha Raddatz that the two women endured "the exact same thing their male counterparts [did] and have to show grit and determination and put one foot in front of the other each day" (ABC 2015a). Although Havers and Griest surely endured more than their male counterparts in sexist treatment, TV news accounts of their accomplishment are absent any mention of that possibility. As commentators glorify Havers's and Griest's achievement, they concomitantly express dismay that because of the ban on front-line combat jobs in place at that time, these accomplished Army Rangers would not be permitted to do the work they had just been trained to do.

But it was not always thus that military women were praised in public discourse. Linda Bird Francke shows that despite general acceptance of women serving in the military—even in combat roles over the course of history—every moment of progress challenging this "last intact all-male domain, save for the priesthood," has been met with military and civilian resistance. Rooted in patriarchal military culture, such challenges to military women have questioned "not whether women could perform combat roles, but whether women should," she argues (1997, 18–19). The experience of WACs, for example, illustrates cultural resistance to women's participation in warfare. Shortly after the Pearl Harbor bombing, the Army formed the Women's Army Auxiliary Corps, which became an official part of the Army as the Women's Army Corps (WAC) in 1943 (Goldstein 2001; Meyer 1996). The Air Force, Navy, and Marines soon followed suit with women's divisions of their own. Joshua Goldstein points out that although WACs were well regarded among their Army peers, public opinion of them was poor due to a media whisper campaign to cast them as "women with low morals" (2001, 92), something I discuss later in this chapter.

Despite cultural and institutional resistance to women warriors, one can find numerous international and transhistorical examples of them, as Goldstein has. However, these are exceptions that "together amount to far fewer than 1 percent of all warriors in history" (Goldstein 2001, 10). Even accounting for multiple changes in militaries worldwide since the mid-twentieth century, "combat forces today almost totally exclude women, and the entire global military system has so few women and such limited roles for them as to make many of its most important settings all-male" (11). But Goldstein notes as well that NATO militaries have been steadily including more women each year and in general progressing along a similar path: "from combat aviation, to combat ships, to submarines, to ground combat" (84). Historical examples do exist of women's mobilization into combat arms leading to improvements in military power, but these are few and far between; typically, they emerge in societies faced by extreme threats that necessitate women being utilized in this way (Goldstein 2001, 70). For instance, the World War I Russian "Battalion of Death" comprised a combat unit of three hundred women and four hundred men that battled and defeated German troops. After the victory, the battalion's women were instructed by their commander, Maria Botchkareva, to regard themselves differently. They "were no longer women, but soldiers," she announced (Goldstein 2001, 76). Botchkareva's distinction marks the perceived incompatibility between femininity and combat that continues to inform public discourse around women in combat, underlying the Warrior Women media niche that I referenced earlier and informing the title of this chapter.

Despite the numerous public challenges to women serving in the military, hundreds of thousands of them have done so in the United States since World War I. The Women's Research and Education Institute (WREI) traces their official, active duty to 1901 and unofficial service back to the Revolutionary War era, when women disguised themselves as men to be able to fight while others followed their husbands to their camps and even into battle (2013, 5). Jeanne Holm's history of women in the U.S. military reveals that during this time women such as Molly Pitcher (an alias for two women, possibly) fought in place of their injured husbands and were glorified for their heroism, while others donned men's or boys' clothing so that they too could fight in the Continental army (1982, 4–5). Holm explains that all wars following this one saw a similar pattern of "rapid mobilization for war and equally rapid demobilization at war's end," which pushed women into and then out of military service. Goldstein maintains that throughout history and across the globe, significant numbers of women have been enlisted into the military "only in times of extreme need in war" (2001, 93). Francke concurs, noting that during "times of national crisis, women are suddenly indispensable to the services. In times of peace, they are just as quickly disposable" (1997, 22).

Not until the military began a process of stabilizing and institutionalizing its recruitment and enlistment practices in 1948 were women granted permanent places in the U.S. military (Holm 1982, 5). The Women's Armed Services Act of 1948 gave women peacetime military service opportunities in the Air Force, Army, Navy, and Marines, and the act came about as the result of pitched battles in Congress. Holm argues that its passage reflected a tacit acceptance of the need for women's labor for rapid mobilization more than it was an endorsement of their right to military service; consequently, it set a 2 percent employment cap on military women (114). Following on the act's heels, in 1951 Secretary of Defense George C. Marshall created the Defense Advisory Committee on Women in the Services (DACOWITS) to recruit more women during the Korean War, a time when the military was encountering enlistment difficulties (Francke 1997; Goldstein 2001; WREI 2013). Francke explains that since the committee's inception, DACOWITS members have been indispensable advocates for women's increased presence in the military and particularly during and after the Gulf War—the focus of her account (1997, 22).[4] Cynthia Enloe argues that DACOWITS has been most influential in shaping the image of the woman soldier as a "still-feminine, professionalized 'citizen-patriot'" (1994, 92).

Other policies governing military women were made and changed after the creation of DACOWITS. In 1967, President Johnson lifted the 2 percent enlistment cap, a move that permitted women to be promoted to higher pay grades and ranks and made the military a more attractive career option for women (WREI 2013, 9). But because policies are not always implemented as intended, in 1971 the DoD established the Defense Equal Opportunity Management Institute (DEOMI) to conduct diversity training meant to reduce racism within the armed services; since its inception, it has expanded its training to "cover every subgroup which was not white, male and Christian" (Francke 1997, 242). Today DEOMI works with the Sexual Assault Prevention and Response Office (SAPRO) to fight sexual harassment, as well, an effort to further protect service members (more on that in chapter 4). Brenda L. Moore attributes the passage of the Defense Officer Manpower Personnel Management Act (DOPMA) during the 1980s with further support for military women; this act stipulates that women officers be treated as equals to men in appointment, promotion, and service separation (2017, 192).

Conscription's end in 1973 prompted a steady rise in the number of women in military service. WREI figures show that as of 2012, 14.5 percent of enlisted service members were women, and 18.5 percent of service women were officers (2013, 17, 18). Among both enlisted women and officers, a significant percentage are women of color: 55.4 percent and 38 percent, respectively (18). Moore points out that the large number of African American women serving is attributable to military efforts to achieve racial equality: "The military has been seen as the only viable avenue for upward mobility by many bright and ambitious African Americans" (1996, 124). If history is a guide, numbers of women in both enlisted and officer ranks are likely to increase now that the combat ban has been lifted and women's combat experience will count toward promotion. Racial imbalances, however, may continue even as more women are promoted based on their combat experience: women (and men) of color—especially African Americans—are overrepresented in the enlisted ranks and underrepresented among officers, a problem that Judith Hicks Stiehm refers to as the "higher the fewer" (1996, 67). Additional evidence suggests that women of color are less likely than white women to choose combat roles for themselves; Laura L. Miller's research on Army women's attitudes toward combat includes an African American noncommissioned officer (NCO) justifying her (and others') reluctance to volunteer for combat: "We've suffered enough already in life. Why would we want to take on anything more?" (1998, 55). Eileen Patten and Kim Parker find that "compared with their male counterparts, a greater share of military women are black and a smaller share are married" (2011, 1). Zillah Eisenstein adds that this "multiracial newly gendered working class" of the twenty-first-century military is compensated poorly, with beginning salaries roughly equivalent to what they would make at Walmart or McDonald's; combat forces therefore consist mainly of those with just a high-school education (2007, 59–60).[5]

Following Goldstein's extensive survey of women serving in combat roles around the world, he concludes that women "have generally performed about as well as most men have. Women in combat support roles, furthermore, have had little trouble fitting into military organization, and have held their own when circumstances occasionally placed them in combat. . . . They can fight; they can kill" (2001, 126). WREI observes that women's performance during the wars in Iraq and Afghanistan has dispelled concerns about how they would perform "under fire," demonstrating instead their "importance and prowess" to counterinsurgency warfare (2013, 17). Between 1948 and the 1990s, Congress, various presidents, and the DoD chipped away at the combat exclusion policy. By 1993, women were officially permitted to occupy Air Force and Navy "combat cockpits"; and in 1994, the Navy "opened combat ships to women," and "the Army, under pressure from its black male secretary, Togo D. West Jr., muscled the white male club of the Army into opening over 32,000 new jobs to women" (Francke 1997, 255). In the intervening twenty years before the combat ban was lifted, various policy changes such as the repeal of the DoD Risk Rule[6] opened more positions to women that moved them closer to or into combat, though the ground-combat exclusion was maintained until 2013 (WREI 2013). The recruiting difficulties that all branches of the military experienced a few years into the wars in Iraq and Afghanistan, along with the aspects of war specific to these countries, probably necessitated a discussion of how to bring more women into combat roles; but even with the ban in place, 11 percent of the fighting forces experiencing regular deployments to Iraq and Afghanistan have been composed of women, according to Tanya Biank. Thus, "today's generation of servicewomen [has seen] more war service than either their fathers or grandfathers" (2014, 5).

Gendering War

Despite a profusion of examples of women fighting in wars great and small, historically combat has been a masculine endeavor, whereas support and peacemaking have been coded feminine—an Othering process based on gender essentialism. Eisenstein pithily summarizes the division this way: "War institutionalizes sexual differentiation while also undermining it. War demands opposition, differentiation, and the othering of peoples. The privileging of masculinity underscores all other processes of differentiation. War is a process by which masculinity is both produced and reproduced. The heroic warrior is the standard. Everyone else is a pussy, a wimp, a fag" (2007, 25). Virtually all feminist scholars who study the relationship between war and gender point to cultural and political practices that persistently naturalize, normalize, and reinforce links between masculinity and war (a very abbreviated list includes Carter 1998; D'Amico 1998; Eager 2014; Elshtain 1987; Enloe 1994, 2000; Goldstein 2001; MacKenzie 2015; B. Mitchell 1996; Peach 1996; Sjoberg 2014). From the phallic symbolism of war weaponry to the narrative of military men protecting women and children,[7] from the feminization of enemy forces as well as those within the U.S. military who cannot hack its physical and psychological intensity, to the "band of brothers" mythology that suffuses it, war, and by extension the militaries that fight wars, is gendered. Kacy Crowley and Michelle Sandhoff observe that "within the military, the most masculine space is combat," because combat is tied to being both a "real soldier" and a "real man" (2016, 2). And because battlefields are public spaces, Lorraine Dowler notes that excluding women from combat "creates a gendered dichotomy of space whereby women are denied access to powerful political spaces" (2002, 162). Such a division reinforces the separation of these spheres, subordinating women beyond the boundaries of the battlefield.

Megan MacKenzie argues that a "band of brothers" mythology has both inspired and maintained the combat-exclusion policy and does so with three truths: "Nonsexual, brotherly love, male bonding, and feelings of trust, pride, honor, and loyalty between men [are] mysterious, indescribable, and *exceptional*. Second, male bonding is . . . both primal and an *essential* element of an orderly, civilized, society. Third, all male units are . . . *elite* as a result of their social bonds and physical superiority" (2015, 3, emphasis in original). This mythology is central to a war logic that relies on "gendered stories and myths about 'real' men, 'good' women, and 'normal' social order" (4)—a "nodal point from which many military policies stem" (18). Women's integration in the armed forces has illuminated the constructed nature of gender norms and military patriarchy, but not by a long shot has it eliminated them. The pseudonymous military officer Billie Mitchell calls the idea that military women have achieved equality with their male counterparts the "gender lie at the heart of military thinking" (1996, 36). On the basis of research of women's experiences at West Point, she argues that the "story of women in uniform is one about living on the edge of one's gender. Military women are not men. They're not women. This is a story about being a woman who's a man. . . . This is about phallic women. To be a successful Army officer is to be, by definition, a man" (40). Mitchell's study reveals how women must adopt masculine qualities in order to adapt to a hypermasculine institution; yet no amount of adaptation will be sufficient because the military's "culture has put so much energy into linking the [military] task and the phallus. . . . The phallus and the work of the soldier owe something to each other. Their discourses of power are linked" (55).

That women warriors pose a threat to military phallic power explains a great deal about why military men have resisted gender integration so vigorously, despite (or maybe because of) women's repeated demonstrations that they are equally capable as the men. Crowley and Sandhoff's interviews with twelve women who served in combat missions in Iraq reinforces Mitchell's points; in order to fit into predominantly male units, these veterans performed masculinity by constructing themselves as "tomboys" and by persistently denigrating femininity (2016, 4). But even this performance was not enough to make them accepted: all twelve were either victims of or witnesses to sexual harassment and assault (8). "Regardless of how tomboyish they were or how much they defined themselves as different from other women, they were still seen as women," Crowley and Sandhoff conclude (12). Kenneth MacLeish concurs.

In his study of life at the Army post Fort Hood, he describes the Army as "a profoundly gendered institution that places men and women, and masculinity and femininity (to the exclusion of other configurations of gender), in compulsory intimacy with and highly structured opposition to one another. The Army, the profession of soldiering, and the making of war are all ostensibly masculine domains" (2013, 18). Like Crowley and Sandhoff, MacLeish observes a process through which military personnel suppress qualities coded feminine, such as empathy and care, so that men and women can more easily "command and inflict violence" as soldiers (18). The female soldiers at Fort Hood are "deeply invested in the masculine homosociality of Army corporate culture," MacLeish reveals, and tend to use "female" as a pejorative to refer to other women. In this context, females are considered to be "disruptive of good order," use their femininity "as a crutch," and are viewed as "generally less capable" than men. Dana, a woman and an engineer, confesses to MacLeish, "I hate females so much" (19). Dana expresses a sentiment characteristic of what Francine D'Amico calls the "warrior mystique": a mind-set that promotes martial masculinity and "subjects women to greater manipulation by those controlling military institutions, thus allowing women to be militarized but not empowered" (1998, 120).

Media Warriors

Whereas denigrating feminine qualities and expressing hatred for "females" even when one identifies as a woman herself appears to be integral to military culture, a very different gender construction emerges in media culture, particularly among representations that Warrior Women comprises. Despite the strong influence of such military cultures on media content, post-9/11 Warrior Women discourses are overwhelmingly women friendly—a shift most likely driven by the need for military women's labor in Iraq and Afghanistan. Looking back at the emergence of the WAC reveals how regard for military women has changed in media over six-plus decades. Since its earliest incarnation as the Women's Army Auxiliary Corps (WAAC) in 1942, the WAC faced a media campaign waged in newspaper and magazine editorials, war reporting, and especially cartoons that expressed a firm belief that women's feminine qualities would prevent them from being able to carry out their military duties. Leisa D. Meyer's examination of the WAC's trajectory shows mainstream media discourses poking fun at women working in the military by using unflattering stereotypical depictions of WACs as not too bright, incompetent, physically fragile, preoccupied with trivial issues, and generally "illogical or scatterbrained" (1996, 26). According to Meyer, the African American press was generally more supportive than the white press was, an editorial perspective informed by WAAC policy mandating that 10 percent of its members be

African American. This policy cast the military as "one of the major arenas in which the fight for racial equality must take place" (30).

Once the WAAC had been incorporated into the regular Army and lost its auxiliary status in 1943, it again faced attacks on its legitimacy, this time with a "slander" campaign accusing the WAC of "sexual immorality" among its members (Meyer 1996, 34). WACs were accused of being sexually promiscuous, even lesbians. "The lesbian was the epitome of the sexually autonomous woman, not even requiring a male presence to satisfy her sexual desire," writes Meyer; she thus became an effective means of impugning the character of the WAC. Even WAC director Colonel Oveta Culp Hobby, a Texas political insider and newspaper owner, "was taken aback at the vitriol of the slander campaign" (51) and particularly its attacks on women's patriotism. This made recruitment more difficult: expressing a wish to join the WAC "could in itself be cause for suspicion, because 'real women' would not want to be 'soldiers' at all" (43).

To counter the slander campaign, Hobby worked with WAC recruiters and PR staff to reframe women's military service as necessary to win the war but not "radical or threatening" (Meyer 1996, 53); they thus emphasized WAC members' devotion to their families and conveyed a message that "military women were not so much stepping out of the home as they were simply meeting the conflict encroaching on their private sphere" (54). What Hobby found in navigating between the ad agency Young & Rubicam's and her own vision of WAC service influences media representations to this day: "women soldiers must not seem to threaten either male power in the military or the notion that masculinity [is] integrally tied to the definition of 'soldier'" (180). Tasker's examination of films, newsreels, documentaries, and recruiting materials about World War II auxiliary military women extends Meyer's work, as she concludes that such representations "centralize the military woman while insisting on her auxiliary status. Her service is typically taken as a sign of modernity, rhetorically contrasted to previous generations of women constrained by a femininity understood as inappropriate to the needs of the present. To this end, tropes of personal transformation are a recurrent feature of the images and narratives" (2011, 70).

Much of what Tasker sees in representations of auxiliary military women presages TV news discourses about women in combat after 9/11, particularly the emphasis on modernity and personal transformation. Segments that rely on the "first woman to . . ." formula (as those reporting on the first women graduates of Army Ranger school do) feature correspondents and commentators detailing both the difficulty of the tasks that women warriors have successfully completed and the ways in which their achievement has changed them. As they glorify women warriors, these news stories congratulate the military, too, for recognizing women's martial competencies and even excellence—a sign of the institution's gender politics becoming more progressive.

Of course, not all news treatments of women in combat operation are celebratory. The 2003 Jessica Lynch rescue story offers a contradictory construction that numerous feminist and media scholars consider to be the nadir of reporting on women in combat after 9/11. TV news stories and a made-for-TV movie about Private Jessica Lynch's capture by Iraqi forces and rescue were crafted as what Tanner Mirrlees calls a "media pseudo-event," propaganda meant to "make US citizens feel good about the war" (2016, 150). This pseudo-event succeeded in duping most of the U.S. press corps by constituting Lynch—a white, working-class woman from West Virginia—as both hero and victim: brutalized by Iraqi soldiers when she was in captivity, Lynch also fought bravely even as she was being captured (Kumar 2004). Tasker asserts that what was memorable about the Lynch incident was the "extent to which the media presence and contested image of the military woman would so explicitly form part of the Lynch story. The American media first promoted the idea of Lynch as warrior and subsequently as victim, a process that morphed into a self-regarding angst about its own myth-making and the amount of attention Lynch was receiving compared to (real) male soldiers" (2011, 215). Laura Sjoberg observes that much of the media coverage about Lynch emphasized her rescue by Army Rangers and Navy Seals from the hospital where she was recovering from injuries sustained in the attack on her supply tank. Lynch was "*fought for* instead of fighting in much of the story—she was helpless, a captive in an Iraqi hospital. The soldiers needed to save her. She was so helpless that she needed to be rescued before the four other prisoners captured along with her. . . . Of course, Lynch had to be saved—*war is about protecting innocent women*" (2007, 85, emphasis in original).

Vital to Jessica Lynch's story is that it was manufactured to mobilize popular support for the war in Iraq. A list of falsehoods fed by the Pentagon to credulous news media includes that Lynch was shooting her gun when she was captured, that she was shot at, that Iraqi troops withheld medical treatment, and that she was tortured at the Iraqi hospital where she was recovering, a situation that necessitated her rescue. Sjoberg and numerous others—even Lynch herself—have pointed out that these parts of the story were untrue. They did serve a larger purpose, however; Sjoberg argues that in casting Lynch as a "woman of extraordinary bravery; as a victim of Iraqi cruelty and sexual violence; and as an innocent woman in need of saving," the military showed that its goal was to "achieve an idealized image of the militarized woman" (2007, 86).

Perhaps not surprisingly, Jessica Lynch is white, whereas other women in her unit whom media accounts barely mention are not: Shoshana Johnson, who was shot and imprisoned in the same attack that injured Lynch, is African American, and the American Indian Lori Piestewa was killed. After Johnson had been rescued from captivity and returned home, she, like Lynch, reported that she had been treated respectfully by her Iraqi captors. Sjoberg suggests that despite Johnson's and Piestewa's stories from the attack being accurate, whereas Lynch's media rendering was not, women of color do not fit the picture of the "ideal, militarized woman"; they are therefore absent from most media renderings (2007, 87). Melissa Brown's analysis of Army recruiting ads reinforces this idea, as she finds that "African-American women are underrepresented in recruiting ads and overrepresented in the military, especially the Army" (2012, 170). "The ideal of militarized femininity created by the armed forces is by and large white," Brown argues. "This may be because to the larger (white) culture, a white woman more generically represents 'women,' and [is] seen as more feminine and thus as more appealing and nonthreatening. As recruiting ads normalize women's military participation and broaden definitions of femininity by expanding women's roles, the omission of nonwhite women may, like the absence of markers of combat, reinforce gender divisions" (171). Like recruiting ads, television news coverage of women in combat also constructs an idealized image of warrior women; but unlike the ads, TV news features a cast of multiracial warriors and white officers. In the sections that follow, I detail facets of the representations that constitute the Warrior Women regime.

Constituting Warrior Women

Consensus among feminist scholars who study gender and war is that masculine dominance and patriarchy characterize war and military service and that many military women internalize the codes that render them subordinate to men. When the statement "I hate females so much" is uttered by a woman, it reveals loathing for biological characteristics that render women as weaker and less competent than men in martial contexts. An essentialist view of gender relations, this perspective has pervaded military life and warfare. Tasker's examination of U.S. news-media accounts of military women between the 1980s and early 2000s reveals "contradictory tendencies to celebrate and pathologize them" as they attempt to situate women within military culture (2011, 205–6). Perhaps because the representations I examine in this chapter were aired during wartime and focused on the topic of combat, they include little or no pathologizing. Instead, post-9/11 TV news stories laud warrior women for their accomplishments as they constitute them as recognizable, grievable martial subjects. As noted in the introduction, I argue that these news segments work together to discursively construct a Warrior Women (sub)regime of representation—one that constitutes women warriors as martial subjects every bit as capable as men and that fits well in the prowoman, post-9/11 militarized regime I examine throughout *Postfeminist War*. To accomplish this discursive work, TV news stories rely mainly on three formats: debates; in-studio commentary, which often includes action scenes from Iraq and Afghanistan or training camps; and on-site reporting that features embedded war correspondents commenting on service women's contributions to combat and reconnaissance missions.

But no matter the format, TV news stories discursively render military women to be, in Judith Butler's (2010) terms, both recognizable and grievable. In so doing, the Warrior Women regime discursively positions women as equals to service men—the martial subjects we have historically been conditioned to recognize and grieve as such. Like the film and television documentaries I have examined, the system of power in these TV news representations produces truths about military women by insisting that combat is central to and ubiquitous in modern warfare, by equating military women to men, and by minimizing those concerns about gender that have posed obstacles to women serving in combat—specifically, physical strength and motherhood. These discourses thus construct a regime of truth around women warriors that underplays the battlefield and sexual violence that permeate women's military experiences as it celebrates them for their martial prowess. To prescribe to viewers which issues are legitimate in determining combat policy for women, TV news programs use the debate format more than any other. In these stories, anticombat spokespersons raise concerns about women being injured or killed in warfare either because some may be mothers and will therefore leave behind damaged children or because they believe women's ability to fight is not on par with that of men. Echoing many other feminist military scholars, Lucinda Joy Peach observes that the "protection myth, which calls into question the propriety of risking the safety of the nation's childbearers by exposing them to the risks of combat, is evident in the military's traditional approach to pregnancy. The military has historically argued that assigning women to combat would hamper combat effectiveness and efficiency because of their conflicting roles as mothers and potential mothers" (1996, 170). This was particularly evident during the Persian Gulf War, according to Managhan (2012), Stabile (1994), and Tasker (2011). And although the argument that maternity should prevent combat duty pops up sporadically across fifteen years of news segments, it is greatly overwhelmed by its converse—sometimes made by women warriors themselves—that just like fathers, mothers put service to country ahead of family.[8]

Most likely to espouse such anticombat arguments in TV news is Elaine Donnelly of the conservative Center for Military Readiness. A onetime member of DACOWITS and, according to Francke, its "influential archenemy" (1997, 39), Donnelly was a frequent guest on debate-format programs across this fifteen-year span. Her success at helping to whip congressional votes to support combat exclusion from 1984 to 1986 and again in 1992 as a member of the Presidential Commission on the Assignment of Women in the Armed Forces reveals her clout on the combat-exclusion issue. Enloe notes that as a member of the Presidential Commission, Donnelly opposed changing the combat-exclusion policy because she believed women were not "meant to be killers" (1994, 104). Donnelly's view (shared by some others in the Pentagon and even by a few DACOWITS members), moreover, was that "women weakened, not strengthened, the defense of the country" (Francke 1997, 39).[9] Donnelly's views and methods were shaped by Phyllis Schlafly, with whom she worked to fight the Equal Rights Amendment (ERA). Using what she learned from Schlafly, Donnelly started her own organization in 1993—the Center for Military Readiness—funded by various conservative organizations, including Concerned Women for America and Schlafly's Eagle Forum (Francke 1997, 40). In her appearances on post-9/11 TV news, Donnelly argues strenuously against lifting the combat ban, mainly because she opposes soldier mothers serving in combat. "We are a civilized nation. We don't need to send young mothers off to fight our wars," Donnelly asserts on one program (CNNFN 2004). Along with Phyllis Schlafly, a few pundits and legislators, and a variety of retired and active-duty military personnel (usually male officers) also iterate evergreen conservative points about maternity, strength differences, and gender mixing that they believe mitigate against women serving in combat.

Despite the availability, public visibility, and mediagenic presence of the anticombat supporters (Donnelly chief among them), they are no match for the parties who push to eliminate the combat ban. The procombat faction comprises numerous retired military personnel, legislators (two of whom are women veterans: Representatives Tammy Duckworth[10] and Tulsi Gabbard), war correspondents, and program hosts such as Ted Koppel of *Nightline*. Combat supporters not only are more numerous than those in the anticombat group but also include women veterans actively advocating for the elimination of the combat-exclusion policy. Among this group, retired Army Brigadier General Pat Foote (president of the procombat Alliance for National Defense) and retired Navy Captain Lory Manning (director of the procombat Women's Research and Education Institute) appear most frequently. Having served in combat roles themselves and witnessed other women doing so as well, these veteran officers and others like them make a compelling case for allowing women in combat arms. This contingent's argument for the elimination of the combat ban coalesces around three main points (which I detail shortly): that women already serve de facto in ground combat, that women warriors perform combat duties as well as men do, and that gender differences between service women and men should be considered minimal and inconsequential. In the sections that follow, I provide representative examples that illustrate the affirmative character of the Warrior Women regime.

"Combat Is Everywhere"

In an appearance on CNN's *American Morning*, retired Air Force Brigadier General Wilma Vaught—a decorated Vietnam War veteran and former member of DACOWITS—provides a commander's perspective on the question of whether women are suitable for combat. Vaught comments that "given the nature of the situation in Iraq, combat is everywhere. And if you're going to do your job, you're in harm's way" (CNN 2005e)—a point made ad infinitum by many others as well to justify doing away with the combat ban. The favored rationale that procombat spokespersons proffer for ending the combat-exclusion rule is that of de facto combat, or combat being everywhere, as Vaught puts it. To this group, the conditions of post-9/11 warfare have rendered the notion of an isolated front line—battles take place there and only there—virtually meaningless. Because IEDs, car bombs, and suicide bombers regularly wreak havoc across U.S.-occupied spaces such as Iraq's Green Zone, combat occurs in spots historically considered to be behind front lines; women should therefore be trained to fight in such conditions.

Goldstein dates the notion of vanishing front lines to the 1991 Persian Gulf War (2001, 95), but others observe that even during the Vietnam War, distinct front lines were all but impossible to maintain. In *Women in War* (2014), the Army nurse and Vietnam veteran Diane Carlson Evans remembers that "the combat zone [was] 360 degrees around you"; there, the only difference between the women and men was that women "could be shot at but . . . couldn't shoot back." This is one reason that the combat-exclusion policy has posed an "untenable paradox," according to MacKenzie. As the policy was being maintained after 9/11, women were dying from what the Pentagon recognized as "hostile operations"; in recognition of their performance in such operations, some women were compensated with combat pay and honored for their valor and contributions to combat (2015, 46). Across the news stories I examine, military personnel, correspondents, and commentators express the impossibility of maintaining both combat-only spaces and the distinction between combat and noncombat roles for deployed military personnel of any gender in Iraq and Afghanistan.

Defining and establishing the boundaries around combat is an important process in constructing Warrior Women's regime of truth. Reiterated assertions about combat being everywhere or 360-degree combat zones or vanishing front lines present these as uncontested or just the way things are in warfare. The CNN Pentagon correspondent Barbara Starr adds additional credibility to this view when she refers to combat supporters' wish to convey "the *reality* of wars like Iraq, where even supply clerks, technicians, medical personnel, truck drivers, military police, all the jobs that some of those nearly 10,000 women do, are jobs that put them at risk, that literally do put them in combat" (CNN 2005g). Referring to the female Army captain and combat-helicopter pilot Toby Johnson, a voice-over from *World News Tonight with Peter Jennings* asserts that "for the men in Captain Johnson's unit in Kuwait, women soldiers are a fact of life" (ABC 2003b). *Nightline* host Ted Koppel recounts,

"When I was embedded with the 3rd Infantry Division, first in Kuwait and then in Iraq, back in the spring of 2003, I must confess I was surprised by the number of women soldiers that were up there with us at what the Army was calling 'the point of the spear.' Intelligence officers, helicopter pilots, fuel truck drivers—the women were everywhere" (ABC 2005a). Statements such as these about facts of life and realities of combat prescribe to viewers what they should understand about actual conditions of warfare and therefore establish a truth about women serving in combat roles in Iraq and Afghanistan: that the contemporary default for women's service is always already combat.

Stories about and by military women reinforce this idea. For example, Representatives Tammy Duckworth and Tulsi Gabbard, both combat veterans, appeared on various news programs to detail the duties that service women perform when deployed: for example, Gabbard explained to CNN's Soledad O'Brien that two female Silver Star recipients received their medals for "operating on the front lines . . . under fire, under extreme duress, shoulder to shoulder with their male and female counterparts and exhibiting great courage and heroism and saving the lives of their brothers and sisters" (CNN 2013a). Gabbard's point was powerfully reinforced by Army Sergeant Leigh Ann Hester (the first woman to be awarded a Silver Star since World War II) as she tersely relayed to *World News Tonight with Diane Sawyer* the story of the battle for which she received her medal: "We were taking fire everywhere. I just remember hearing the pings of the bullets going by me and hitting the ground beside me. I shot one guy. I saw him fall" (ABC 2013b). Or there was this *Nightline* exchange between interviewer Deborah Amos and Army Private Theresa Broadwell about a firefight in Iraq:

AMOS: With three American soldiers already down, machine gunner Broadwell had to cover her lieutenant, as he jumped out to try to rescue the fallen Americans.

BROADWELL: They hadn't stopped the truck yet when we started taking fire.

AMOS: How did you know when it was time to shoot?

BROADWELL: As soon as I heard them shooting at us. And it was . . . you really don't have time to think about it. It's just—it just happens.

AMOS: Broadwell was awarded the Bronze Star and a Purple Heart for her role in the firefight—a war hero at twenty. (ABC 2005a)

These segments emphasize that despite the exclusion policy, service women bravely soldier on as they add the "already" to this post-9/11 truth about Warrior Women.

Representations such as these also make women warriors recognizable, in Judith Butler's terms, because they illustrate in quite graphic terms how precarious life becomes on the battlefield and how dependent soldiers are on one another. Private Broadwell, for example, becomes a hero because she puts herself in harm's way to rescue her fellow troops and thus illustrates that "one's life is always in some sense in the hands of the other. . . . Reciprocally, it implies being impinged upon by the exposure and dependency of others" (J. Butler 2010, 14). Other soldiers featured in news segments are also depicted as enmeshed in networks of military personnel, while some explicitly call out their dependency on their compatriots. A CNN story from June 2005, for example, reported on a Marine unit in Fallujah, Iraq, that had lost three female members the previous day in an attack that injured eleven more. After featuring comments from three women in the unit, the reporter turns to Sergeant Trent Padmore, burned as he pulled some of the blast survivors to safety. Asked about his female peers, Padmore tells reporter Jane Arraf, "I personally know that we need them here, and I'm glad that they are here. . . . I've been in firefights with at least three of them, . . . and they all conducted themselves professionally. They're Marines. . . . I really wish people would stop calling them female Marines because they're Marines. That's what they are" (CNN 2005f).

Constructing military women as "no longer women, but soldiers," and therefore recognizable as combat warriors, TV news discourses engage in an iterative process of transformation that Butler describes as "solicitation." In this context, women ask to be recognized, but not for what they already are; rather, they "solicit a becoming, . . . instigate a transformation, . . . petition the future always in relation to the Other" (J. Butler 2004a, 44). The Other here is the figure of the masculine warrior who has dominated popular and media cultures seemingly since time immemorial. But by elevating to visibility service women's presence in combat zones as well as their bravery and sacrifices there, Warrior Women representations enable their transformation to recognizability by diminishing their status as Other to this martial realm. Additionally, the segment just discussed exemplifies grievability, which works in concert with the precariousness at the heart of these concepts. Sergeant Padmore's distress palpable, his reminiscence about his fallen comrades expresses both sadness for their deaths and admiration for the martial skill they exhibited while alive. He grieves the women as Marines and wants no gender distinction made for them. In Padmore's and the rest of this segment's commentary, precariousness, recognizability, and grievability are intertwined in a discursive construction that casts women as warriors.

As news reports establish that combat zones are ubiquitous in Iraq and Afghanistan and that women, too, fight heroically and die in them, they further naturalize the disappearance of front lines using passive-voice reiterations of their disappearance and metaphors that suggest that the processes by which front lines have disappeared are either unknown or naturally occurring. This is more than an academic issue: not identifying the agents responsible for such a change and suggesting that ubiquitous combat zones come about simply as a result of natural processes situates this essential aspect of warfare outside of discourse, where other naturally occurring phenomena seem to reside. Representing combat and warfare as outside of human intervention discourages critical scrutiny and instead encourages viewers to accept them as inevitable, unchangeable aspects of human nature and social organization. For example, when the CBS News reporter David Martin intones, "it has been said repeatedly there are no front lines in Iraq" (CBS 2005a), he renders absent both the decision-makers and the decision-making processes that determine where the U.S. military fights and for what reasons. Martin's use of passive voice is so common in TV news as to be passé, as is the point made by the NBC reporter Jim Maceda, that "in this insurgent war, front lines have melted away" (NBC 2005b). Front lines that melt away like ice from a Minnesota lake suggests that a natural process—not military policy created and executed by human agents—is responsible for their disappearance. These news programs' framing of front lines discourages exploration of the issue of how they come to be there in the first place.

Despite how TV news programs render war, it is neither inevitable nor naturally occurring: front lines are not simply here today and gone tomorrow as a result of natural forces. Instead they result from the concerted political and economic calculations of legislators, military policy makers, and presidents. Once these parties decide to make war, they need media to affirm the decision and legitimate subsequent attacks: a process that numerous scholars have documented among U.S. media (as I discuss in the introduction). In news discourses, the combat-is-everywhere truism recognizes women as warriors poised to fight anywhere as it situates war policy outside the realm of discourse; but it further obscures the consideration of war, front lines, and warriors themselves as political constructions. Those fighters designated as insurgents, for example, lack the credibility—and thus the recognizability and grievability—of U.S. troops, no matter their gender identity. Naturalizing these aspects of combat in this way also serves to rationalize policies that make war appear to be inevitable and therefore justify its perpetuation. Additionally, this discursive treatment clarifies that military women's combat labor is both necessary and important to waging this new brand of war. Captain Lory Manning says as much when she tells NBC's Jim Miklaszewski that legislation being debated at that time, 2005, to ban women from combat-support units would "devastate the Army," as it then comprised 27 percent women, many of whom are routinely deployed for combat-support missions (NBC 2005a).

Judith Butler argues that these media representations act as trajectories of affect; as such, they orient audiences to understand, sympathize, and even empathize with their subjects in particular ways. TV news coverage, for example, "positions citizens as visual consumers of a violent conflict that happens elsewhere, at least in the United States where geographical distance from our so-called enemies allows us to wage war without close domestic scrutiny of our actions" (J. Butler 2010, xv). When the women are everywhere, as is combat, it becomes easier for viewers to avoid scrutinizing the processes, people, and policies that bring wars into being and maintain them; this strategy, then, "naturalizes the effects of war as a presupposed background for everyday life" (xiv). Although this coverage hints at this fact, neither reporters nor guests point out that front lines are as ideological as they are material—a discursive strategy that naturalizes both front lines and the process that designates them in the manner Butler explains.

While combat being everywhere sounds a cautionary note about front lines that encourages combat training for service women, this trope does other, political, work as well. Its apparently nonpartisan message and reportorial tone mask its place in neoconservative rhetoric circulated by Bush administration officials as a way to legitimate tactics associated with the GWOT and particularly to justify invading Iraq. During the run-up to the Iraq War, Douglas Kellner reports that President Bush and the neocons surrounding him "regularly described the 'war against terrorism' as World War III, while U.S. Secretary of Defense Donald Rumsfeld said that it could last as long as the Cold War and Dick Cheney, speaking like a true militarist, said it could go on for a 'long, long time, perhaps indefinitely.'" This neoconservative logic, Kellner continues, created "an Orwellian nightmare" that would "plunge the world into a new millennium of escalating war with unintended consequences, and embroil the United States in countless wars, normalizing war as conflict resolution and creating countless new enemies for the would-be American hegemon" (2005, x). That a discursive strategy of encouraging combat training for women could subtly reinforce neoconservative fearmongering by other means reveals how readily martial postfeminism may be pressed into the service of a specific political agenda—all the while appearing to stand outside of politics and discourse as nothing more than a practical training consideration.

"America's Daughters Are Just as Capable of Defending Liberty and Freedom as Her Sons"

Voiced on *ABC News* in 2013 in response to the end of the combat ban, Representative Tammy Duckworth's assertion in this subheading pithily expresses the perspective of the great majority of the guests, pundits, and correspondents who discuss women in combat during their TV news appearances: service women are martially capable in equal measure to service men and have therefore earned the right officially to serve in combat. This strategy comprises three reiterated points: that service women and men possess similar, if not identical, militarily significant qualities (what I call *equivalence*); that dangers of warfare are gender neutral; and that women's military careers are needlessly hampered by the combat-exclusion policy. (In conversations about military careers, some guests refer to a "brass ceiling" that limits women's promotion to top ranks.) These rationales are proffered at various times by most everyone who appears in post-9/11 TV news coverage of women in combat, their words working together with visual imagery from Iraq and Afghanistan of women serving alongside men and undergoing grueling physical training regimens.

Equivalence. To establish equality between women and men, TV news stories offer reassurances that service women and men are similar, if not identical, to one another in militarily significant attributes. For example, we learn that women enlist in the military for the same reasons men do and, once enlisted, that they are equally capable as men. When CNNFN's Muriel Siebert asks Captain Lory Manning why women enlist in the military, Manning replies, "Well, I think it's kind of for the same reasons the men do. Education, I think, is a very big factor. Money for college, skills trading, and this good old standby, the reason I joined, to travel. To get out and see the world" (CNNFN 2003). Commentators also express reasons for enlistment that go beyond practicality and into the symbolic: retired Lieutenant Colonel Karen Johnson defends women's desires to join combat missions on *The Early Show* by reminding anchor Hannah Storm, "To be an American citizen you have a right to be able to participate in the military and to serve the military as a full and responsible citizen. And as women, we are patriotic. We care about our country, and we're willing to fight and to die for our country" (CBS 2005a). On *NBC Nightly News*, Grace Barnett, the first woman to enlist in Army infantry, explains her reason for wanting to be in combat this way: "Serving the country that I love, and that—that gets you right here [*she points to her heart*]. It—it's very much part of my blood" (NBC 2016).

While the women featured in these discourses are being patriotic and practical, they are also prochoice about combat, emphasizing that women should be allowed the option of training for and fighting in combat missions. Perhaps the most credible advocates of this position are military women themselves, who explain that they possess the attributes necessary to successfully execute the tasks involved in such missions. "In my eyes, God created everyone equal, regardless of gender," the West Point cadet Chelsea Haviland explains to ABC News' Elizabeth Vargas. She continues, "So, if you're a female and you chose to be in the Army, you chose to put yourself in harm's way. So why separate between men and women?" (ABC 2005b). This segment pits Haviland against Jesse Sladek, another West Point cadet. Sladek concurs with Haviland that women are as capable of men in combat service, but she objects to women being assigned to combat roles; she believes the sight of women being injured or killed in combat is too upsetting to both women and men and would therefore weaken the combat effectiveness of all.

Haviland and Sladek's exchange is typical of how Warrior Women discourses equate women and men: those who question women being in combat do so not because they perform differently in combat but on the basis of arguable, even dubious, issues such as the one voiced by Sladek. These voices are ultimately drowned out by the procombat chorus, however, which reacts with stoicism after members of their unit are injured and killed (as the CNN segment featuring Sergeant Padmore illustrates). Brigadier General Wilma Vaught's assertion that a combat death is a combat death no matter the gender of the soldier is exemplary of the way meaning is ascribed to women warriors. "I think that there is no difference between the loss of a daughter or a son," she tells CNN; "and our women—I've talked to many of our women who have served or are serving in Iraq, and they're very proud of what they're doing. And they are a part of a unit. If that unit deploys, they want to deploy with that unit. They want to serve and be a full part of soldiers in our military today" (CNN 2005e).

Choosing to serve in combat arms does not automatically qualify women (or men) for this line of work, of course. But if viewers are skeptical that women have the physical and psychological strength required of men in combat units, they will be met with reassurances from people on the procombat side that women are indeed up to the tasks that combat requires. During one episode of *Nightline*, for example, Deborah Amos voices over scenes of women in boot camp with an observation: "Female soldiers bond the same as males. It begins at boot camp. At Fort Leonard Wood, Missouri, 29 percent of the twenty-five thousand Army recruits who arrive here each year are women. They join for a variety of reasons: for education, for adventure, for their country. Here, they are turned into soldiers" (ABC 2005a). This *Nightline* episode includes clips of various service women who have received combat medals and others who are simply proud to serve. One telling exchange takes place between Amos and Colonel Ashton Hayes, a military police officer who has served with women MPs. Hayes tells Amos, "If the women meet the standards, they become soldiers. And they just kind of blend into everybody being a green person." Confused, Amos asks, "A green person?" Hayes replies, "Or tan, depending on your uniform." "It's the Army's way of saying that everyone is a soldier first," Amos concludes (ABC 2005a).

Being a soldier first and putting the mission above all else is an imperative expressed variously across Warrior Women and affirms to concerned viewers that like men, women can do this as well. An *NBC Nightly News* segment about the increasing number of women fighting and dying[11] in Iraq and Afghanistan features an interview by the reporter David Gregory of the parents of Emily Perez, the first female West Point graduate to die in Iraq. "Her parents, Daniel and Vicki, remember a born leader," intones Gregory. Daniel Perez continues by recounting that "Emily always led from the front. She never shirked any of her responsibilities. She was a soldier's soldier." Later, Daniel adds, "What Emily showed me was that it didn't make a difference whether you were a man or a woman. She was their equal." Gregory concludes, "A soldier's soldier, a woman, fighting an enemy that makes no distinction" (NBC 2006). Or as Lieutenant Deborah Mesa puts it as she participates in a study at Fort Stewart, Georgia, that determines combat fitness standards for women and men: "A soldier isn't defined by gender; a soldier is a soldier" (CBS 2014).

Neutrality. References to gender neutrality mark the second discursive strategy justifying women's combat service. David Gregory, for example, voices a notion that abounds across Warrior Women coverage: the enemy does not make gender distinctions, and neither should the U.S. military. After all, as Colonel Laura Richardson observes, "It doesn't matter what unit you're from or where you—where you are in this country, they can reach out and they can get you." The NBC reporter Ned Colt follows up, "The dangers here are not gender sensitive, and increasingly neither is the military" (NBC 2004b). Noting that in Iraq "American servicewomen have suddenly found themselves in combat," the CBS reporter David Martin points to Sergeant Lee Ann Hester, whose valor in combat resulted in being awarded the Silver Star. "When the shooting starts, gender doesn't matter," Martin tells viewers (CBS 2005a).

The idea that enemy combatants and their weapons are gender indiscriminate relates to another notion that Warrior Women representations take on: unit cohesion or the band-of-brothers effect. One day after the announcement about the combat ban's demise, *The Today Show* featured Matt Lauer interviewing Army colonel and NBC military analyst Jack Jacobs. After Lauer establishes Jacobs's credentials (receiving the Medal of Honor for "heroic actions" in the Vietnam War), he asks Jacobs how the military will react to the change in policy. Jacobs's assessment is a positive one. He brushes off any suggestion that women weaken the military, noting that there were unfounded complaints of this nature after women were permitted into the service academies. He tells Lauer that there is no need to worry about combat training double standards because maintaining these standards is something good leaders will do: "there's no reason why both men and women can't maintain the same high standard of physical fitness." Jacobs makes similarly quick work of the idea that men fight to protect the other men they serve with as a band of brothers and that this bond would be "irreparably compromised" with the addition of women to their units. Jacobs answers, "Well, I think it's already been proved that that's not the case. There have been plenty of instances in which combat outposts and forward operating bases have been attacked and women have fought alongside men. . . . When people are trying ardently to kill you, it really doesn't matter to you who is on your left and on your right as long as they're doing their job. We fight to accomplish the mission. We fight for the country and most of all, we fight for each other" (NBC 2013b).

This sentiment is echoed in numerous clips, including one from CBS News about the Marine Corps. Because it comprises mostly infantry units, this is the branch with the fewest women and the most intensely masculine mythology. Scenes from 29 Palms, a Marine desert training camp, show a multiracial group of women and men training together under physically demanding conditions to determine fitness levels necessary for combat. Corporal John Wood tells the reporter Jan Crawford, "We all know how to work together. And . . . they go hand in hand, the training together as well as being able to pass those physical standards. And once you have those two together, there should be no reason to not trust the Marine to the left or right, whether they be male or female." Following Woods's comment, the camera switches to Corporal Tevin Guion, who adds, "The way I'm just going to look at it is not only do I have my brother in arms, but I have my sister in arms that I have to protect as well" (CBS 2015). Allaying fears that mixed-gender combat units will weaken cohesion and combat readiness, stories such as these normalize women's presence in combat by neutralizing gender differences that, historically, have worked to keep women off the battlefield.

Equality. A third and final strategy that these news narratives use to construct "America's daughters" concerns workplace equity. The profusion of stories featuring warrior women performing as well as men might prompt viewers to wonder why women are not being recognized for their combat labor. Multiple news stories address this question and do so by focusing on the notion of equality of opportunity. Warrior women themselves say they want to make the military their career and need to be able to do so on a level playing field, which combat experience provides. The CBS reporter Anna Werner queries Lieutenant Deborah Mesa about this issue: "There are probably some women out there who are saying, 'Why on Earth would you ever want to wind up in combat?'" Mesa replies, "It's all a matter of the individual—who, whether it's a male or female—what career path they want to take in the military" (CBS 2014).

Segments such as this one (and many others) reduce combat policy to the level of individual career choice, a move that obscures combat's morbid potential by equating combat service to a civilian profession—office work, for example—where employees are not required to prove their competence through violent acts. In this context, military service is just another job, a message that aligns with both DoD recruitment appeals and JAMRS discourses that emphasize the professional development and technical competencies fostered by military jobs (Goldstein 2001, 93). This technocratic perspective is reflected in Warrior Women discourses, which suggest that the military is a meritocracy where real career advancement is possible only when combat has been a part of a service member's experience—a box to check rather than a life-altering (or ending) experience.

Television news shows use "equality of opportunity" and references to general workplace fairness to familiarize viewers with the career problems military women face when prohibited from serving in ground combat. Eliminating the combat-exclusion policy will allow women to be promoted for their combat service, thereby removing a major obstacle to career advancement—what is known as the "brass ceiling" and what Enloe notes is the "spikiest barrier" to military promotion (1994, 94). For example, in January 2012, Jonathan Karl of ABC News commented on a Pentagon policy change that preceded full elimination of the combat ban. Explaining that the Pentagon was opening up fourteen thousand combat-related jobs such as those in "intelligence, logistics, and communications," Karl calls the policy a "first step toward equality of opportunity" for women in the military but a long way from "*true* equality" for women (ABC 2012). Karl's comments echo those of other reporters who emphasize the importance of women achieving this type of parity with military men while they simultaneously express doubts about how complete such equality may be: Karl concludes this segment by reassuring viewers that women will not be next to men in foxholes anytime soon.

TV news stories personalize equality of opportunity in multiple stories that showcase different women's military accomplishments. Just after the ban on women serving in combat roles had been lifted, *CBS Evening News* featured the story of Colonel Christine Stark, who, when "she started in the Army [in the early 1980s], wanted to be an officer in the infantry." Stark had to "settle" for the military police, one of the few places where she could be a troop leader. Even after she had completed two tours of duty in Afghanistan, where she was shot at, "her gender kept her from being assigned to front-line units." Stark tells the interviewer David Martin why she resented the restrictions: "I'd been born and raised to think I could do anything, and then to be told that because of my gender, I couldn't have certain positions . . . ," she trails off. Following Stark's regretful reminiscence is a shot of Secretary of Defense Panetta and Joint Chiefs Chairman Dempsey signing the order, accompanied by a voice-over noting that although it comes too late for Stark to serve in combat, it is "a triumph nevertheless." Martin asks, "Is there a sisterhood in the Army that's doing high-fives now?" Stark replies, "There absolutely is. This has been a landmark decision." Martin concludes his interview with Stark by asking, "Do you have any doubts about women being able to succeed in combat arms?" Stark responds with an unequivocal, "No. I don't have any doubts." In the final shot, David Martin, wearing coat and scarf and standing outside (of the Pentagon, presumably), sums up the order's impact by implicitly referencing the brass ceiling. Solemnly he concludes that although women make up 14 percent of the military, they are only 7 percent of the generals (CBS 2013). A CNN story about four women suing the Pentagon to allow them into combat arms includes this comment from one of the women, Marine Corps Reserve Captain Zoe Bedell: "The policy limits my future in the Marine Corps. I would be assigned to positions based on my gender rather than my qualifications or accomplishments. This doesn't make sense to me personally or professionally and frankly doesn't make sense to the military" (CNN 2012).

Like Bedell, news commentators take issue with the combat-exclusion policy on the grounds that it disadvantages women—many of whom have performed heroically in combat—and weakens the military. For example, MSNBC's Rachel Maddow introduces a segment about the ban with this story:

> In 2009, Major Mary Jennings Hegar, a combat-helicopter pilot in the California Air National Guard, was on a medevac mission in Afghanistan when her aircraft was shot down. She was wounded on the ground. She had fifteen pieces of shrapnel in her right arm and leg, but she still returned to retrieve three wounded soldiers on the ground. She returned fire in that attack once she was shot down. She was awarded the Distinguished Flying Cross with Valor for her actions that day in 2009. But she could not seek the kind of leadership positions that the military usually affords you because you have experience like that, because the Defense Department did not officially acknowledge her experience in combat. Seriously? Yes, seriously. (MSNBC 2013c)

Maddow's introduction is exceptional for enumerating the injuries and fighting that Hegar experienced in combat.[12] In contrast, most news stories cast combat service as a credential to earn toward promotion and fail to portray the violence and destruction that characterize it. Scrubbing combat of its morbid particularities allows an equality argument about permitting women into combat arms that likens these roles to office work or other civilian jobs that do not require employees to risk their or others' lives. Constituted in this way, a military career that includes combat missions can appear simply as an exciting means of climbing a professional ladder.

Expanding military service into a career is a hook used in recruiting advertisements intended for women, which bear a striking similarity to the TV news stories I examine. After the removal of the enlistment cap in 1967 and in preparation for the end of conscription, all branches of the military began to change recruitment tactics, and all, to a greater or lesser extent, employed advertisements intended to encourage women to enlist. Christiane Amanpour observes about this historical moment, "young women were definitely part of the marketing plan" ("Women in War" 2014). Lorry Fenner notes that during this period, the military also made attempts to "attract quality women of higher intelligence rather than men in the lowest categories of intelligence" (1998, 14); recruiting ads thereafter emphasized pay and benefits that came along with service in hopes that well-educated women would respond. These 1970s-era recruiting ads used second-wave feminist appeals including wage equity, work opportunities, and financial independence. The voice-over for one TV ad from this period describes the Air Force as "a *now* place to be," with "exciting, glamorous" scientific and research jobs "open to a girl." Another ad, this one for the Navy, features African American women, jazzy background music, and a hip-sounding male voice-over explaining that women "make the same pay as a man doing the same job and get the same advantages as a man. It's opportunity, advancement, good pay, equality. The new Navy" ("Women in War" 2014). Jeremiah Favara traces this tactic's legacy to contemporary recruitment materials, where ads featuring women use the "language of gender equality while framing the military as an inclusive and equitable institution" (2016, 1).[13]

Melissa Brown's analysis of recruiting ads from the end of conscription through 2003 reveals that whether or not these ads are intended for women, they routinely feature women and thus make "it more imaginable for some women and their parents/communities that 'normal' (i.e., feminine or heterosexual) young women can be part of military institutions." However, Brown notes that although recruitment images may feature women in training or flying planes, they have been "absent from the scenes of combat action" (2012, 155). Recruitment ads are changing to reflect the combat-exclusion policy's elimination: not only is a Marines recruiting ad released in May 2017 the first from the Marines to feature a woman, but it depicts her in scenes that include crawling and swimming through a grueling training course and then engaging in desert combat (U.S. Marines Corps 2017). And though this video differs from the ads that Brown examines by depicting a woman in combat, its white protagonist hews to a pattern of featuring mainly white women to construct an idealized vision of military femininity—a virtual erasure of women of color, and particularly African American women, who disproportionately populate enlisted ranks (M. Brown 2012, 171). TV news is more heterogeneous than this; combat segments typically feature women of color in footage of training or of battle sites. The retired officers who participate in studio debates and advocate for allowing women in combat roles, however, are white. This representational pattern racializes equality in the Warrior Women regime by implying to viewers that women of color may not be officer material and thus raises the question of whether equality of opportunity in officer ranks extends only to white women.

Constructing service women as equal to men with regard to combat capability is not simply a shift in the way news reports talk about these women; it signals a move upward for women in the military hierarchy, one that allows them to shed the "female" designation and ascend to the level of being proper soldiers—a process of maturation, of growing up. The implication here is that the military is a meritocracy that welcomes qualified women into combat arms as much as it does qualified men. Once women have gone through the specialized training they need for the variety of combat roles that await them, they will be greeted as peers and equals to the men who have always served in combat. This process and the cultural implications that follow from it parallel the postfeminist expectations of young women and girls that Angela McRobbie sees in public discourse that celebrates their achievements and potential for success; that is, contemporary discursive constructions of girls and young women focus more on their "capacity, success, attainment, enjoyment, entitlement, social mobility and participation. The dynamics of regulation and control are less about what young women ought not to do, and more about what they can do" (2009, 57).

At first glance, this move appears to be a progressive one that simply works to encourage women to stay on course, to keep fighting these social and political battles for equal opportunity. But McRobbie cautions that "what seems to underpin these practices is a suggestion that young women have now won the battle for equality, they have gained recognition as subjects worthy of governmental attention and this has replaced any need for the feminist critiques of what [Chandra] Mohanty [2003] labels hegemonic masculinities" (2009, 57). And although this figure of a young woman appears as one who warrants all manner of investment, she can also be mobilized for a more troubling purpose: to embody meritocratic values (57–58). Among the constructions of Warrior Women, postfeminist renderings of equal opportunity work to mask not only the military's patriarchal hierarchy, which remains intact despite the inclusion of women in combat roles, but also the misogyny that fuels sexual violence and discourages effective policies for preventing it (the subject of chapter 4). Warrior Women's celebratory discourses about combat parity thus have a dangerous side—one that deflects attention from military-specific sexual violence by suggesting that once women ascend to the level of combat warriors, they have achieved the martial version of having it all.

"You Have to Be More of a Woman than You Have Ever Been"

In retired Army Brigadier General Pat Foote's response to the host of CNNFN's *The Flipside*, who asks how she advises women who want to serve in the military, she explains that she tells them, "You have to be more of a woman than you have ever been in serving in this man's army." She continues, "By that, I mean you have to bring the very positive attributes of your womanhood to the table, and with humanity, with competence, with technical proficiency, and with great care for those who are charged to your responsibility, you have got to apply all of your woman skills to doing the job. Never try to be one of the boys. It will never work. You are not one of the boys; you are a woman who is bringing her skills to the table" (CNNFN 2004). Although Foote's advice may seem paradoxical, it reflects the way gender difference is treated in TV news segments about women in combat after September 11, 2001, and enhances the pitch for martial equality of opportunity addressed in the previous section. That is, while news stories do not shy away from raising questions about how women's attributes and differences from men may affect combat operations, they tend to downplay any significant or negative impacts that gender differences may have. This is Foote's meaning: by being as good or better than men, military women dispel concerns that gender differences pose legitimate obstacles to their being assigned to combat arms. Physical strength differences, unit cohesion, and maternity—both the potential for and the actuality of it—are the three rationales perennially used to exclude women from combat, and all are brought up in the Warrior Women regime. By far, however, most guests, commentators, and reporters work to diminish the role these factors may play in women's combat performance. In this way, Warrior Women challenges the band-of-brothers mythology that justifies the combat-exclusion policy—particularly allaying concern that women are "not natural soldiers, . . . [are] physically inferior to men, and . . . would ruin the bonds necessary for combat missions" (MacKenzie 2015, 2). In Warrior Women discourses, gender thus becomes "a red herring," using Pat Foote's apt analogy (CNNFN 2004).

Physical Strength. When Secretary Panetta announced the end of the combat ban, he issued a qualifier: "Not everyone is going to be able to be a combat soldier, but everyone is entitled to a chance" (Fox News Channel 2013a). Giving women a chance to be in combat takes on mantra status in Warrior Women, where it works to diminish the importance of physical strength differences to ground combat effectiveness. Albeit in an unusually comedic fashion, an exchange between the first female combat pilot, Air Force Colonel Martha McSally, and Army Lieutenant General Jerry Boykin (noted as a member of the conservative Family Research Council) on *Fox News Sunday* exemplifies this dynamic. In response to Boykin's claim that lifting the combat ban is a social experiment that will have dangerous results, the host, Chris Wallace, asks McSally whether she is confident "women can meet the same physical standards for ground combat that men do." Undaunted, McSally replies,

Look, we know the bell curve of men is stronger than the bell curve of women, but they overlap. And so the current policy basically says that no women can meet the standard and, therefore, all men can. So that's like saying, General Boykin, Pee Wee Herman is okay to be in combat, but Serena and Venus Williams are not going to meet the standard. The bottom line is treat people like individuals. Physical strength is one element of ground combat, but all those other qualities I've mentioned, like aptitude and courage and discipline and leadership, are also what women bring to the fight. (Fox 2013a)

McSally's exhortation to evaluate women as individuals when they enlist in combat roles echoes throughout Warrior Women discourses to such a degree that it takes on the status of wartime common sense (even Chris Wallace ends up agreeing with her). Air Force Lieutenant Colonel Karen Johnson's reply to Elaine Donnelly's assertion that women's lack of upper-body strength endangers everyone in combat situations is another in this verbal repertoire. Johnson concedes to the CBS host Hannah Storm and Donnelly that "some women are not [able to lift fellow soldiers and carry them]." However, "some men are not [either]. But many women are able to. I met a seventeen-year-old woman who can press five hundred pounds. I can lift patients and take them down stairways out of a hospital that's burning. That's my job" (CBS 2005a).

To illustrate that some women do indeed possess the physical strength to lift and carry heavy items, body armor, and even fellow soldiers, numerous news stories cut in scenes of women training to do these very tasks. The CBS story featuring Lieutenant Deborah Mesa shows her being physically monitored as she performs such combat activities as lifting a simulated injured soldier out of danger—"one hundred five pounds of weight through a tank hatch while wearing seventy pounds of combat gear." The reporter Anna Werner notes that in that exercise Mesa is lifting more than her own weight. "Oh, yeah, definitely," Mesa replies confidently. "How do you do that?" Werner asks her. "All legs," says a smiling Mesa (CBS 2014). ABC's treatment of "Army pioneers" Griest and Havers proceeds in a similar fashion, although the scenes of them and their male counterparts going through Army Ranger training—"that legendary course designed to break you mentally, physically," as Martha Raddatz notes—make Mesa's work look tame by comparison. Wearing camouflage uniforms and sporting buzz-cut hair, these muscular Rangers appear on the training course swimming while weighted down with heavy packs and crawling on all fours through mud with another soldier hanging beneath them—scenes making them indistinguishable from the male Rangers. After a series of such shots from Ranger training, Raddatz confirms that both women have met the same grueling standards as the men, then cuts to a shot of male Second Lieutenant Erickson Krogh; Krogh assures viewers, "I have no issues or qualms with them serving next to me in combat" (ABC 2015b). This, too, is an important part of Warrior Women's discursive formula. Men— often officers—appear at the end of a segment to affirm the claims of military women and reporters: yes, these women perform competently as warriors and should be considered as such.

Unit Cohesion. As these news stories confirm that women are up to the tasks required of them in combat, they also serve to reassure nervous viewers that women's presence in combat missions not only will not damage the cohesiveness of the group but may actually enhance it. Statements by military men such as Krogh's just quoted make multiple appearances in Warrior Women discourses, adding credibility to the argument that warrior women will improve, not hurt, unit cohesion. An exchange between Canadian Army General Rick Hillier and Anderson Cooper on CNN's *Anderson Cooper 360 Degrees* illustrates how officers legitimate this argument. Part of the process of opening combat positions to Canadian military women in 1989, Hillier voices emphatic support to Cooper and the other guests for the policy change. Hillier explains that although the Canadian military did eliminate the push-up requirement to qualify for combat (because, Hillier says, "I never met a Taliban commander who was frightened of somebody doing push-ups"), it maintained a requirement that soldiers be able to carry at least one hundred pounds. Further, Canadian combat training requires that soldiers "carry that weight for a long period of time. They could carry their weapons, and when they were finished that long period of time, they could carry a buddy on their back, man or woman, of their rough size, because they might be injured or wounded. And they could dig a trench. And they could scale a wall. And they could bring the fight to the enemy, after all of that, in a high temperature or climate. That's the kind of fitness that we wanted, and that's what we got from all of our soldiers, male or female." Hillier continues by describing important benefits that accrue with women in combat operations:

> Just simply out in villages amongst the population of Afghanistan, our male soldiers simply could not speak to the females that were in the area. You simply cannot do that. Our female soldiers could talk to them, could obtain all kinds of information, sometimes very actionable intelligence. [They could] actually disseminate our own messages themselves, start to build a rapport with the people that we were there to help, and they could do things that male soldiers simply could not do, simply because they were female. And at the same time, they could do everything else that we asked them. There were many pluses. (CNN 2013a)

According to most of the guests (particularly military personnel) who appear on TV news programs, physical strength differences and changes to group cohesion pose no substantial problems to combat effectiveness. In most regards, women perform as well as men in combat conditions, and they offer important additional skills such as being able to elicit "actionable intelligence" from Afghan and Iraqi women.

Motherhood. As TV news stories minimize concerns about women's strength and effect on unit cohesion, they also work to ameliorate the vexing contention that soldier mothers reduce combat effectiveness. This represents a departure from what others have seen in media representations from earlier times. For example, as I note in chapter 2, Tasker (2011) finds soldier mothers portrayed in television and film treatments of military women as problematic and disruptive to patriarchal, hetero family norms. And Stabile's analysis of news coverage of military women during the 1991 Persian Gulf War reveals a preoccupation with white, married soldier mothers, concerned with "not how to feed [their] children, but with whom to leave them" (1994, 127).

What Tasker and Stabile see in media constructions of soldier mothers follows from U.S. military policy, which since 1948 has focused on how motherhood can affect women's combat performance or deployment potential (Peach 1996, 170, 182n2).[14] And although today's service women are more likely than their male peers to be single parents—according to a Pew Research Center report, 12 percent of women and only 4 percent of men are single parents (Patten and Parker 2011, 6)—post-9/11 news stories display little evidence either of recognizing this fact or of being preoccupied with any other aspect of soldier mothers. Those guests who argue that motherhood should be combat disqualifying make unsupportable, even illogical statements or see their position challenged by others for inherent sexism. In one segment, for example, Elaine Donnelly inadvertently refutes her own claim that the United States is a "civilized nation" and should therefore not deploy mothers when, two sentences later, she asserts, "and yet we are the strongest military in the world" (CNNFN 2004). Donnelly's claim is untenable: if the United States has the strongest military in the world and maintains its status as a civilized nation all the while deploying mothers, it would be irrational for the military to stop doing so and risk either weakening its strength or losing its "civilized" status (or perhaps both).

On other programs, guests who raise motherhood as combat disqualifying find themselves challenged with individualistic feminist arguments. For example, when CNN's Judy Woodruff asks Alan Carlson of the Family Research Council why he believes women should be excluded from combat, Carlson replies, "One of the oldest and most basic of human instincts is to protect children, protect childhood, and to protect motherhood. And as we open more and more combat possibilities to women, we're putting more and more young mothers in harm's way." Retired General Wilma Vaught counters that "we need to consider the desires of the women involved and their concerns" and continues,

Last week I visited with the Piestewa family out in Arizona, whose daughter was killed. And I can tell you I never heard them say once that their daughter should not have been in the Army, that their daughter, even though she had children, that she should have made a different choice. They are just tremendously proud of her. And so I think we're dealing with a different issue here. And further, we have many men now who are single parents. And you know, if we're going to consider this, we have to consider both men and women, where in a previous era this wouldn't have been the case. Women are comfortable with what they are doing. (CNN 2003)

The credibility of Vaught's response is strengthened by her status as a decorated military veteran with firsthand experience meeting with the families of soldier mothers, a contrast to the civilian Carlson, whose response comes across as uninformed and paternalistic.

Phyllis Schlafly of the Eagle Forum comes in for similar treatment in an appearance on MSNBC's *Hardball*. After naming three soldier mothers who were killed, injured, or captured in Iraq, she angrily argues, "There is no threat that faced our country that required us to send single mothers of infants out to fight the evil empire. I think this thing is shameful to our country. I don't think this is a career opportunity for women. I think this is an embarrassment to our nation. And the policy that would send these young mothers of infants out to fight the enemy, I think, is a tragic assault on motherhood, on children who are left behind." Karen Johnson of the National Organization for Women and a retired Air Force officer, forcefully disagrees with Schlafly:

First of all, about 6 percent of the military are single fathers. What about sending single dads into combat? I certainly think it was shameful to have the war in Iraq, and that anyone was injured in that war is terrible because we didn't have any proof of any real threat to the United States. However, beyond that, women have been serving in the military for decades in combat roles. And not particularly in the U.S. but certainly in the Russian military during World War II, we had combat fighter pilots. . . . We—I'm a retired Air Force officer—have served admirably as females, and we can do any job that we need to do.

The host, Mike Barnicle, jumps in at various times to challenge Schlafly as well, noting that women choose combat roles and are not forced into them. Yet Schlafly returns repeatedly to conservative, essentialist talking points that even this early into the war sound archaic and patriarchal (MSNBC 2003). A veteran of media debates such as this one, Schlafly does not back down. Nor does her Family Research Council counterpart, Alan Carlson. But the conservative positions that these two organizations' representatives espouse on women in combat are overwhelmed in quantity and martial credibility by the chorus of procombat voices. That even the issue of maternity cannot be marshaled effectively by anticombat advocates is another indication that this representational regime favors women serving in combat—a position amplified by *Army Wives'* depiction of Joan Burton, among other media treatments.

In elevating military women to be equals with their male counterparts and rendering gender difference positively, TV news stories construct women warriors as recognizable martial subjects. Featuring them in war footage works to further achieve recognizability for warrior women. Thus, women's appearances on TV news screens alongside their male counterparts, framed by the name of the operation they're involved in (Operation Enduring Freedom, for example) and network logos, "spangled in red, white, and blue," as Norman Solomon describes them, situates them in a context meant to "exude pride in a nation resurgent" (2005, 144). Similarly, scenes that feature women competently using their weapons, operating machinery, or piloting helicopters underscore that women can and do act skillfully in this world even as these constructions fetishize the technologies that warriors handle (such scenes probably do double duty as product placement for military-equipment manufacturers). Fetishizing weapons of war is just one technique that Stahl reveals plays a prominent role in militainment, which serves to legitimate, even glorify, U.S. service members and encourage viewers to support them all, no matter their gender. Thus, the numerous segments that show military women operating military equipment—piloting a Blackhawk attack helicopter or undergoing biometric monitoring to measure combat worthiness, for example—or that discuss them in voice-overs while such equipment moves about the screen mark them as troops worthy of the same rhetorical support that male troops receive. Production elements and rhetorical strategies of militainment therefore do additional work of making women warriors recognizable, grievable martial subjects, vital to this network of supporting, warrior hands.

• • •

In March 2017, an unusual photo spread appeared in *Vogue* magazine as part of its 125th anniversary celebration: twenty-five photos of women warriors stationed at Hawaii's Joint Base Pearl Harbor–Hickam. The photographer Jackie Nickerson introduces the project by explaining that she "wanted to make pictures that empowered women, that captured women who were strong, who are part of defending the USA. They did not disappoint" (Codinha 2017). Images that compose "Armed Forces" are dramatically different from the photos of emaciated, disaffected fashion models who typically adorn the pages of *Vogue*; in place of them are multiracial, muscular, even butch warriors. Several are cancer survivors; one advocates for victims (of what we do not know); two serve on fast-attack submarines. None smile. All look tough. All but one are foregrounded standing by or sitting at the machinery they operate. The single exception is Army Reserves Sergeant Kawaiola Nahale, a competitive swimmer, who in two photos is immersed in a swimming pool, her muscular body sporting a competition swimsuit, while a swim cap adorned with two American flags and goggles wrap around her head. *Vogue*'s place atop the hierarchy of women's fashion magazines signals the worthiness of the photographic subjects chosen to grace its pages: we can say with confidence that women warriors have now achieved recognizability.

These *Vogue* photos bear striking similarities to images of warrior women from TV news, which in turn parallel those found in TV and film documentaries and books about warrior women. This tripartite collection of images and words serves to expand the repertoire of meanings historically articulated to warrior women, representing gender difference at a historical moment in which war news dominates the media environment. As I have noted in previous chapters, Stuart Hall (2001) argues that representational regimes do important work constructing difference at specific historical moments. Following Hall, I have argued that the images and words from all of the sites that feed into the Warrior Women regime constitute women as recognizable martial subjects and affirm their place in both the military and combat operations. In this way, Warrior Women attenuates gender difference—those attributes that have served historically to contrast military women to men—as it reinforces racial imbalances that traverse military ranks.

Over the course of fifteen years after September 11, 2001, representational practices of television news contributed to the Warrior Women regime mainly using three overlapping, mutually constituting discursive patterns: one sets up the context of modern warfare as always already combat; the second raises the status of military women to mark them as equals to military men, long assumed to be naturally combat capable; and the third plays down the significance of gender differences that have historically served to keep women out of combat arms—mainly maternity and lesser physical strength. During this period, the Pentagon eliminated the ban on women serving in ground combat, a move commended by those who appeared in the majority of news programs that covered this important change in military policy. The patterns in TV news representations of military women probably play a role in grooming viewers to expect women in combat arms, thus attenuating resistance to women in this type of military service at a time when their labor is badly needed. But Tasker reminds us not to "romanticize or simply celebrate [military women]. It is clear that to a large extent a place appears for military women as and when their labor is required"; moreover, in "our current historical context of open-ended war and ongoing military interventions, that labor has been integral to American assertions of military authority" (2011, 15). Eisenstein notes that although "women in the military may make the military look more democratic—as though women now have the same choices as men—. . . the choices are not truly the same. . . . At present, this stage of patriarchy often requires women to join the army in order to find a paying job or a way to get an education" (2007,

20). To wit, almost all of the women enlisting in the military in 2003 reported that they were doing so in order to receive job training and education benefits (Eisenstein 2007, 21).

As long as military women are ready and willing to serve in combat, the public appears poised to support them. Laura Miller's extensive interviews with Army women, for example, reveal that most of them support voluntary service in combat arms for qualified women (1998, 61). And Rosa Brooks cites a Pew poll that shows military women benefiting from military service: 87 percent report an increase in self-confidence, while 93 percent feel that their military service has "helped them 'grow and mature as a person'" (2016a, 30). These sentiments are reinforced in the vast majority of news segments in my sample and reflected among the public as well. A poll conducted jointly by the Pew Research Center and the *Washington Post* several days after Secretary Panetta's announcement showed that 66 percent of the U.S. public supported the elimination of the combat-exclusion policy, while only 26 percent opposed it. Men and women in all racial categories were equally supportive of the change in policy, and 58 percent reported that the change would improve women's military opportunities (Pew Research Center 2013).

For all these reasons, Eager believes that, "from a theoretical perspective, the repeal of the combat exclusion policy is a victory for liberal feminism" (2014, 180). Feminists appearing in TV news programs, such as Senator Tammy Duckworth, would likely agree with Eager, as would many academic feminists (D'Amico 1998). But this is only part of the story. Although liberal feminism certainly contributes to Warrior Women's ideological underpinning, it is not the sole force that does so, and its prominent role in discussions of women in combat does not necessarily represent a victory. As MacKenzie asserts, "The decision to remove the combat exclusion has very little to do with women. Instead, the policy change serves to recover a battered military image, rewrite the history of women's roles in Iraq and Afghanistan, and falsely portray the military as a gender-inclusive institution" (2015, 196). Like MacKenzie, I am not particularly sanguine about the combat-exclusion policy's impact on feminism. Instead, I see the repeal of the combat ban being a victory for postfeminism, specifically the *martial* postfeminism that I examine in the chapters of this book. In combat news, martial postfeminist ideology produces postracial discursive constructions of women warriors mainly cleansed of the violence and destruction integral to war; martial postfeminism, moreover, depoliticizes militarism.

Ruth Marcus provides an example of this problem in her *Washington Post* column, as she comments on an appearance by the *Lean In* author and Facebook COO Sheryl Sandberg at the U.S. Naval Academy. Reporting on Sandberg's pep talk to a gathering of military officers, Marcus calls out the Pentagon's recalcitrance in promoting women to officer ranks. Although she notes archly that accomplishing that "is going to take a whole lot of leaning in, not just by women but by the institution itself" (Marcus 2014), she fails to note the incommensurability between the standards for promotion in professions that Sandberg writes about and those used for military women: combat labor is in no way comparable to, say, IT work, and making it appear to be so constructs a dangerous and false equivalence. Like so many others, Marcus and Sandberg do the insidious work of the "warrior mystique," specifically "soften[ing] the military's image as an agent of coercion and destruction, and . . . promot[ing] the myth of the military as a democratic institution, as an 'equal opportunity employer' like any other, without reference to its essential purpose: organized killing for political objectives" (D'Amico 1998, 122). Attempts to gloss over the military's raison d'etre do news consumers a grave disservice and suggest that even civilian news organizations work on behalf of military interests; in this case, they also work to advance the complementary ideologies of martial postfeminism and banal militarism.

As I have shown in previous chapters, postfeminism and postracism mutually constitute the ideology that underlies representations of military marriage, family life, and motherhood; they do so as well in representations of women warriors. For example, the female officers who appear in TV news programs to support women serving in combat roles are all white, whereas the footage of combat training and operations that accompanies discussions about women serving in combat typically includes scenes in which African American, Asian, and Latina women work alongside white women. Such images suggest that the military has achieved a level of racial diversity similar to what we see splashed across and celebrated in numerous popular culture sites. But as Catherine Squires (2014) contends about the postracial mystique, representations of racial diversity do not remedy racism in practice. Thus, however accurately the racial diversity of Warrior Women reflects the disproportionately low numbers of women of color serving in officer ranks, it also reinforces and perpetuates a racial power imbalance that is found in all branches of the military. Further, it conveys an additional message that those women permitted to exercise military power as officers will be white, while those enlisted and in the infantry forces that the officers command and perhaps lead into combat will be people of color. Finally, Warrior Women does not begin to address the systemic racism in the civilian world that makes military service one of the few occupations in which women of color can expect to see regular career advancement.

In this regime of representation, military women of color signal both that the military is a racially diverse organization and that women of color are as patriotic as their white counterparts in their desire to serve their country. Colonel Ashton Hayes's suggestion earlier that combat training melts away racial and gender differences to reveal green- or tan-uniformed people who are otherwise identical warriors mirrors assertions of color blindness associated with postracialism: the "I don't see color" defense for why one cannot be racist that Eduardo Bonilla-Silva refers to as "color blind racism" (2002). The postracial discourses of Warrior Women obscure intramilitary racial power imbalances and racism that add another layer of oppression to military women's experiences, rendering invisible the racial makeup of the objects of U.S. military violence: the brown-skinned, largely Muslim populations of Afghanistan and Iraq. This is neither incidental nor insignificant; as Eisenstein points out, "The conceptual deficit that disallows the naming of racialized gender as central to the reconfigurations of power allows its decoy status for anti-democratic rule" (2007, xvii). Scenes from TV news that showcase military racial and gender diversity, therefore, also mask the racism, imperialism, and militarism that drive decision-making about whether and where to go to war.

Martial postfeminism is composed of these postracial discourses as well as liberal feminist discourses that emphasize how gender equality improves the military by allowing individual women to shine as warriors. TV news programs in my sample of post-9/11 coverage of women in combat repeat ad infinitum that in combat operations women are as capable as men of performing well. Because women are already serving in de facto combat conditions—are fighting-and-dying just as men are—these segments encourage us to reward warrior women for their competence and sacrifices and therefore recognize them as martial subjects. But even as the Warrior Women regime encourages viewers to critically examine the combat-exclusion policy and push for its repeal, it discourages exploration of broader policies about warfare and does not ask why people are fighting-and-dying in Afghanistan and Iraq at all. This move is typical of the depoliticizing work that postfeminism does. In the context of news about the military, such depoliticization obscures important considerations about combat operations—their goal of capturing, destroying, and killing, for example, or how combat works to perpetuate questionable wars such as those in Afghanistan and Iraq. In place of a robust discussion of such issues is a highly constrained, martial postfeminist focus on whether women should be permitted in combat arms and thereby ascend to officer ranks.

Decontextualizing and depoliticizing war in its coverage of women in combat, TV news represents a general trend in manufacturing consent for war that Robert W. McChesney links to the media political economy. The political economy factors that I explicate in the introduction come into play in combat news, too, and especially in efforts to promote war by humanizing the troops. As McChesney puts it, "embedded reporting in combination with full-throttle jingoism on U.S. television news made it difficult for journalists to do critical work" (2008, 108). Christiane Amanpour, CNN's top foreign correspondent at the time, concurs, regretfully adding, "I'm sorry to say, but certainly television and, perhaps, to a certain extent, my station was intimidated by the [Bush] administration and its foot soldiers at Fox News. And it did, in fact, put a climate of fear and self-censorship, in my view, in terms of the kind of broadcast work we did" (quoted in McChesney 2008, 109). McChesney notes further that "U.S. journalism, especially in coverage of wars, tends to run in packs" (111), a prominent feature of the reporting I examine for this chapter. That is, rather than scrutinizing the Bush administration's rationale for war in Iraq by investigating alternative reasons for it—one being "the imperial drive encouraged by the existence of a massive military-industrial complex" (114)—TV news programs amplify troop-supporting sentiments by promoting women's combat service and thereby sidestep addressing more controversial topics. This tendency is particularly noteworthy because it contrasts starkly with the coverage that sexual assault receives for most of the same fifteen-year period, as I discuss in chapter 4.

Warrior Women diversifies war reporting by integrating service women's experiences into stories about combat and occupation, thus marking these women's lives as precarious as well as grievable. But troublingly, this regime's discursive constructions of women warriors also normalize and naturalize militarism. Returning to my late father's song, I want to propose deploying it in a different context. Now that its question of whether women can "win this war" has been settled—at least in the world of TV news—I would urge journalists to insist that war makers answer the song's question after a slight shift in emphasis: no matter the gender of the warrior, we deserve to know "what the hell *are* we fighting for?"

4

"This Wasn't the Intended Sacrifice"

Warrior Women and Sexual Violence

Women serving in the U.S. military today are more likely to be raped by a fellow soldier than killed by enemy fire in Iraq.
—Representative Jane Harman, 2008

Rape is used by political beings for political purposes. To effectively work against rape, and support those who have been raped, we must confront the myths of manhood as we simultaneously support those who have been victimized, and hold accountable those who do the victimizing.
—Rus Ervin Funk, 1997

In July 1992, National Public Radio relayed the following account of Jacqueline Ortiz's military service in Operation Desert Storm:

> Jacqueline Ortiz was a mechanic with the Army's 52nd Engineer Battalion, stationed eighteen miles from Iraq during Desert Storm. Two days into the war, Ortiz was attacked.

JACQUELINE ORTIZ (ARMY MECHANIC): On January the nineteenth, 1991, at ten o'clock in the morning, I was sodomized by my company first sergeant. I immediately reported the incident to my supervisors. Unfortunately, my claim fell on deaf ears. After I was attacked, I had to look at this man almost every day for two and a half months later. I was refused medical attention for all this time.

Ortiz, the mechanic in Desert Storm, says she wakes up screaming from nightmares. She throws up almost every day, so often that the enamel on her teeth has been eaten away.

ORTIZ: I would have rather been shot by a bullet and killed that way than to deal with what I have to deal with daily. (NPR 1992)

Ortiz recounted her assault to NPR in a report on female veterans testifying to a Senate committee. "Acts of sexual violence, including rape, are common, and the military has not done enough to protect its female members," NPR's reporter concluded. The problem did not disappear after these veterans testified, and almost twenty-five years later, civilian news media were reporting on another story about the military's culture of sexual harassment and abuse—this one starting with the Marines and then growing to encompass other branches. In this case, a Marine whistleblower calling himself War Horse revealed that a Facebook group—Marines United—had been created by male Marines to share "naked and compromising photos of their [female] colleagues"; the photos included the women's names and the units they served in, as well. Marines United had more than thirty thousand members when its existence was made public (Gibbons-Neff 2017). A flurry of news coverage accompanied the exposé, reporting on tawdry details such as the "raunchy and sexually violent comments" that members made about the photos (Martin 2017). Following these revelations, one news report's headline announced, "The Marine Corps Has a 'Toxic Masculinity' Problem" (Ward 2017)—an issue I will return to in this chapter.

When the DoD issued its annual report on sexual assault in the military for 2016, it revealed that this sort of cyber abuse is becoming more common. Writing in *Task & Purpose*, an online news magazine for veterans, Jared Keller noted that the report found that at least twenty-six hundred active-duty service women in all branches of the military "have been subject to some form of nonconsensual exposure" of sexually explicit photos, à la Marines United (2017). Marine women reported being subjected to this more than did women serving in other branches. Brian Purchia, a spokesperson from Protect our Defenders, an organization working to prevent military sexual violence, argues that this latest incident shows that "the military still has a long way to go in ending the epidemic of rape and sexual assault, holding assailants accountable, preventing and punishing retaliation, and eradicating rampant misogyny and harassment within the ranks" (quoted in Keller 2017). Purchia's words are unusual for their identification of misogyny as a factor in military sexual violence, and still they may understate the situation.

Between 1992 and 2017, when the Marines United story broke, tens of thousands of service members across all branches of the military and service academies were sexually assaulted and harassed. Some incidents became high profile, such as the Navy's Tailhook assaults (which occurred in 1991 but became public in 1992 with the testimony of Lieutenant Paula Coughlin), while the majority of the others flew under the civilian public's radar. In 2014, the NOW Foundation estimated that five hundred thousand service members over the preceding twenty-five years had been raped, sexually assaulted, or subjected to "unwanted sexual touching." In addition to the psychological and physical toll on the victims, the financial costs incurred are mind-boggling: the Rand Corporation calculates that in 2012 alone, $3.6 billion was spent by the DoD to cover "medical and mental health services" and victims' lost earnings (NOW Foundation 2014). In 2016, 4.3 percent of service women and 0.6 percent of service men—about 14,900 total—experienced sexual assault, according to the DoD's Sexual Assault Prevention and Response Program (SAPRO) annual report on military sexual assaults (DoD SAPRO 2017, 13). The 2016 numbers reflect a decrease in reported sexual assault incidents since the 20,300 it reported in 2014 (DoD SAPRO 2017, 9).

Although sexual assault was a problem in the military long before post-9/11 troop deployments, instances of it increased greatly among troops stationed in Afghanistan and Iraq: between 2002 and 2004, service women made more than one hundred reports of sexual assault, including rape, in the Central Command region of Afghanistan, Iraq, and Kuwait (Eisenstein 2007, 29). Because sexual violence is notoriously underreported, this figure probably reflects only about 20 percent of the attacks that occurred there: according to Protect Our Defenders (2017a), 81 percent of victims of military sexual assault in 2016 did not report their attack. As reports of sexual violence continued to rise after 9/11, some public figures—legislators, for example—began referring to sexual assault as an epidemic.[1] Despite this, the DoD did little to recognize the magnitude of the problem or attempt to solve it until 2005, when it established SAPRO.

In this chapter, I track TV news discourses about military sexual violence, examining how they fit within a wider representational context of post-9/11 war reporting. What emerges is that with two notable exceptions—revelations of assaults of multiple Air Force Academy cadets in 2003, and in 2013–2014, efforts by members of Congress to pass legislation intended to change the system in which military sexual violence is prosecuted (the Military Justice Improvement Act, for one)—TV news outlets gave the problem little attention and implicitly aligned themselves again with DoD priorities. Not until the release of *The Invisible War* in 2012—a documentary film exposé of military sexual violence—did these organizations apparently consider the problem newsworthy, covering it intensively throughout 2013 and tapering off by about a third in 2014. But however numerous, almost all these stories showcased individual Congress members and legislation they were debating to address the problem and not strategies for preventing military sexual violence. Television news reporting about military sexual assault thus ebbs and flows (mostly ebbs) in accordance with specific events—arrests of high-ranking perpetrators or reports of multiple assaults in the service academies, for example. Although the stories that do appear are sympathetic to survivors and eventually somewhat critical of the military's failure to address the problem, they fail either to investigate sexual assault as an institution-wide, structural problem or to analyze its roots in misogyny and toxic masculinity[2]—even when there are numerous signs pointing to both. In this way, I argue, sexual assault coverage in TV news both draws from and advances martial postfeminism—specifically in reporters' refusal to engage with either the military's structural sexism or feminist scholarship and activism around sexual violence and rape culture. Not doing so leaves intact both the military's patriarchal hierarchy and the warrior mystique that continues to inform war reporting even in the face of a serious and widespread problem such as this one.

• • •

The Department of Defense's inattention to sexual violence deterred most, but not all, media outlets from investigating the problem. In 2004, the *Denver Post* reporters Amy Herdy and Miles Moffeit produced an investigative series, "Betrayal in the Ranks," and introduced it with this stark description: "Thousands of women have been sexually assaulted in the United States military. Thousands more have been abused by their military husbands or boyfriends. And then they are victimized again. This time, the women are betrayed by the military itself. They are discouraged from reporting the crimes. Pressured to go easy on their attackers. Denied protection. Frustrated by a justice system that readily shields offenders from criminal punishment" (2004, 2). Featuring the stories of more than thirty women and framing their experiences as both representative and part of a larger problem, "Betrayal in the Ranks" was the first extensive journalistic investigation of the problem to appear after 9/11. It set the tone for subsequent reporting by implicating the military in creating conditions that victimize women and enable their attackers to get away with little or no punishment. As the preceding passage reveals, victims are punished more often than their assailants are.

Another exposé came from Helen Benedict in the indispensable 2009 book *The Lonely Soldier: The Private War of Women Serving in Iraq*, which builds on her 2007 research on military sexual assault published in *Salon*. After interviewing over twenty women Iraq War veterans, Benedict notes in the 2007 article that "every one of them said the danger of rape by other soldiers is so widely recognized in Iraq that their officers routinely told them not to go to the latrines or showers without another woman for protection." The unintended consequence of this advice can be death by dehydration. Colonel Janis Karpinski recounted to Benedict that some female soldiers refused to drink liquids during the day because they feared "being raped by male soldiers if they walked to the latrines after dark." According to Karpinski, three women died this way in 2003 when serving in Iraq, where summer temperatures can exceed one hundred degrees. Military sexual assault thus puts service women in what Sheila Jeffreys terms "double jeopardy": like service men, they can be killed or injured in warfare, but to a disproportionate degree, they also "face sexual violence from their own side" (2007, 16).

Filled with agonizing stories of women's assaults and mistreatment by the military justice system, Herdy and Moffeitt's and Benedict's accounts, along with several others, were circulating in news media (mainly print) during the early years of the wars in Afghanistan and Iraq. Though news organizations of all kinds had access to these accounts, they failed to make military sexual violence the subject of investigation and connect the scattered reports of various assaults. This pattern exemplifies what Frank Baumgartner and Sarah McAdon found in their study of thirty-six years of reporting on college campus sexual assaults: that newspaper stories use episodic rather than thematic framing and therefore sacrifice analysis of "broader ideas, such as rape culture and victim-blaming, on statistical trends, or on rape or campus rape as a general problem" (2017). Baumgartner and McAdon see a shift toward more thematic coverage since 2014, however, and note that examining "'boring' trends and patterns may help address the problem of campus sexual assault even more than the occasional focus on high-profile cases." But despite reports that started with the service academies' rampant sexual violence and eventually expanded to include incidents in every branch of the military, TV news outlets failed to cover this thematically or even to maintain a critical stance toward the military that would allow for more substantial investigation of this destructive and long-standing problem.

Rather than thematic reporting, a radio silence mostly greeted the subject of military sexual assault in war reporting after 9/11. Those few TV news stories that did appear overlooked signs of military sexual violence being both systemic and structural and minimized the gendered character of that sexual violence with an intense focus on Congress members and dramatic moments from legislative debates over methods for prosecuting military sexual assaults and harassment. This coverage worked together with reporting on women's suitability for combat (the topic of chapter 3) to further affirm women's place in the military either by not focusing on the sexual violence that so many were encountering or by condemning sexual violence without pushing investigation into what military-specific factors could cause and perpetuate such abuse. In this regard, the following exchange between the director of *The Invisible War*, Kirby Dick, and the MSNBC anchor Andrea Mitchell is instructive. After Mitchell asks Dick whether lifting the combat ban will help to solve the problem of sexual assault, he replies, "Well, it's a good thing, because, obviously, any kind of equality is good. I think it will lessen harassment, but the real problem here is most of these assaults are caused by serial predators, men who assault again and again. Putting women in all parts of the military, that will not address that problem. The military has to go after these men and investigate and incarcerate and prosecute them with the same will that it fights a war" (MSNBC 2013b).

Reflexive assurances such as Dick's that combat equality may have a positive impact on sexual assault are scattered throughout the fifteen-year period of TV news coverage of military sexual assault that I examine in this chapter. The whole exchange illustrates how television news representations around sexual assault work together with combat coverage to constitute warrior women and model to the civilian public how to understand and respond to this additional, internal threat to them—women whom these discourses elevate to the level of recognizable, grievable warriors. Although TV news organizations were slow to take up the issue and then sparse with coverage until late in this fifteen-year period, they nevertheless played an important role in establishing that women warriors must also contend with enemies *within* military ranks as they train to and eventually fight against the more familiar ones from without.

The combat-exclusion policy comes into play in this discursive regime mostly in commentary such as Dick's that lauds the ban's elimination for its potential to decrease the incidence of sexual assault. Far fewer commentators appear in these news stories to take the opposite position and argue that lifting the ban will lead to more sexual assault (due to women and men working in closer proximity to one another than before the ban was lifted).[3] In these patterns that oscillate between silence and explicit messaging, TV news instructs viewers about how to understand the scale and nature of military sexual assault as well as remedies for it: congressional solutions that modify reporting and prosecution processes are acceptable, whereas attending to misogyny or toxic masculinity is not, despite their prevalence in all branches of the military and negative impacts on service members of all genders. This discursive process contributes to Warrior Women's pedagogy around grievability (à la Butler), especially, by both suggesting what it is about this situation that is worthy of our concern and empathy and circumscribing political solutions to the problem.

Television news stories reflect and amplify the military's positions on sexual assault that emerge in *Army Wives*, in media appearances by numerous military personnel during this fifteen-year period, and in the military's own sexual assault materials going back at least two decades. The news stories hew, moreover, to what Meghana Nayak has found in DoD reports on military sexual violence, particularly in how they regard such violence "as an anomaly even while the military's very mission and presence relies on masculinist norms that perpetuate such violence" (2009, 147). As with coverage of women in combat, TV news stories about sexual assault work within the confines of the warrior mystique, refusing to consider—even after numerous examples in their own reporting suggest it—that "women's increasing presence in the military does not change the institution's fundamentally gendered structure, which at its core is coercive, hierarchical, and patriarchal" (D'Amico 1998, 122). Military sexual assault has apparently vexed TV news organizations, which have responded to it with sporadic, mainly tepid criticism of the military's treatment of sexually violated troops. What results for many assault survivors is military sexual trauma, the subject of the next section.

Traumas of Military Sexual Violence

The catch-all term "military sexual trauma" (MST) has been used by the Veterans Health Administration (VA) since 1992 to refer to the collection of psychological and physical symptoms caused by sexual violence during military service. The VA now requires treatment for MST, and its duration can be for as long as is necessary for a veteran to recover. Margaret Bell and Susan McCutcheon explain that MST may result from "any sexual activity during military service in which a Service member is involved against her or his will—he or she may have been pressured into sexual activities (for example, with threats of negative consequences for refusing to be sexually cooperative or with implied better treatment in exchange for sex), may have been unable to consent to sexual activities (for example, when intoxicated), or may have been physically forced into sexual activities." Such activities include but are not limited to "unwanted sexual touching or grabbing; threatening, offensive remarks about a person's body or sexual activities; and threatening and unwelcome sexual advances" (2015, 323). The VA's definition and mandate that veterans be treated for MST arose from testimony by Jacqueline Ortiz and others that I excerpted at the beginning of this chapter. Starting in 2000, the VA began MST screening among all veterans seeking health care; the results of that screening indicate that about one in four women and one in one hundred men have experienced sexual violence during the course of their service. Resulting health problems typically include "PTSD, depression and other mood disorders, and substance use disorders," as well as secondary health problems "and/or difficulties with issues like homelessness" (Bell and McCutcheon 2015, 324).

One factor that can exacerbate MST and further complicate its treatment is the likelihood that a victim may be subordinate to the perpetrator in the system of rank and authority. As Francine D'Amico points out, "When the boss/officer, usually a man, is one's military 'superior,' the potential for the abuse and sexual harassment of the employee/soldier, usually a woman, differs from that in the civilian employer-employee relation. His power over her has multiplied not only because of his gender and job title but also because of his rank" (1998, 124). How commanders proceed after receiving a report of sexual violence has been mostly at their discretion, and many of them have reacted negligently, if not criminally so. Survivors have been fearful to report because they have seen what happens to others who have. "When the perpetrators are of higher rank, or otherwise in the victim's chain of command," Marie Thompson observes, "that victim's safety and confidentiality can be compromised; their perpetrators are often free to continue committing crimes both in and out of military service." Even worse, she adds, "factors associated with duty locations and unit cohesion [make] transfers . . . difficult and/or unlikely. Many [victims] fear dangerous reprisals for reporting. Frequently victims are told, 'it did not happen' or are further scrutinized and blamed for offences" (2014, 134).

What Thompson describes is echoed in Helen Benedict's work and Herdy and Moffeitt's series, as well as the documentaries *The Invisible War* and *Service: When Women Come Marching Home* (2012). In addition, Human Rights Watch dedicated an entire report to the widespread problem of retaliation meted out against military assault survivors who report the crime (62 percent say they have been retaliated against). The report introduces the problem with this devastating list: "Spat on. Deprived of food. Assailed with obscenities and insults—'whore,' 'cum dumpster,' 'slut,' 'faggot,' 'wildebeest.' Threatened with death by 'friendly fire' during deployment. Demeaned. Demoted. Disciplined. Discharged for misconduct" (2015, 3). Given such treatment and impunity for those who do the retaliating, it is not surprising that only one in four victims report their assault to a superior officer: Human Rights Watch notes that those who report are "12 times more likely to suffer retaliation for doing so than to see their offender, if also a service member, convicted for a sex offense" (3).

Military sexual assault and the resulting trauma are pervasive, destructive to survivors, and harmful to combat preparedness and unit cohesion.[4] Yet, despite the problem's prevalence and deleterious consequences, TV news outlets were slow to recognize and cover it. Using LexisNexis to search, I could find only one mention of the term "military sexual trauma" in fifteen years of TV news coverage, and it is so brief as to risk going unnoticed. In a CNN interview featuring Representatives Tammy Duckworth and Tulsi Gabbard discussing changes they wish to see in the reporting system, Duckworth names MST as a problem but does not follow this with any further discussion of it (CNN 2013b). Media inattention to the problem of sexual violence, reports that view trauma as "collateral damage," and those that "identify the locus of the 'disease' lying solely with the warrior" exemplify what Marie Thompson believes must change if we are to see improvement in or, better yet, elimination of MST (2014, 135). *The Invisible War*'s moving accounts of MST align with what Thompson calls for and also provide a stark contrast to the negligent treatment it receives in TV war reporting—a discursive practice that allows the military's rape culture to flourish.

Military Rape Culture

In the groundbreaking book by Emilie Buchwald, Pamela R. Fletcher, and Martha Roth that conceptualizes and defines rape culture, the authors define rape culture as "a complex of beliefs that encourages male sexual aggression and supports violence against women. . . . In a rape culture, women perceive a continuum of threatened violence that ranges from sexual remarks to sexual touching to rape itself. A rape culture condones physical and emotional terrorism against women and presents it as the norm. In a rape culture, both men and women assume that sexual violence is a fact of life, as inevitable as death or taxes" (2005, xi). Their definition resonates with survivors' and observers' accounts of their military service experiences and underscores that because sexual violence can be woven seamlessly into cultural practices, it therefore poses hazards to a wide range of people, usually women and anyone else who may be construed as feminine. Although Buchwald et al.'s definition assumes a gender binary in which men are perpetrators and women are victims, men are also subject to sexual violence (mainly by other men)—and particularly when they serve in the military, as the VA's figures on MST reveal. This aspect of rape culture has been especially difficult for victim advocates to address given the cultural stigma associated with male victims of sexual assault, and news reports make only brief and fleeting mention of it.

Despite the long-standing culture of rape within the military, news outlets seem loathe to integrate investigation of it into their war reporting. And on those occasions when TV turns up the volume on military sexual violence, TV news reports exhibit patterns similar to those found in coverage of such violence in the civilian population and documented by feminist scholars for several decades: journalists avoid consideration of the violence as systemic as they sidestep a feminist analysis of the misogyny and masculine dominance that create the conditions for sexual violence to occur. Moreover, in accounts of military sexual assault, reporters focus a disproportionate amount of attention on Congress members and legislative fixes for the military's system of prosecution. These patterns parallel what Buchwald et al. find in newspaper and TV reporting on sexual violence. That is, it tends toward covering "particularly brutal sex crimes and dwell[s] on their lurid details" while playing down or ignoring "the reality of relentless, everyday sexual violence" (2005, xiii). This is particularly so in coverage of military sexual violence. Scattered reports that it is rampant have circulated in public discourse since at least the early 1990s; yet after 9/11, reporters and commentators express bewilderment about its prevalence and continued existence and thus disregard the long history of the military's rape culture.

Because reporters shy away from a feminist analysis of gender in this context, and specifically toxic masculinity, they will likely continue to revisit this bewilderment. TV news organizations' unwillingness to push beyond superficial, perfunctory reporting thus results in discursive silences around the gendered power relations that produce and sustain military rape culture—a pattern that emerges first in coverage of the service academies and training programs.

Training in Sexual Violence

Even before 9/11, reporters were faced with indications that sexual violence had been long standing and institutionally perpetuated starting with the systems of military education and basic training. Stories about the abuse of service academy and military college cadets appear as far back as 1994, when Susan Faludi published a *New Yorker* article about the experiences of Shannon Faulkner—the first woman to be admitted to The Citadel, South Carolina's military college and bastion of southern, white masculinity (Faludi later incorporated Faulkner's story into her book about masculinity in the United States, *Stiffed* [1999]). Although the Citadel is a military college and not a service academy, like the other senior military colleges in the country, it trains cadets mainly as part of the Reserve Officers' Training Corps (ROTC). The training—and, more importantly, the hazing—that goes on in both types of institutions can be brutal and, in some cases, criminal.

When news about cadet assaults at the Air Force Academy began to emerge in 2003, war correspondents were unprepared to address how military educational institutions and training rituals might play a role in perpetuating sexual violence, despite sexual harassment and assaults being common in the service academies (where both increased in frequency during the 1990s [Goldstein 2001, 97]). The NOW Foundation notes that "sexual harassment and sexual assault at the military academies have been a fact of life for both women and men cadets for decades," with women being the "primary targets" (2014). Susan Jeffords relays stories about the sexual abuse of West Point cadets, which include their finding "shaving cream-filled condoms in their beds" and "obscenities scrawled on their walls," being called "whores" by the men, and being sexual assaulted in their own dorm rooms (1991a, 106). Buchwald et al.

write that attacks at the service academies and military colleges "remind us that even young men who are considered an elite group regard their women classmates as potential sexual prey" (2005, xiii).

Sexual abuse and rape at the Army's Aberdeen Proving Grounds came to light in 1996 when twelve NCOs were charged with assaulting almost fifty women they were commanding during their training (Thompson 2014, 132). An indication of the problem's persistence, in 2012 a similar story emerged about basic-training instructors sexually abusing upward of forty trainees at Lackland Air Base in Houston, Texas. About the Aberdeen case, Carol Burke writes that as more women enter military training, a growing gendered power differential "between trainers and trainees, and . . . lack of mediation or effective oversight" can result in sexist forms of abuse (2004, 20). The sequence of military training is fundamentally sexist, as well, based as it is on warrior-culture initiation rites. According to Burke, these proceed from "infantilization and feminization . . . to practices designed to rid the adolescent of all traces of the female. To the extent that the military brass have permitted training to operate as a male rite of passage, they have furthered a culture hostile to women" (20). Because the service academies and training facilities breed and then feed sexual predators and those who enable them into the military system, and especially the officer corps, they play a crucial role in maintaining the structures that produce and maintain rape culture. Without focused attention to eradicate the practices that encourage misogyny and homophobia at these sites, we should not expect the officers and other personnel they produce to view these systems as problematic, let alone be involved in acting to change them.

As Buchwald et al. point out, the service academies are elite institutions, in part because admissions are extremely competitive. All but one—the Coast Guard Academy—require students to be nominated by a member of Congress, thus strictly limiting the number of students who can be admitted in a given year. And men continue to be overrepresented at all the academies; for example, the Air Force Academy's 2016 graduating class comprised 22.4 percent women (U.S. Air Force Academy, n.d.), while West Point's 2015 enrollment figures show that just 19 percent of cadets there were women (NCES, n.d.). That these institutions' students must be accomplished and bright (not to mention politically well connected) to be admitted perhaps makes them unlikely to come to mind first when the subject of military sexual violence arises. But given their track record, they should. In 2014, for example, the *Christian Science Monitor* reported on a Pentagon study of academy students' experiences with sexual harassment and assault. Focus groups revealed that 80 to 90 percent of women said that they had been subjected to "sexist comments" during the past year. When queried further, many of the women said, "we're surprised it's not higher." This is a bad portent: according to SAPRO, "There is a strong positive correlation between the experience of sexual harassment and the eventual sexual assault of people in military units" (Mulrine 2014).

An insider-outsider feminist analysis of sexual violence at the Air Force Academy by Lorraine Bayard de Volo and Lynn K. Hall (a former cadet) situates on a continuum of violence the training activities and rituals that cadets must participate in. Their illuminating study points to problems in several areas, including militarization processes and the academy's "adversative method of education (in which new cadets endure extreme physical and mental stress)." This method, de Volo and Hall find, "normalize[s] aggression against those identified as feminine" by devaluing femininity and naturalizing women as "targets of harassment and aggression" (2015, 866, 867). In combination with militarization, adversative education encourages officers to idealize masculine-coded attributes of "toughness, strength, bravery, controlled aggression, and mastery over emotions. Conversely, characteristics broadly identified as feminine were devalued: tenderness, weakness, fear, passivity, and emotionalism. Cadets maintained this gender hierarchy on a daily basis, often in mundane ways—small-scale actions that might well be excused as trivial if not understood as cumulative as well as coconstitutive with other forms of violence" (874). But in spite of the history of sexual harassment and abuse at the service academies and SAPRO reporting on them,[5] these elite, masculine-dominated institutions mainly escape media scrutiny, with the exception of early in the post-9/11 period.

The first TV news coverage of sexual assault from this time focused on the Air Force Academy in reports about a cadet being charged with sexually assaulting another. These stories were quickly followed by more, revealing that dozens of cadets were coming forward to report being sexually abused there. News outlets treated these assaults as aberrant and remediable with a change in leadership. Referring to revelations about widespread academy assaults and their aftermath as a "sex scandal" is one means of signaling that reporters see academy sexual violence as anomalous, as the anchor Ann Curry does in her introduction to a *Today Show* segment: "The military has now charged a cadet with sexual assault in connection with a sex scandal at the Air Force Academy" (NBC 2003b). Even setting aside TV news programs' need to have attention-grabbing headlines, the term "scandal" is not particularly apt if reporters intend to gain insight into military sexual assault. The first definition for scandal in *The American Heritage Dictionary* is "any act or set of circumstances that brings about disgrace or offends the morality of the social community; a public disgrace" (Morris 1981, 1158). So, although it is accurate that the cadets' *allegations* offended the morality of the Air Force Academy social community and evoked outrage, the actual sexual violence apparently made no impact on the morality of the academy, as evidenced by the persistence of the violence— something brought to light by the allegations. Scandal terminology thus discourages viewers' examination of these assaults as symptomatic of a larger problem in the education and training of officers.[6]

After Curry reports the details of the cadet's attack and her subsequent treatment (being "disciplined for fraternizing, drinking, and sexual activity"), this NBC segment fails to follow up on that part of the report suggesting that a widespread problem existed: "Meanwhile, dozens of other female students complained they were victims of similar assaults and were punished for coming forward" (NBC 2003b). The fact that starting in 2003, over fifty cadets came forward to accuse upper-class cadets of sexual assault indicates that such violence is not an aberration but a regular occurrence indicative of the existence of rape culture.

To be clear, I am not claiming that news reports utterly ignore the academy attacks, numbers of victims, or the weak punishments administrators face. These issues get plenty of attention as discrete issues. Instead of complete inattention, what I document are failures that follow from reporters presenting sexual violence as scandalous: that it is a failure to understand such violence as a persistent threat for a disproportionate number of service women and cadets and to investigate the banal processes that perpetuate sexual violence (as de Volo and Hall [2015] have). For example, the same *Today Show* segment reported that a "sophomore cadet here at the Air Force Academy is accused of rape, sodomy and providing alcohol to minors; serious charges that could result in a court-martial and further tarnish the reputation of the Academy" (NBC 2003b). The month before, the reporter Linda Douglass of *World News Tonight with Peter Jennings* provided a similar introduction to one academy rape victim: "This young woman is one of fifty-six women who say they were raped repeatedly when they were cadets at the Air Force Academy." And then the program cut to another cadet listing what happened to her and some of her peers: "Sodomy. Just all, all kinds, assault, rape. Just, just nasty things. Nasty." From there the camera cut again to Douglass, who quickly shifted to mentioning Congress, where "outraged Senators accused Air Force brass of ignoring assaults on women" (ABC 2003c).

ABC's treatment is like other sexual assault stories that appear during this fifteen-year period: after reporters enumerate criminal acts and establish the numbers of victims, their focus shifts to officialdom—in this case, Congress and "Air Force brass." Of course, these groups bear collective responsibility for solving the problem. Burke, for example, maintains that the Air Force Academy's oversight board was aware of a sexual assault problem there but did not do much about it until it became public in 2003 (2004, 51). However, such singular focus on the upper echelons discourages investigation of what these stories signal: that service academies are producing and enabling sexual predators who will graduate to the officer corps. This maneuver thus sidesteps the issue of how and where to effectively intervene into military training and education in order to prevent further perpetuation of sexual violence and the resulting trauma. Reporting Air Force Academy sexual violence as a scandalous aberration may attract eyeballs, but it glosses over both the mundane and insidious dimensions of sexual violence in military training and education, as well as its history.

A *Today Show* segment from February 2003 begins to lay out the magnitude of the Air Force Academy's problems in an interview with Dorothy Mackey, a former Air Force captain who founded an organization to counsel military sexual assault survivors, and Senator Wayne Allard, a member of the Senate Armed Service Committee. Mackey resigned from the military after being sexually assaulted: "In the first five years of my Air Force career, I was actually raped three times. I also witnessed as U.S. military members had purposely targeted young women to get them drunk and then either rape or gang rape them. When I took this to the legal office, they refused to even investigate it. And in my last year of the service, I was tag-team assaulted by two superior officers who were, in fact, the complaint system, one of which was a former Air Force Academy graduate." Mackey continues, "Ultimately, I had to resign my commission because I didn't want to be raped again by one of the individuals. And I could not find help inside the service. I virtually was told to go away or shut up or I was on my own. I'd gone even to the Justice Department three times and tried to get their help and people on the outside, and they refused to help me. Fortunately, I found a really good attorney, and she took my case" (NBC 2003b). What Mackey relays about her experience—including reporting to officers who refused to investigate and a reporting system itself staffed with assault perpetrators—is typical, according to *The Invisible War*'s poignant survivor stories. Senator Allard, who at that time was pushing the secretary of the Air Force to investigate the academy, notes that the problems there date to 1991, when "they had some problems with sexual harassment": "We thought that perhaps maybe they'd put some procedures in place that would take care of the problem" (NBC 2003b). Tragically, this was not the case.

Although TV news outlets failed to see sexual violence as structural in their Air Force Academy reporting, they finally started to comprehend this more than a decade later, when news emerged that several officers leading sexual assault and prevention departments had themselves been charged with sexual assault or domestic violence. For example, after Senator Gillibrand's Military Justice Improvement Act was defeated for the first time early in 2014 (it was defeated twice in total, as of 2018), reports juxtaposed news of that against arrests of the commanders, such as in this headline of NBC's *Today Show* on March 7, 2014: "The Senate has voted down a change in the way sexual assault accusations are handled in the military even as two high-profile cases highlighted the growing problem" (NBC 2014). And it was a problem: Between

2005 and 2013, the firings of almost one-third of military commanders were for "sexual offenses," according to Kate Harding (2015, 89).

Given the almost total inattention to the implications of future military officers being trained amid rape culture, it is not surprising when officers look the other way or even perpetrate sexual violence themselves. TV news programs' treatment of this aspect of sexual assault provides a glimpse into how ill equipped war correspondents are to cover such a serious topic that falls outside the bounds of standard reporting in this context: body counts, battles won and lost, sites for troop deployments, and so forth. Such negligence can have grievous consequences: by not learning about rape reform from feminist activists and scholars, TV news reports play a role in continuing, rather than solving, the problem of military sexual violence. But even amid a rather indifferent response to this aspect of the problem, TV news stories do attend to survivors. Numerous segments across fifteen years that feature service women telling their assault stories to sympathetic reporters bring to light the pervasiveness of sexual violence in the lives of women warriors and the institutional failures of the military to help them—the subject I address in the next section.

Survivor Stories

Although TV news stories seem loathe to probe the issues that produce and perpetuate military rape culture, they do commendable work when they feature survivors recounting their sexual assault stories. Certainly "lurid details" appear in their accounts (which may be unavoidable due to the nature of sexual assault), but overall, commentators and reporters appear to be supportive of survivors and avoid either disbelief or casting blame. Such supportive treatment reflects the influence of what Lisa Cuklanz refers to as a feminist-driven "rape reform movement," which has since the 1970s worked to sensitize reporters who cover sexual violence (2000, 7). As Benedict's analysis of "sex crime" news coverage reveals, such a sympathetic perspective on victims has not been automatic on the part of reporters and editors, historically speaking. Much of the news coverage that Benedict examines reproduces rather than challenges rape myths such as "women provoke rape" (1992, 15). A key difference between military and civilian sexual assault survivor stories is that those with a military focus include reassurances that even after being attacked, survivors want to continue on with their military service—their sense of patriotism and duty intact.

On occasion, however, a story appears and illustrates how intractable rape myths can be in a post-9/11 media environment. A comment made by the Iraq War veteran and Congress member Tulsi Gabbard, for example, could be construed as victim blaming and has particular resonance for a military context. In an exchange concerning sexual assault reporting and the chain of command, the CNN host Candy Crowley asks the veterans and Congress members Tammy Duckworth and Gabbard how the system should be changed to treat victims fairly after they report an attack. In a problematic non sequitur, Gabbard asserts, "These predators seek out people who are weak targets." Duckworth agrees with her, and Gabbard continues, "I was not a weak target, so it's not something that I experienced personally" (CNN 2013b). That predators go after "weak targets" is problematic for its suggestion that a victim asks for her assault by dint of being perceived as weak; it perpetuates the myth that in one way or another, rape victims encourage their own attacks. It is an odd statement, more so because it is preceded by Gabbard's insistence that the system to report and prosecute be refashioned to center on victims, "from the moment that the victim makes that report, all the way through to the point where the perpetrator is prosecuted and charged and punished." In the remainder of her appearance, Gabbard is vociferous about her support for an amendment to the Uniform Code of Military Justice as well as for punishing commanders who retaliate against victims who report. Considering this context, I draw the conclusion that even for someone who supports military rape reform—as Gabbard does—the myth of the victim who somehow invites her assault is a powerfully insidious one.

Victim blaming fits with postfeminism, as well. A postfeminist ideology is individualistic rather than collective, and as many scholars have noted, this focus results in suggestions that women who experience problems of any sort have only themselves to blame. "I was not a weak target, so it's not something that I experienced personally" illustrates this perfectly, as it simultaneously deflects from examining the toxic masculinity that motivates sexual assaults. Fortunately, Gabbard's expression of postfeminist victim blaming is the exception and not the rule. News accounts that feature these stories are generally sensitive and supportive, casting survivors as patriots and warriors forced to fight their own peers on this intramilitary battlefield.

Following three brief clips of cadets relating details of their assaults, for example, ABC introduces a *20/20* segment on the Air Force Academy's "explosive new sex scandal" this way: "They were the country's best and brightest. Proud to be chosen for the Air Force Academy. But they say they were living with the enemy. Outnumbered, overpowered, sexually assaulted, raped and warned never to tell" (ABC 2003a). Using a similar frame, the reporter Cecilia Vega of ABC's *World News Tonight* establishes that "Stacey Thompson wanted so badly to be a Marine, she enlisted before she was even eighteen." "That's the thing I'll never forget is I was excited. I wanted to do this," Thompson confirms; she then goes on to recount to an incredulous Vega her story of, first, being sexually harassed when she was stationed in Japan and then, after reporting the harassment to her commander—the man who was harassing her—a sergeant in her direct chain of command raping her as well (ABC 2014).

The experience transforms Thompson into an activist, with more detailed accounts of her story appearing in several print media outlets as well as on the CBS News website.

NBC (2012) frames similarly but gives more extensive treatment to the survivor Claire Russo, whose disturbing story the network replays in several different programs. "Claire Russo always wanted to serve her country. Even as a little girl, she dreamed of becoming a Marine," the reporter Natalie Morales announces. "Why the Marine Corps?" Morales asks. Russo replies, "When I was ten and when I was eighteen and when I was twenty-three, . . . the reason never changed. They were the toughest." Morales details Russo's path, noting that "she went through Officer Candidate School, graduating fourth in her class. Her father, Ken Wilkinsen, watched her commissioning with pride." But then Russo's life changed. "The exemplary Marine attended the Marine Corps Ball at a San Diego hotel. She went with her cousin Tom, a Navy officer, who introduced her to Captain Doug Dowson, an F-18 aviator. Dowson bought her a drink and said he'd take her to a room party." Russo then reveals to Morales the events of and after that night: Dowson drugged and then raped her. "Really the next thing I remember is being on the ground in the bathroom. He was holding me down and sodomizing me. And at that point, I was just crying and begging him to stop." Russo's rape was followed by a dramatic intervention by Zach Paton, an NCIS agent friend of Russo's cousin, who insisted that Russo go to a civilian hospital for a rape exam and then report the attack to civilian police. "It was very apparent," Paton tells viewers, that the Marine Corps was "going to take no action," despite the collection of "forensic evidence, testimony, and photos" that Paton was prepared to make available for the investigation. Whereas the Marines were not interested in investigating Russo's case, the civilian district attorney was. Her story concludes when the DA obtains a warrant and searches Dowson's house, where Paton and police officers discovered "hidden cameras and hundreds of hours of video of Dowson having sex with seemingly incapacitated women. And then Paton discovered something else. Just seven months prior to Claire's assault, a female aviator, Captain Naomi Boyum, who's since left the military, had a similar incident with Dowson. She says she told her commander but felt pressure not to file a report. The DA charged Dowson with Claire's rape. He pleaded guilty to sodomy before his civilian trial began and was sentenced to three years in prison."

Russo is not the only service woman in this segment with a story about sexual assault. Following the account of Russo's experience, Natalie Morales interviews Darchelle Mitchell, Andrea Neutzling, Laura Sellinger, and Kim Wellnitz, each of whom relates distressingly common details in her narrative about military sexual assault: Morales explains that "the petty officer [Mitchell] says raped her was acquitted, and it was her Navy career that suffered." Mitchell tells her what happened following her report of the rape: "My request to reenlist was denied, and my assailant, he was advancing in the middle of all of it." "He was promoted?" asks Morales. "He was promoted," Mitchell confirms. Laura Sellinger describes what her sexual assault response coordinator told her: "Don't expect anything to happen from this. You need to find a way to get over it." The exchange continues with Morales relating that Sellinger's commander refused her request not to disclose the rape and announced it to her squadron—an act that triggered further harassment. "And now I'm dealing with I'm a slut, I'm a whore. I've never been so hollow," Sellinger tells a sympathetic Morales. The other women relate similar stories of victim blaming and impunity for perpetrators. For instance, Wellnitz's rapist was honorably discharged and a few years later convicted of raping two teenage girls (NBC 2012).

Morales concludes the segment by switching back to Russo, asking her, "That young, patriotic girl who was you back then, who loved to hear the national anthem and got emotional whenever you would hear it, do you still feel that way?" Russo confirms, "I do. I—I love this country. But, you know, there's a wound that will never heal. I gave the Marine Corps everything. And it took from me something that I'm never going to get back." Brian Williams picks up after the segment concludes, asking Morales, "How is Claire Russo doing?" Morales tells him, "She is an incredible woman, so strong, as you saw in that piece. She actually left the Marines, and she went a few years ago to help the Army launch the first Female Engagement Teams in Afghanistan under then General Petraeus, and now she's a . . . fellow on the Council on Foreign Relations, where she's doing a lot of great work helping again with the military and establishing a role for women in the military" (NBC 2012).

The head shot of Russo recounting her rape appears in another NBC story the following year, this one about "sex scandals" in the military: one occurring at Fort Hood, where an investigation had revealed that the Army sergeant first class in charge of sexual assault prevention had been coercing women stationed there into prostitution, assaulting one of them; and the other in the Air Force, where the officer in charge of sexual assault prevention had been arrested and charged with "sexual battery for allegedly molesting a woman near the Pentagon." A voice-over asserts that these incidents and a Pentagon report on sexual assault show that it is "out of control," based on the figure that twenty-six assaults had gone unreported the previous year. "The victims remain silent, fearing the military's male-dominated culture and justice system are stacked against them," we learn. The next sequence of clips features Russo describing how she woke up to being sodomized on the bathroom floor, choking back tears as she says she was "begging him to stop"; Russo in dress uniform, receiving her commission from a male officer; and Russo again in dress uniform, saluting the officer standing across from her. The voice-over relays that her attacker was convicted in a civilian, not military, court. "The only thing that makes my story extraordinary," Russo asserts, "is that I got justice" (NBC 2013a).

These survivors' accounts and others like them garner respect and sympathy from reporters and commentators, who emphasize the warriors' toughness for having endured assaults on their bodies and on their character by peers and officers. The military-specific twist given to survivor stories is the reassurance—repeatedly elicited by reporters and given by survivors—that they remain committed to military service. This point is reinforced in imagery that marks the women as recognizable warriors. Shot sequences feature women in uniform, both dress and combat, in commission ceremonies, and boarding planes en masse for deployments, scenes that solidify the women's rightful place in military culture. Even those who opt for work outside the military, as Claire Russo does, express a desire to retain aspects of a soldier's life. That news organizations believe it necessary to solicit these assurances is noteworthy for how they further facilitate the transformation to grievable, recognizable martial subjects. The words of victims and scenes of them performing military duties affirm the military as an institution, implicitly folding its martial goals into this representational regime as they do so. Despite the sexual violence these women have endured, they continue to be both recognizable and grievable *as warriors*—so tough that even sexual violence cannot weaken their resolve to complete their mission.

Minimizing Masculinity, Displacing Responsibility

Although survivor stories and those about abuse in military educational institutions offer ample opportunities for reporters to interrogate the gendered power differential driving sexual violence, they fail to undertake such an investigation. Instead, while reporters and their guests criticize the military's approach to preventing and prosecuting sexual assault, they stop before they get to an analysis of gender. The reporter Martha Raddatz illustrates the tactic in a *World News Tonight with Diane Sawyer* segment, headlined "Military Sex Scandal." After reporting on the charges of sexual assault against two officers heading up sexual assault prevention offices, Raddatz voices, over an image of a four-square grid, that "there have been decades of promises." Each square contains a head shot of a white, male military spokesperson who, in succession, expresses that there is "zero tolerance" for sexual assault and harassment in the military. Further observing that although some of the "countless hours of military training and messaging" under way to stop sexual violence are "serious,"

Raddatz calls other efforts "seemingly absurd." She skeptically examines a hand-sanitizer bottle in the shape of a hand that reads, "Keep your hands to yourself," then catches a toy football tossed to her from off-camera; she smirks wryly while holding it up to the camera and reading from it, "Don't fumble, get consent." Quickly the camera switches to Representative Jackie Speier, who asserts, "In the end, the training is not going to do the trick. We aren't convicting, we aren't prosecuting, and we aren't kicking people out." In apparent agreement with Speier, Raddatz concludes the segment, "Indeed, the number of cases of unwanted sexual contact in the military has soared 35 percent in just the past two years, making this a problem, say critics, which needs an entirely new approach" (ABC 2013c).

Despite Raddatz's call, an entirely new approach does not emerge from any of these TV news stories (or, apparently, from the DoD), although there is much discussion of the need for one. In the interview with Dorothy Mackey mentioned earlier, for example, Katie Couric notes that the academy had implemented some programs, including a "street smart program . . . for freshmen to protect themselves, a twenty-four-hour rape hotline and amnesty program which . . . encourages the reporting of assaults." She asks Mackey, "Why don't you think these things are working?" Mackey replies, "Because I've had seven academy cadets so far call me and tell me that they're not working. And, in fact, the—those programs, while they may appease the American public, unfortunately, they're actually not working. They're almost kind of smoke and mirrors" (NBC 2003b).

Though Mackey does not elaborate on why she believes the academy's attempts do not work, I would argue that they fail because they place the burden on cadets to protect themselves and locate remedies in the reporting system—in other words, after sexual violence has occurred. As has been the case in civilian colleges and universities, rape prevention becomes the responsibility of potential victims rather than of those who perpetrate such violence. To be clear, I believe these aspects of the academy's program (as well as those on civilian college campuses) are important; they are, however, only partial remedies—necessary but not sufficient. Sarah Jane Brubaker's analysis of sexual assault data from both military service academies and civilian universities shows that programs placing responsibility for prevention on the shoulders of potential victims and not addressing perpetrators actually discourage victims from reporting their assaults in either civilian or military institutions (2009, 66–67). Add to that the chance that the commanders to whom reports should be made are themselves perpetrating sexual assault, and it stands to reason that military sexual trauma is "so ubiquitous—if victims were reporting their assaults to sexual predators, no wonder they weren't getting justice" (Harding 2015, 90).

Illuminating the Enemy Within

After covering the Air Force Academy, most of a decade passed before TV news outlets turned in earnest to reporting sexual assault—despite being clued in about the gravity of the situation by survivor-guests such as Dorothy Mackey. The release of *The Invisible War* (2012) prompted the second, and most substantial, episode of post-9/11 military sexual assault reporting. After the film premiered at the 2012 Sundance Film Festival, it went on to win two Emmy Awards (one for Outstanding Investigative Journalism) and a Peabody Award and was nominated for an Academy Award. Probably owing both to its evocative scenes (in one memorable moment, for example, retired Brigadier General Loree K. Sutton calls the military a "target-rich environment" for sexual predators) and to the publicity strategy of the director, Kirby Dick, and the producer, Amy Ziering (which included screening the film to policy makers such as Secretary of Defense Leon Panetta and members of Congress), television news outlets could not ignore *The Invisible War*. Rather than ignore it, in fact, they apparently outsourced their own reporting to the filmmakers.

Apropos of this point, Dick explains in one interview that documentaries such as theirs can remedy the "decline of investigative journalism and newspapers across the country. Around the country, there's a real need for documentaries to fill that role"—particularly with a subject that the military had "covered up for many, many years" (J. Kim 2012). Dick believes the film has done this, even breaking a story that other news organizations had missed: that of rampant sexual violence against women stationed at the elite Marine Barracks Washington (MBW). Marines assigned to MBW are considered the very best; among their duties is accompanying the U.S. president to various public functions. Perhaps because their elite status makes them believe they can get away with it, many of these male Marines also assault their women peers with impunity (*Invisible War* 2012). Pushing the film's intervention further, Dick took to a news forum himself the year after the film's release, penning a *New York Times* op-ed piece published on the first day of a Senate Armed Services Committee hearing on military sexual assault. In it, he asserts, "The military has a problem with embedded, serial sexual predators. . . . These predators select and befriend lower-ranking victims; often they ply their victims with alcohol or drugs and assault them when they are unconscious. . . . There is a way to stop these predators: we should prosecute and incarcerate them. But here the military fails entirely" (2013).

I discuss *The Invisible War* at length in this section to underscore its importance in both expanding the Warrior Women regime and shifting TV news outlets' attention, albeit temporarily, to military sexual violence. Between 2001 and 2012, they aired 45 segments on this topic; between 2013 and 2014, they aired 122, 91 of which were aired in 2013. Of these, there were 108 different stories;[7] 79 appeared in 2013, and 29 in 2014. Of these, 63 percent in 2013 and just under 52 percent in 2014 referenced Senate legislation, mainly in interviews with Senators Gillibrand and McCaskill, video clips of them during dramatic moments in their bills' deliberation and evolution, or a combination of both. Scenes of Gillibrand and McCaskill dressing down male military brass testifying in front of the Senate Armed Services Committee in 2013 not only circulated across broadcast and cable TV news channels alike but migrated to YouTube, where they have received thousands of views.

Together, Dick and Ziering's film and appearances expand the representational context of sexual assault coverage both to emphasize the depth and breadth of the problem and to challenge the military to solve it. In the process, the film works to construct new truths about the structural nature of military sexual assault. Along with illuminating aspects of how the military is structured to reproduce a sexual violence status quo, *The Invisible War* focuses on the wrenching experiences of a group of service-women survivors (some of whom are part of a class-action suit against the military).[8] All of these survivors report being treated with derision and disbelief after they report their assaults. Some, such as the Coast Guard veteran Kori Cioca, face further trauma when they seek treatment from the VA, which for Cioca makes the tasks of refilling her medication and scheduling physical therapy onerous. Many of the women consider suicide after their assault; some, such as the former Marine first lieutenant Ariana Klay, raped while serving at the MBW, attempt it.

In visible distress, Klay and her husband, Ben, relate the brutal details of her story of abuse, which starts almost immediately after she begins her assignment. Once she arrives at MBW, several of Klay's male peers tell her that they consider the women working there to be "walking mattresses," whose sole purpose is to be "fucked." Not long after receiving the misogynistic threat, Klay learns firsthand that the men are serious when one of her fellow officers rapes her. Upon learning of the attack, the rapist's friends tell Klay that she will be killed if she reports it. Despite the death threat, Klay does report the rape, only to see it covered up by other MBW officers. This is the series of events that precipitates her suicide attempt, the devastating consequences of which the film captures vividly. After the film's release, both Ariana and Ben Klay appear briefly in TV news segments as they testify to Congress about the horrific repercussions of military sexual violence in their lives.

Klay's story is not an outlier. Other women in the film describe how, in addition to being assaulted, they are treated with contempt after reporting their attacks to their commanders: refusals to investigate, accusations of lying, and retaliation against them—some even charged with adultery (a dischargeable offense). What is more, the film reveals that 33 percent of service women who were raped did not report their attack because the commander was a friend of the rapist, and 25 percent did not report because the commander himself was the rapist. *The Invisible War* pushes for two major changes: moving reporting procedures outside the chain of command and improving the prosecution system to ensure that perpetrators will be tried and, if found guilty, punished with dismissal. It also encourages the DoD to enhance both survivor support services and SAPRO's sexual assault prevention efforts; it stops short, however, of suggesting that rehabilitation programs acknowledge and then treat the toxic masculinity driving sexual violence in the academies and in the military itself.

Dick and Ziering do not leave the film's potential impact on its audiences to chance. In one interview, for example, they urge viewers to get involved and offer several avenues for doing so: visiting the #NotInvisible website and signing a petition there to "demand change"; hosting "a screening . . . to spark conversation, awareness, and change"; donating to the Artemis Rising Invisible War Recovery Program; and "join[ing] the conversation" on *The Invisible War* Twitter feed to protest military sexual abuse (J. Kim 2012). Currently the website for *The Invisible War* links to Protect Our Defenders, which has taken over #NotInvisible and offers numerous support and legal services as well as a social media community and political advocacy. Dick expresses hope that the film has therapeutic value as well. Just prior to PBS's airing of *The Invisible War* in May 2013, the *Independent Lens* blog posted an interview in which Dick describes viewers being "outraged and moved and compelled to want to take action and help." Even the people who appear in the film "have said the experience of participating in the film has significantly changed their lives for the better—it's been surprising, therapeutic and empowering—they no longer feel invisible and discarded and ashamed. They feel validated, and it's renewed their faith and trust in others" (Dick, quoted in *Independent Lens Blog* 2013).

This combination of the documentary's affective rendering of sexual assault survivors' experiences and presentation of options for activism makes *The Invisible War* unusually influential: policy makers have attributed the film with moving them to act, and it has been used in training workshops throughout the military. The documentary compelled then–Secretary of Defense Leon Panetta to make remedying sexual assault one of his top priorities, and he "immediately institut[ed] significant policy reforms," according to *The Invisible War*'s website (Protect Our Defenders, n.d.). New York's Senator Kirsten Gillibrand is perhaps the most open about how the film pushed her to become a strong advocate for advancing *The Invisible War*'s agenda. Gillibrand reports that she found herself so "gripped with anger and disgust and determination that [she] was going to do something about" military sexual assault (Zremski 2014). After viewing the film, Gillibrand drafted the Military Justice Improvement Act, designed to fix the flawed prosecution system that allows so many assault perpetrators to go free. Although Gillibrand's legislation was defeated in favor of that of Missouri's Senator Claire McCaskill, which allows prosecutions to remain at the discretion of military commanders, her numerous appearances saturated television news programs and propelled to visibility the issues illuminated in the documentary.

The Invisible War's efforts to publicize and remedy military sexual assault successfully increased both the volume of stories and the intensity with which news programs focused on the subject. Albeit late in coming, in many ways this attention is noteworthy for how it publicizes a problem that victims and advocates had been struggling to illuminate. The fact that almost every story in this two-year period mentions the magnitude and contours of the problem—tens of thousands of service members being assaulted each year, many of their cases dismissed or overturned by commanders—is laudable, as are the numerous stories that give voice to survivors (which, as I discussed earlier, TV news stories aired a number of even before the appearance of *The Invisible War*). This sort of focused attention is significant for establishing the scale of the problem as well as the trauma it causes. As I noted earlier, these are strategies advocated by feminist rape reformers to validate sexual assault survivors' experiences and therefore aid in their healing. Such aspects of this coverage illustrate that TV news representations can at times comfort the afflicted when compelled to do so.

Nevertheless, TV news outlets limit themselves in how much they will afflict the comfortable—in this context, sexual assault perpetrators. After *The Invisible War*'s release, TV coverage hewed to a standard formula of focusing on individual senators and their legislative dramas, using pithy sound bites circulated widely through the year's coverage. Senators Gillibrand and McCaskill became the faces associated with tackling military sexual assault, and clips of them uttering their signature phrases during Senate Armed Services Committee hearings that feature all-male military brass testifying about rampant sexual assault under their leadership appear in most of the coverage during 2013 and 2014. Gillibrand's oft-repeated words emerge as she establishes the seriousness of sexual assault to the officers, telling them that commanders must be made aware that sexual assault is a crime. "Not every single commander necessarily wants women in the force. Not every single commander believes what a sexual assault is. *Not every single commander can distinguish between a slap on the ass and a rape*," she calmly insists (my emphasis indicates the sentence that gets the most airplay, e.g., Fox News Channel 2013b). McCaskill earns coverage for both an exasperated "are you frickin' kidding me?" in response to the officers' ignorance about the extent of the problem across all military branches and her characterization of sexual violence: "This isn't about sex. This is about assaultive domination and violence" (e.g., ABC 2013a).

Although it is gratifying to watch this group of men be dressed down by female senators, the sound bites dominate the coverage and effectively work as a substitute for a deeper, feminist analysis of the problem. McCaskill's assertion, for example, works as broad cover for ignoring gender. Like *Army Wives'* Claudia Joy Holden's insistence that rape is about exercising some vague form of power, McCaskill's statement, while strongly worded, is incomplete for its refusal to identify the misogyny and toxic masculinity that motivate "assaultive domination and violence." Clips featuring these phrases and other moments of legislative drama that fill the news hole tell TV news audiences that this is as far as they will go with their coverage, despite plenty of signs that suggest military sexual violence should be investigated specifically as an exercise of gendered power (something *The Invisible War* begins to do). Important as it may be to understand legislation designed to change the systems for reporting and prosecuting military sexual violence, it need not and should not eclipse other reporting on the topic. But TV news reports during 2013 and 2014 saturated the airwaves with discussions of Senator Gillibrand's bill, the changes it would make to the Uniform Code of Military Justice—including how it would remove sexual assault reporting from the chain of command—and how Pentagon brass were responding to the legislation.

This coverage takes an even more dramatic turn as it reports on Senate deliberations after McCaskill introduced a more military-friendly bill that competed with Gillibrand's. On MSNBC, for example, the host Luke Russert implies that the senators' conflict is a catfight when he addresses the subject of their bills to Representative Tulsi Gabbard:

> RUSSERT: There is a battle now happening in the United States Senate between Kirsten Gillibrand and Claire McCaskill about what exactly legislation should look like.
>
> [McCaskill] said to *USA Today*, quote, "Under Kirsten's scenario, those cases would not go forward. This new regime of lawyers would have all the power around these prosecutions, and they would also be the last word."
>
> The Missouri Democrat said she's also had to make the case to undecided lawmakers that voting for our reform doesn't make you antiwoman.
>
> Do you think that people that don't support the Kirsten Gillibrand legislation are antiwoman? Is that a fair characterization? And is that a bad split for the Democratic Party?
>
> GABBARD: Well, I'm actually going to take your question just one step back because it's important for everyone to understand, wherever they fall in this issue, this is not just a woman's issue. There are more men who have been sexually assaulted in the military than there have been women. (MSNBC 2013a)

Gabbard's attempt to reframe sexual violence as "not just a woman's issue" degenders violence in a manner reflected in so much of this coverage. Senator Gillibrand reiterates this point at various times, as does Anu Bhagwati of the

Service Women's Action Network in her frequent appearances, such as the following one on Fox News Channel's *Lou Dobbs Tonight*. In a series of clips from the Senate Armed Service Committee meetings that generated many dramatic moments, Bhagwati testifies, "Just over half of victims of sexual assault in the military are male. So, fourteen thousand of those twenty-six thousand victims last year were male. It seems shocking, I think, for people to first hear that, but when we realize that rape and sexual assault aren't about gender, [we see] they're about power and control" (Fox News Channel 2013b).

Gabbard, Gillibrand, and Bhagwati all hint at the value of using a gender lens to better understand the problem, but they subsequently obviate it with reiterated implications that men being victims too mitigates against the need to critically examine the gender constructions and performances of perpetrators of sexual violence. Not only does this suggest that only women are gendered, but it overlooks feminist work on rape and sexual violence that has been conducted on behalf of men as well as women. Additionally and importantly, it obscures the performance of masculinity by sexual violence perpetrators, known variously as toxic, hegemonic, or misogynistic masculinity. This sort of omission in public discussions of sexual assault and rape is common, according to the rape researcher Kate Harding. Passive-voice constructions such as "Sally was raped" or Gabbard's "There are more men who have been sexually assaulted in the military than there have been women" avoid addressing assault perpetrators. Harding argues that this works to represent rape as "an abstract threat to women, the way climate change is a threat to the earth—it's a frightening specter we all live with, and we must change our own behavior in hopes of warding it off, but you can't really pin it on anyone in particular. You've heard of 'victimless' crimes. Rape is perhaps the only perpetratorless crime, in our collective imagination" (2015, 36).

Though absent from TV news accounts, feminist researchers and rape reformers have long critiqued and attempted to intervene into the constructions and performances of masculinity that lead some men to be sexually violent. Research by Jackson Katz, Michael Kimmel, Myriam Medzian, and John Stoltenberg, for instance, illuminates dangerous myths about manhood used both to socialize men and boys and to shape popular culture, where all manner of artifacts encourage them to act on these myths. But none of these feminists—or any others, for that matter—appears in TV news coverage of military sexual assault, an omission that Benedict warns reporters and editors about when they cover "sex crimes." Under the category of systemic reforms that she recommends for news organizations is "Stop Disregarding Feminism." Signaling its importance to her project, Benedict concludes her book with this recommendation: "Finally, the press must stop being afraid of feminism. At the moment, the mainstream press is so unwilling to consult feminist sources that it has effectively crippled its chance of covering sex crimes properly, for it is in the fields of feminist sociology, medicine and anthropology that an understanding of these crimes lies" (1992, 266). Citing the historian Roy Porter, Benedict identifies two feminist "formulations" that he believes are particularly helpful for obtaining deeper understanding of rape: that "rape cannot be fully understood in terms of individual rapists, but only in terms of masculine values at large," and that "rape is more an expression of misogyny than of pent-up sexual desire" (quoted in Benedict 1992, 266). Porter's and Benedict's assessments are informed by the feminist rape-reform movement, which has been reformulating how rape is treated legally, politically, and socially for at least four decades. Cuklanz observes that these feminist activists are in general agreement that "rape is a result of gender inequality in economic, political, and social terms," although they may disagree about "how these inequalities variously contribute to the problem of rape and the likelihood of meaningful change within a patriarchal and capitalist system" (2000, 11). However widely held these beliefs are among rape reformers, Cuklanz identifies a disjuncture between them and news media, which she argues are "poorly suited to the expression of feminist reformulation of rape and rape reform" (2000, 15). This does not have to be the case, though, as *The Invisible War* illustrates.

Gender and Sexual Violence

To prevent sexual violence, some contemporary rape reformers and educators concentrate on revealing those constructions and performances of masculinity that enact it. To reiterate a theoretical point from the introduction, gender is produced in and through discourse and performed; it is not an expression of biologically rooted attributes. Thus, people with any gender identity may perform masculinity. However, because of the disciplinary function of discursive gender practices, masculinities tend to be performed by those who identify as men and boys. Media and popular culture discourses constitute meanings around gender performances, in part by rewarding some and disciplining others to the margins of social acceptability—sometimes violently. To wit, according to the Southern Poverty Law Center, trans women of color are "almost certainly the group most victimized by hate violence in America"; in the first few months of 2015, their murder rate averaged about one woman per week (Terry 2015). (President Trump's August 2017 tweet banning transgender troops from the military is another unfortunate example of vilifying gender-nonconforming people.)

Media are not the only, but they are likely the most ubiquitous, producers of discourses that prescribe and proscribe performances of various masculinities. As Jackson Katz's research reveals in the documentary *Tough Guise 2* (2013), film, television, and video game representations all privilege and reward tough, violent, muscular men as they constitute meaning around masculinity; on the other hand, tender, nurturing performances of masculinity are difficult to find in mainstream media representations. Even advertising intended for men reinforces a system that legitimates and distinguishes from femininity performances of masculinity that equate it "with violence, power, and control (and femininity with passivity)," according to Katz (2011, 262). Martha McCaughey's research on the "caveman mystique" (2008) shows how this construction of masculinity gains credibility and disciplinary authority from human behavior and evolution (HBE) theories of sex differences and especially popular media interpretations of them. Perhaps the most disturbing of these interpretations is the one that is most relevant here: that for evolutionary reasons, men are biologically programmed to rape—a notion with enough popular culture traction to have become a truism excusing violence and misogynist behavior.

Clearly, the performances of masculinity that align with caveman attributes or advertisements are neither socially neutral nor benign, particularly for anyone who exhibits qualities coded feminine. "When dominance and power define masculinity," Myriam Medzian asserts, "men rape as a way of putting 'uppity' women in their place." She observes further that "many men feel deeply threatened by the achievements of the women's movement. Some react to the greater freedom, independence, and power of women with rage and violence, including rape, battering, and killing" (2005, 161). Medzian's point is relevant to military sexual assault, suggesting that service men who sexually assault women peers do so out of resentment over their masculinist domain being integrated by individuals they consider subordinate to them. Such violence and harassment against women who integrate male-dominated organizations of all kinds are distressingly common (see, for example, Brubaker 2009, 64–65).

But what are we to make of service men who assault other military men? As Marie Thompson observes about public responses to men being victims of military sexual violence, this issue "continues to befuddle even those committed to mitigating this issue." Comments made by Senator Lindsey Graham during Senate Armed Services Committee hearings on sexual assault that identified only "female members of the military" as victims of sexual violence therefore exemplify "the powerful challenges faced in disrupting ideals of hegemonic masculinity, particularly as the gendered composition of forces across rank and duties in the contemporary military continues to shift. Ignoring men as victims of these crimes limits any measures meant to address the problem because our interventions fail to escape our own paradigmatic confines" (2014, 133). The paradigmatic confines that Thompson refers to stem from a binary, men-rape-women, view of sexual assault. In addition to being essentialist and simplistic, this view does not include sexual predators who attack other men. But to understand and work to prevent sexual violence wherever it occurs, we would be wise to follow the example of rape researchers who focus on perpetrators' gender performances. Because 98 percent of rapists are men (Harding 2015, 36), and men are typically socialized to perform masculinity rather than femininity (although what constitutes proper masculinity changes historically, geographically, and culturally), examining discursive constitutions of masculinity that reward sexually violent behavior, such as those found in the military, would be a good place to focus research and investigative reporting.

Men who rape other men nullify the gender-binary paradigm by being equal-opportunity attackers, as it were. According to Michael Scarce, they tend to be hetero and white, and "virtually every study indicates that men rape other men out of anger or an attempt to overpower, humiliate, and degrade their victims rather than out of lust, passion, or sexual desire" (1997, 17–18). Just as "men's rape of women is a hateful act designed to reinforce male supremacy," Rus Erwin Funk asserts, "so is men's rape of men" (1997, 222). Along with other feminist researchers and antirape educators, Scarce and Funk concur that to prevent rape, it must be redefined as "an act of misogynist violence, expressed as a hatred and devaluation of all things feminine." Male rape is thus "very much bound up with the gendered oppression of women" (Scarce 1997, 234).

Military Masculinity and Sexual Assault

The Invisible War explores the problem of military sexual assault by exposing its scale and ineffective systems of redress. But it delves no further into examining cultural systems that produce serial predators who, the film argues, run rampant—and mainly with impunity—throughout the military's ranks. However important improved reporting and prosecution processes are, they constitute only part of an effective response to sexual violence, and neither is a *preventative* measure. When faced with other problems designated as epidemic—diseases, for example—news media typically respond with public-service announcements meant to prevent their spread. Think about stories that appear every winter with advice about how to prevent rhinovirus (aka the common cold) or reminders to get a flu shot or vaccinate our children. Yet when news outlets encounter something that most of them eventually refer to as an epidemic in the military, they are strangely silent on the subject of prevention, going only so far as to simply mention changing "military culture" or some variation thereof.

Feminist research and personal accounts of masculinity's role in sexual assault are out there for motivated reporters to learn from, some of them even published by the Department of Defense. For example, writing about the Tailhook attacks after reading the DoD's 1993 report on them, Cynthia Enloe observes that the report concluded that a "potent mixture of bureaucratic decisions and masculinized social pressure . . . turn[ed] men in military units into assailants" (1998, 57). The men's behavior became misogynist after the various pilots' units started sponsoring hospitality suites at the Las Vegas hotel where the convention was held (suites previously sponsored by weapons manufacturers) and were "encouraged by their commanders to look at one another as fierce competitors" (58). The competition turned criminal when the aircraft pilots—"tailhookers"—saw themselves being a "particular breed of men, that they were especially brash, and [should] chase after women if they were going to perform successfully as fighter pilots" (58). Just after the Marines United incident became public, the former Marine Alexander McCoy recounted aspects of his recent boot-camp experience that he believes led to harassment and abuse of women: "My fellow male Marines and I were taught to look down on our female counterparts. . . . My drill instructors called female Marines sluts and told stories about women's supposedly poor personal hygiene out in the field. The message we got was clear: Female Marines are disgusting and worthless and physically unsuited for the service" (2017). McCoy views such antipathy not as inevitable in a masculinist organization such as the Marines but rather as a result of "tolerating a culture where female Marines are treated with contempt, defined solely as sexual objects unworthy of the job and as distractions to the men" (2017). In a *Washington Post* column about the Marines United incident, Kathleen Parker consults two retired Marines who served in Vietnam for their thoughts on what drives such harassment. One of them offers an insightful reading of the connection between combat and sexual violence: "Marines embrace the warrior archetype more than other branches. The shadow of this is patriarchy, misogyny and brutality. We are trained to be killing machines, deadening all emotion except anger. We're told we don't have the luxury of sensitivity, so we objectify everything, including women" (2017). Sheila Jeffreys echoes other feminist scholars when she adds that "sexual domination is integral to military masculinity as is shown in the history of sexual violence against women that has been carried out by militaries historically and today" (2007, 16). (Susan Jeffords argues that sexual violence is not incidental to women's military service but an integral—and preventable—part of it [1991a, 105].)

All of the foregoing accounts echo Michael Scarce's research on sexual violence between men. Scarce notes that "all-male environments"—military organizations and prisons, for example—encourage the men in them to act violently as they establish hierarchies of authority: "rape and sexual violence epitomize this exertion of power" (1997, 35). What is specific to military organizations, Scarce observes, is an induction process, which "breaks men down psychologically, systematically trains them in aggressive and violent combat, teaches them to objectify their opponents as nonhuman, and enforces a rigid code of prescribed masculinity that is valued above all else[.] Similar to life in prison, rape between military men typically results from internal power struggles and the establishment of authority within a broader realm of male superiority" (46–47). The brutal system that Scarce describes is maintained by what he calls a "cover-up mentality . . . congruent with the preservation and maintenance of military organizations" (45). Sacrificing individual desires for the greater good is part and parcel of maintaining military order but results in "majority rule governance where the minority [sexual assault victims] is not only left unprotected, but stifled in a silence that prevents any challenge to institutional order" (45). Based on an examination of DoD and congressional reports and other materials pertaining to sexual violence in military ranks, Meghana Nayak's analysis echoes Scarce's in that she suggests that "military efforts to combat sexual violence are paradoxical given the central role that masculinity and violence play in the existence of the military" (2009, 153).

Given the integral part that performances of violent masculinity play in discursively constituting the military, it is no wonder that military officials have responded to rampant sexual violence within their ranks with virtual silence. Over the course of fifteen years, TV news reporting parallels the military response in either not reporting on the issue at all (several years saw no stories aired about sexual assault) or refusing to acknowledge misogynistic masculinity and its role in sexual violence—even as news outlets significantly increased coverage of some of the issues raised by *The Invisible War*'s exposé. Official silence such as this can have damaging, long-term consequences and is thus, in its own way, rhetorical.

Silence about sexual violence emanating from the military and TV news organizations, for example, serves to discipline survivors, their advocates, and viewers and exemplifies what Catherine Warren labels "institutional silence." In her study of sexual abuse by physicians and the silence about it by the various actors that the institution of medicine comprises (e.g., professional associations), Warren observes, "Silence works as a tool of domination in institutions. While many understandings of silence come from its ritualistic application—the Quaker religious silence or transcendental meditation— silence in institutions often has an instrumental rather than ritual purpose. . . . Any institutional domain has areas it vigilantly ignores. These black holes are nodal points of power. The capability of keeping an area silent and virtually unexamined is an important, if not an ultimate, key to power' (1996, 3–4). Silence around the sexual abuse of troops benefited the DoD by obscuring a problem that could have choked off the stream of recruits needed for multiple, long-term deployments to Afghanistan and Iraq from 2001 onward. When silence on military sexual assault emanates from TV news organizations, it is another means of demonstrating bureaucratic affinity with the DoD during wartime, something that with few exceptions the U.S. press corps was keen to do—particularly in the first half of this fifteen-year period. As I discussed in chapter 3, TV news outlets' support for the military and war in general extends to supporting women serving in combat roles, too; substantial investigation of military sexual assault would complicate efforts to cast military service for women as a positive, even glorious, experience. A thorough, historical examination of military sexual assault would, moreover, require adopting a feminist lens—a feature that is almost wholly absent from mainstream news media.[9]

Along with Warren, Cheryl Glenn views silence as rhetorical, particularly as it pertains to reinforcing institutional power relations. In this context, she concludes, silence may be used strategically both to maintain a power differential that benefits people at the top of a hierarchy most and to discipline those at lower levels should they speak out about injustice or abuse (which often takes the form of sexual assault and harassment). Glenn argues that the "alpha group in every social situation determines (and tries to control) the speech, speaking patterns, and silences for the women and men in the beta, gamma, (and lower) groups in every social situation. Given that most if not all social situations are framed in hierarchy, both women and men inhabit some measure of silence within a muted group, speak in double-voiced discourse, and consider their words and silences against the dominant system of communication" (2004, 30). These are apt words for describing how silence perpetuates military sexual abuse, as are the conclusions of Warren's case study of medicine's "brotherhood of silence" (1996, 158). For example, when doctors, supervisors, employers, and professional societies were confronted by women and girls accusing their physicians of sexually abusing them, they utilized a combination of silencing strategies that were both passive (ignoring complaints and evidence of sexual abuse) and active (destroying evidence, blaming victims, and disparaging those who spoke out). The military's response to reports of sexual assault that broke out of their silent "containment" parallels those of medicine, as we have seen: individual victims have been blamed, demoted, and further harassed in a process that allows the institution to deny wrongdoing or acknowledge its culture of misogyny.

What Glenn and Warren argue about strategic uses of silence is reflected in Stuart Hall's observation that "representation works as much through what is not shown, as through what is" (1997, 59). Absence, in other words, works productively in regimes of representation. Truths about military women produced by the Warrior Women regime thus emerge from what is missing from TV news representations, as well as what is manifest. In the case of sexual assault, what news stories neglect for the first decade or so following 9/11 is acknowledgment of the pervasiveness of military sexual violence. What is persistently absent in the entire fifteen-year period is any recognition of the dangerous performance of masculinity responsible for it. These two absences across an expanse of TV news representations reveal a great deal about media organizations' priorities for war reporting after 9/11, not to mention their attitudes toward feminist analysis of military rape culture. They refuse, in other words, to have theory in an epidemic, as Treichler puts it, even when the theory could lead to a cure for the military's toxic masculinity problem. Absent such a substantial, theoretically informed change to military thinking and practice, prevention of military sexual violence will be slow in coming, if it happens at all—the subject I address in the next section.

The Pedagogy of Women Warriors

Through accounts of incidents from the previous year, SAPRO's annual report reveals any changes in the scope of the sexual assault problem and explains what the DoD is doing to mitigate it. These days, the report's release typically prompts only brief mentions in TV news stories, where the issue of military sexual assault has become so normalized that only the "man bites dog" stories, such as the Marines United incident, receive much scrutiny. Within the DoD, however, the problem continues to merit attention precipitated in part by *The Invisible War*, which has been used to train officers and specialists in sexual assault prevention. Using the documentary this way illustrates how investigative journalism can be explicitly pedagogical by publicizing an issue and then influencing policies that govern it. Among numerous examples of this are that the VA now considers MST a serious condition that merits treatment for as long as veterans need it. And these days, service men survivors of sexual assault have options for treatment that include anonymous weekly group chat sessions at SafeHelpRoom.org.

TV news coverage of sexual assault works with combat reporting to mutually constitute a pedagogy around women warriors—one that fits with the broader martial context of this post-9/11 moment. We learn, for example, not only that women warriors will encounter combat everywhere but that they are likely to confront prolific sexual harassment and sexual violence as well. Additionally, TV news discourses take their cue from the DoD and *The Invisible War* to guide public understanding of the fallout from sexual assault as well as how to regard proposed solutions for it (legislative remedies, changes to reporting in the Uniform Code of Military Justice, and so forth). The truths constructed here contribute to the body of knowledge produced and circulated as part of the Warrior Women regime and work to "enable and constrain the range of desires, actions, and identities available to us as gendered beings," much as do the civilian antirape discourses that Nicola Gavey examines. About these, she argues that "the truths propagated within such knowledge can be said to play a constitutive role in shaping the possibilities for gendered action that create the cultural conditions of possibility for rape" (2009, 96–97). By ignoring connections between militarism, masculinity, and sexual violence in a military context, we cannot "undermine the cultural formation of masculinities that are too easily capable of sexual violence," as Gavey puts it (97). That is, while TV news programs illuminate the harrowing circumstances of survivors' attacks and subsequent treatment, they demonstrate adherence to the representational status quo of sexual assault. As Cuklanz (2000) and Sarah Projansky (2001) show, since the 1970s, mainstream media offerings exhibit at least a minimally sympathetic view of sexual assault survivors. In the twenty-first century, this perspective is neither controversial nor even especially critical.

Survivors in these Warrior Women discourses are represented within boundaries that are constituted in part by the political economic relationships of TV news organizations and the Pentagon, relations that constrain representations in particular ways. Of course, all representations are constrained by numerous factors; but to my mind, one of the most important aspects of Warrior Women representations is how images and words construct women warriors as grievable. Affective renderings of service women's experiences with sexual assault in the Warrior Women regime offer viewers opportunities to engage with these warrior survivors on a personal level and to grieve with them, as Judith Butler has described the process. These constructions encourage viewers to align themselves with DoD-approved projects meant to alleviate the suffering of military women who have endured sexual violence. The expressions of grief depicted in these Warrior Women work as Butler contends; they offer "a sense of political community of a complex order . . . by bringing to the fore the relational ties that have implications for theorizing fundamental dependency and ethical responsibility. If my fate is not originally or finally separable from yours, then the 'we' is traversed by a relationality that we cannot easily argue against" (2004a, 22–23).

Conditions of grievability with which news viewers are presented align with what is likely to be a DoD-approved construction: women are recognizable as warriors and grievable, therefore, because they could be harmed or even killed in the line of duty; they are vulnerable to attack from within and without. What TV news accounts obscure, however, is both an accounting of the violence that women warriors are themselves responsible for as they perform their military duties and the larger martial objectives that they work in service of. This larger context for warrior women's actions is typically absent—an omission that perhaps makes it easier to grieve them as vulnerable humans and not the killers that their military service trains them to be: after all, *they* kill for peace, as Anastasia Breslow explained in chapter 3.

Postfeminism also constrains these representations of military sexual assault, much as it does in the popular film and television from the 1980s and '90s that Sarah Projansky analyzes. In other words, these narratives about rape indicate a "partial acceptance of some feminist arguments about rape" by acknowledging it "as a social problem and accept[ing] the need for reform of rape law, court practices, and social and familial attitudes toward rape." At the same time, these narratives implicitly convey a message that feminism is "'already successful' and thus no longer necessary" (2001, 11–12). We have seen a partial acceptance of feminism in the proliferation of stories during 2013 and 2014 about Congress members and the reform legislation they favored to prosecute military sexual assault perpetrators. But like the texts that Projansky examines, TV news representations of military sexual assault resist feminist arguments about the need to interrogate both dangerous performances of masculinity and how various cultural institutions enable and reward them. This is the flip side of TV news representations promoting warrior women as martially equal to men, as I discussed in chapter 3: they forestall a deeper analysis of the role that gender plays in military sexual assault, such as that reflected in decades of feminist activism and scholarship, and leave intact the military's system of patriarchy and masculine dominance that perpetuates its rape culture (for more on this topic, see Mesok 2016). If women are legally permitted to serve in combat arms, then no further gender analysis is needed—an assertion similar to saying that Barack Obama's election brought racism to an end.

The martial postfeminism that informs and results from this pattern of absences, explicit statements, and focused attention guides viewers through the Warrior Women regime, obscuring more radical, feminist perspectives on sexual violence while illuminating others that are less challenging to the military's status quo. What it illuminates, I believe, are those alterations to military justice, reporting, and screening systems that are deemed acceptable by both Pentagon policy makers and legislators. Although brought about by the concerted efforts of the documentary's creators, public and military policy makers, and perhaps most importantly, sexual assault survivors and their advocates, changes implemented to redress sexual violence in the wake of *The Invisible War* have not been as dramatic as some of these actors (namely, Senator Gillibrand and Representative Speier) had hoped. I include myself in this group. As one who has spent *many* hours viewing news and documentary accounts of sexual assault, I sincerely hope that these changes to the system will improve it as well as prevent further violence. But I am not sanguine that significant improvements to prevention of sexual violence (as the Marines United incident signals) will come about absent work that undermines and ultimately eliminates the misogynistic, toxic performances of masculinity responsible for military sexual violence in the first place. Instead of encouraging the (admittedly difficult) work of *preventing* military sexual violence, TV news programs follow legislators, some military leaders (such as the former defense secretary Panetta), and even *The Invisible War*'s creators to push relentlessly for prosecution.

Although improvements to the prosecution system are certainly important and even necessary, we would be wise to regard with skepticism such a singular focus on this aspect of solving military sexual violence. One important consideration here concerns racial bias in prosecution and incarceration that makes African American service members more likely to be punished than their white counterparts are. Activism by the Black Lives Matter movement and research by Michelle Alexander in her book *The New Jim Crow* (2011) reveal that the U.S. civilian prison system reproduces apartheid-like conditions for people of color and particularly African Americans, who are disproportionately convicted and imprisoned for drug offenses, in particular. Alexander argues that postracial thinking enables these conditions when she writes that the "color-blind public consensus that prevails in America today—i.e., the widespread belief that race no longer matters—has blinded us to the realities of race in our society and facilitated the emergence of a new caste system" (11–12).

A similar situation apparently exists in the military, as well. Findings from a report titled *Racial Disparities in Military Justice* published by Protect Our Defenders prompted a *USA Today* headline announcing, "Black Troops as Much as Twice as Likely to Be Punished by Commanders, Courts" (Brook 2017). The report's authors show that although "military leadership has vigorously opposed any suggestions that the commander-controlled justice system is hindered by conflicts of interest or bias and has gone to great lengths to tout the fairness of the system," it is anything but fair to African American service members. Indeed,

> data shows that, for every year reported and across all service branches, black service members were substantially more likely than white service members to face military justice or disciplinary action, and these disparities failed to improve or even increased in recent years.
>
> Depending on the service and type of disciplinary justice action, black service members were at least 1.29 times and as much as 2.61. times more likely than white service members to have an action taken against them in an average year. (Protect Our Defenders 2017b, i)

De Volo and Hall show that between 2004 and 2015 (when their study was published), only four Air Force Academy cadets were convicted of sexual assault, and all were African American despite African Americans being "only 7 percent of cadets, which calls into question whether race operates at USAFA to produce certain understandings of force and consent such that certain men are more readily understood as rapists" (2015, 866n21). Their findings align with those regarding service members who are serving outside of USAFA, as well. The Protect Our Defenders' report reveals that in an average year, African American airmen (the Air Force continues to use this masculine term to refer to everyone in this branch of the service) are 71 percent "more likely to face court-martial or non-judicial punishment . . . than white airmen" are (2017b, i). These disturbing figures indicate that while TV news reports (and other advocates) push for a "law and order" solution to military sexual assault, they are immune to neither the postracial nor the warrior mystique.

• • •

The warrior mystique, like its postracial sibling, is reinforced by martial postfeminism in U.S. news media. This chapter has examined martial postfeminism in TV news discursive practices that construct women's experiences with military sexual violence. In representations that focus on military education and training along with survivors' stories, this regime constitutes meanings around the problem of rampant sexual assault in such a way as to evoke sympathetic, even empathetic, responses to victimized women as warriors, first and foremost. By emphasizing sexual assault's negative impacts on women's military careers, news discourses provide reminders of the value of these warriors and the negative repercussions that losing their myriad contributions can have on a post-9/11 military. However, even as they treat survivors kindly, these discourses discourage examination of the institutional structures and systems that produce and reproduce conditions in which sexual violence flourishes: the sexist rituals that form the adversative education model of the U.S. Air Force Academy, for example, or the free rein that many in the officer corps have to dismiss charges and retaliate against victims who report that they have been attacked or harassed. And in TV news organizations' stubborn refusal to broach the topic of toxic masculinity's role in motivating and perpetuating military sexual violence, they remove themselves from the problem-solving process initiated by Dick and Ziering's production and circulation of *The Invisible War*. Although it is not perfect, the film brought to light the military's thriving rape culture—a culture that has had enormously destructive impacts on its victims, some of whom have killed themselves as a result of their attacks.

As I have illustrated throughout this chapter, a key characteristic of martial postfeminism is its aversion to understanding toxic masculinity and how it motivates military sexual violence. The proliferation of this brand of postfeminism through TV news accounts of such violence suggests that these representations will continue to play only a limited role in comforting those who are afflicted by it. At the very least, this failure is problematic because, as Michael Kimmel contends, "part of transforming a rape culture means transforming masculinity, encouraging and enabling men to make other choices about what we do with our bodies, insisting that men utilize their own agency to make other sorts of choices. To ignore men, to believe that women alone will transform a rape culture, freezes men in a posture of defensiveness, defiance, and immobility" (2005, 156).

Some activists have begun such a transformation effort. In response to Marines United, hundreds of active-duty and veteran female Marines started a group (for now, women only) that they call Actionable Change, which, according to a letter sent to the Marines and excerpted in the *Washington Post*, intends to end misogyny in this branch, "where women are devalued, demeaned, and their contributions diminished." The letter continues, "In a culture that prizes masculinity, it is easy to mistake barbarism for strength. Brutality for power. Savagery for ferocity. . . . Yet we respectfully disagree with the notion that to fight and win our nation's battles, we must preserve an institution where men are permitted or even expected to behave like animals, and women trespass at their peril" (quoted in Lamothe 2017). Actionable Change's push to end misogyny by extricating from the performance of masculinity qualities that the Marines prize—"strength," "power," and "ferocity"—attempts to radically change that branch's misogynist masculinity. And if such a dramatic transformation can happen in the toxically masculine Marines, then surely such a detox regimen is possible in the other branches as well.

My main concern, though, is not whether Actionable Change will see its quixotic vision realized. Although I hope it will and then will detoxify the other branches as well, this group and others like it do not address the larger issue of militarism and how the U.S's. martial objectives produce and reproduce it throughout the world. What Actionable Change is aiming to accomplish, therefore, is reformation of an institution that urgently needs a substantial transformation. I share Mesok's assessment that "movements that seek equality and justice from a nation-state responsible for global violence but that do not critique the structures that facilitate unchecked state and military power are limited in their potential" (2016, 68).

I would extend this critique to the news media I have examined here as well. Although their generally sensitive treatment of sexual assault survivors is commendable, media organizations do not approach the issue of toxic masculinity, which Actionable Change does (if not by name), or how it is deeply embedded in military structures—its institutional character, in other words. For real change to come about, this is a necessary first step, and it must be followed by another, even more difficult one: extricating news outlets and their corporate parents from the military-industrial complex that profits from domestic and international militarization. This is more easily said than done, of course, and I realize that because of the mutual benefits that accrue to the MMIC's constituent elements, this is even more quixotic a goal than what Actionable Change is trying to accomplish. Nevertheless, it is a worthwhile feminist goal—one that is vital for democracy.

Conclusion

Banality's Fatalities

The WNBA's Minnesota Lynx beat the Chicago Sky 110–87 at home the night of September 1, 2017, an easy win that unfolded after an opening ceremony paying tribute to a Minnesota National Guard "homegrown hero"—one of almost twenty military women whom the season saw at center court receiving applause and roars of appreciation from fans and players alike. This homegrown hero was clad in camouflage uniform and boots and resembled the woman on the mural of the American Legion building, described in the introduction of this book. This homegrown hero received her plaudits and autographed basketball with solemn-faced humility, strode confidently off the court, and disappeared into the crowded arena.

Sixteen years out from 9/11, such pregame military tributes have become so common as to go without notice for many of us, I imagine, though apart from women's sporting events, they typically involve military men.[1] That military women are receiving more attention and appreciation for their service in various public and media venues signals a trend illuminated in the preceding chapters of this book, where I have argued that a martial postfeminist regime of media representation has served to banalize and even obscure militarism and war. But there is a fatal side to such banality, which martial postfeminism—woven through civilian media accounts of military and war after 9/11—works effectively to mask, and at a precise moment when civilians cannot afford to be sanguine about militarism and the prospects for war with Iran and North Korea that loom on the horizon.

The Lynx example and the others I have illuminated in the preceding chapters make up a post-9/11 martial regime of representation—one that constructs women's relationships to war and the military both by constituting and circulating truths about their experiences and by attempting to regulate the affective responses of media audiences to them. Although Paige Eager correctly notes that "no single feminist lens can capture all the theoretical and empirical complexities of U.S. military women's lived experiences" (2014, 183), I contend that martial postfeminism is the most accurate label for the collection of themes found in the myriad *media representations* that constitute meaning around women in and around the military. Martial postfeminism is, moreover, a logical outgrowth from this discursive regime, undergirded as it is by the ever expanding and profitable MMIC.

A martial postfeminist regime serves as an interpretive framework that works through images and words legitimating women as grievable, recognizable martial subjects. Whether warriors, mothers, or spouses of military personnel, the women who populate this regime are cast as socially worthy as a result of their myriad relationships to martial activities. Even after they leave the military, some of these women use their service to engage with public life in a different way. The numerous veterans who appear on TV news programs to promote women's combat service or to excoriate the military for its silence around sexual abuse are testament to this dynamic, as are those who decide to run for public office and leverage their military experience into electoral credibility.

Consider the narrative in campaign videos for the former Marine lieutenant colonel Amy McGrath, running for the House of Representatives in Kentucky's sixth district: these quickly went viral during the summer of 2017 and made both McGrath and the videos the subject of news stories. The first, "Told Me," begins with McGrath in a leather bomber jacket, jeans, and white oxford-cloth blouse striding in front of the nose of a fighter jet. "When I was twelve, I knew exactly what I wanted to do when I grew up," she declares. The next shot tracks a fighter jet flying amid dark clouds, followed again by McGrath walking along an airstrip: "I wanted to fly fighter jets and land on aircraft carriers because that's the toughest flying you can do." The video proceeds with McGrath explaining that as a teen she contacted her elected representatives, who, if they responded at all, told her that women were not allowed to serve in combat. After she entered the Naval Academy, the law changed, enabling McGrath to fulfill her dream. "I love our country," McGrath exclaims as she segues into a list of what she was able to accomplish in her twenty years as a Marine: eighty-nine combat missions bombing Al-Qaeda and the Taliban, first Marine woman to fly in an F-18 in combat, and she "got to land on aircraft carriers."

McGrath's enumeration of her combat credentials precedes a shot of her announcing that she is now running for Congress against Andy Barr, "[Senate Majority Leader] Mitch McConnell's handpicked congressman"—on record as saying he would support the repeal of the Affordable Care Act (aka Obamacare). McGrath objects to Barr's pledge to vote to "take health care away from over a quarter million Kentuckians," and tells viewers. "This is my new mission: to take on a Congress full of career politicians who treat the people of Kentucky like they're disposable." The next shot features McGrath, hand in hand with her husband, as they and their three children walk blissfully through a meadow, long grass waving in the breeze. Although people have told her that a Democrat cannot win in her district, a resolute McGrath, standing on the airstrip with the jet behind her again, assures them, "We'll see about that" ("Told Me").

Running for the House of Representatives in New Jersey, Mikie Sherrill expresses similar sentiments on her campaign's website: "Naval Academy graduate, Navy pilot, and former federal prosecutor—Mikie Sherrill is running for Congress to fight back against Donald Trump and to fight for our future." Further down the page, we learn more about Sherrill: "I am a former Navy helicopter pilot, a former federal prosecutor, and a mother of four. I have spent most of my life fighting for our country and our values. As a mother, you'd better believe I will continue to fight to ensure our children have a bright future" (MikieSherrill.com, n.d.). Sherrill's and McGrath's campaign rhetoric follows a formula becoming common for veteran women attempting to enter civilian electoral politics: an emphasis on how a combination of stereotypically feminine qualities and military service makes female veterans better able to fight for their constituents than are the legislators (men, usually) whom they hope to replace. Running in 2014 for a seat in the House of Representatives, the Arizona veteran Wendy Rogers asserted as much: "Women vets have a unique perspective. . . . We have the nurturing and the compassion components uniquely blended into the service to country, [a] mission-minded outlook" (Kucinich 2014).

Absent the ideological work accomplished by the post-9/11 martial regime of representation that I have examined—particularly through Warrior Women—the military halo effect leveraged by McGrath, Rogers, and Sherrill, among others, would probably not be possible. Over the course of sixteen years and running, this regime has constituted military women of various kinds in the way that Rogers describes. Commercial media outlets have articulated this contradictory mix of nurturance, compassion, and militarism to the bodies of women, who perform it without any apparent cognitive dissonance. Robin Andersen notes that "the greatest contradiction and challenge to war and its representations in the twenty-first century . . . [is] how to make war, which at the most basic level is defined by suffering and death, an acceptable practice in contemporary democratic society" (2006, xvii). With constructions of women in and around the military and war, U.S. media negotiate that contradiction adroitly; when doing so in this context, they also demonstrate that championing women is tantamount to advancing militarism and promoting war.

Herman Gray makes a similar point while focusing on the increasing visibility of racial difference in various forms of media, and his point is germane for the representational regime I have examined in this book as well: "The cultural politics of diversity seeks recognition and visibility as the end itself," Gray asserts (2013, 772). He continues, arguing that "the connection between the promise of seeing more diversity in media and post-9/11 attacks on the United States links the regulatory role of race and difference with the discourse of homeland security and global terrorism. Domestically the discourse of racial diversity serves as an alibi for racializing and securing the 'homeland' through increased surveillance, incarceration, and militarization in the name of national security" (774). I would extend Gray's point to racialized constructions of women in post-9/11 civilian media, which work in a similar fashion to obscure militarism and its repercussions in the name of gender equality. Increasingly visible women in hybrid, news, and documentary media accounts of war and the military also serve to regulate affect around grief, acting prescriptively to mark some groups of people as grievable and recognizable as martial subjects, while others—because they are either invisible or treated to disapprobation—are not. In the following pages, I recap the main themes that have emerged from the analyses found in the preceding chapters and then discuss some of the political implications for this post-9/11 martial regime of representation's rosy perspective on women's involvement in war and the military.

Gendering Propaganda

Now out of commission, Lifetime's serial drama *Army Wives* still stands as a rich example of a television network yoking itself to the DoD and Army through strategic alliances that provide realism to attract eyeballs and advertisers to war stories unfolding in real time. In the case of *Army Wives*, we see how stories inspired by real-world events and people can be crafted in such a way as to be as identifiable for Army spouses (mainly wives) as they are for civilian audiences. The high ratings the program received over its seven seasons is evidence of that, as are the accounts of women watching the program that have been documented in the *New York Times* and in anecdotes from the creative and executive producer Katherine Fugate (Lee 2007; Fugate 2008).

Examining the program's origin and narratives in light of President Bush's troop surge to Iraq along with his and his successor's subsequent efforts to navigate military operations for which public support was progressively weakening, provides an interpretive context for *Army Wives*—one that suggests it played a role in helping its millions of viewers negotiate meanings around war and military life. In story lines that centered around deaths and injuries of family members, deployment-induced strains on marriage and filial relations, psychological devastation wrought from service in war zones, heroism, and corruption, the program personalized the travails of war and military life. Performed by a conventionally attractive cast, these stories not coincidentally aligned with propaganda campaigns emanating mainly from the Bush White House and the DoD about the wars in Afghanistan and Iraq and provided a rationale for why, despite all the deaths and spectacular failures there, the U.S. public must stay loyal to their aims. Under the guise of being all about love, these gendered, racialized stories about military service and family life during wartime also served as propaganda paralleling that emanating from news media during this time, particularly in how the program obscured, rendered invisible, or killed off those who questioned or dissented from *Army Wives'* prowar, militaristic messages. It is no wonder, then, that the program proudly touted its cast members' and production staff's work with the Army's Entertainment Liaison Office. This alliance provided the program with the martial verisimilitude it needed to attract millions of military and civilian viewers weekly, as well as to stay within the good graces of the Pentagon. Lifetime will likely celebrate this profitable, quasi-marital partnership for years to come.

Militarizing Motherhood

Army Wives modeled how a TV network could leverage its entertainment brand to expose a large audience of affluential women to gendered military propaganda, thus feminizing the terrain on which negotiations for meaning around wars in Afghanistan and Iraq, as well as military marriage and family life, take place. In chapter 2, I turned to more traditional sites for the proliferation of propaganda—news media—to examine post-9/11 constructions of mothers in and around the military. In this maternal portion of the regime, truths circulated around Security Moms and mothers with children in military service that worked to militarize motherhood. Print and television reporters and editors accomplished this mission by amplifying and legitimating claims about patriotism and dissent that emanated from prowar Astroturf campaigns orchestrated by Bush-administration-aligned prowar think tanks and innocuously named front groups, some employing the "third party technique," a common PR strategy of putting a client's words in the mouth of someone who appears to be independent of that client's interests. (This and many other PR tactics are described by Sheldon Rampton and John Stauber in their perpetually relevant book *Trust Us, We're Experts!* [2001] Military-specific tactics are detailed by Tanner Mirrlees in *Hearts and Mines* [2016].)

Whether cast as Security Moms or mothers of service members, women appearing in these news accounts did so after going through a media-generated winnowing process that divided their mothering along lines of cultural propriety. But just as the process of drawing military front lines is never politically neutral, neither is the process of determining who is doing motherhood properly and who is not. In this case, a combination of news narratives, DoD marketing programs, and PR messaging constituted the discursive terrain on which women were instructed in the art of counterintuitive mothering: showing support, that is, for wars that threatened to kill or injure their children and therefore undermine their maternal power over life. When the grieving Gold Star Mother and self-professed Peace Mom Cindy Sheehan stepped into and started to dominate this portion of the regime, capturing public hearts and minds as she told her story, the commitments of civilian news outlets became quite clear: to silence and discredit this war-opposing mother and any others who might question the Bush administration's war on Iraq. Maternal subjects constructed from these discourses limited proper mothering to those practices legitimating militarism and war; impermissible in this context were questions or challenges to either. And of course, nowhere to be found in such discourses constituting meanings of motherhood were mothers in the lands that U.S. military forces have invaded and occupied. Suffering Afghan and Iraqi mothers are neither recognizable nor grievable in this representational regime that instructs only select women on how to do motherhood during wartime.

Celebrating Combat

Just as news outlets provided instruction in proper military mothering and constructed maternal subjectivities that supported both war and militarism, they played a role in constituting women as warriors and every bit as competent in combat as the men with whom they served. Discursive techniques for establishing such martial equality were marked by a navigation of gender that constructed women not as females (held in low regard in military culture) but as warriors, performing what Gayle Tzemach Lemmon refers to as a "third gender." In her account of women's Cultural Support Teams (CSTs) on "special-ops battlefields" in Afghanistan, Lemmon locates the third-gender concept in a military journal article encouraging the DoD to constitute and train all-women CSTs to accompany special operations units on counterinsurgency missions that required them to interact with Afghan women and men. Such teams, the authors argued, could accomplish more than groups of service men could because Afghan men viewed U.S. service women as uniquely gendered: "not threatening, like American men or subject to the cultural restrictions of Afghan women, but a third group with whom they could interact in a respectful and forthright manner" (Lemmon 2015, 12).

The third-gender concept is apt for understanding not only how CST team members may be viewed but also for how TV news outlets situated military women vis-à-vis combat. Using discursive strategies that emphasized the fluidity and mobility of combat zones to create the notion that combat can be everywhere, promoted women's equality on the battlefield, and attenuated gender differences (particularly those that have historically posed obstacles to women serving in combat), the post-9/11 TV news narratives I have examined worked together to construe women as qualified to serve in combat. Further, they did so from a postracial, postfeminist perspective that glossed over the myriad ways in which race and gender intersect to differentially advantage some women, as they reproduced a hierarchy featuring in studio debates only white women officers while women of color appeared in combat training or on patrol in war zones.

Such postfeminist, postracial renderings of women warriors fit within patterns of reporting that depoliticize and decontextualize war, which numerous scholars have documented about these wars in Afghanistan and Iraq. News stories that aired during the fifteen-year period following 9/11 not only exhibited general patterns of echoing talking points produced by the Bush and Obama administrations and DoD but also promoted combat as a means by which women could and should gain equality with men. TV news outlets' consistency in cheering women on to battle suggests that they used the issue of combat suitability to deflect from investigating either the rationale or geopolitical implications of the United States' war making and subsequent occupation of two countries. Women warriors thus offered TV news organizations an enticing figure around which to express and legitimate a prowar stance through appeals to egalitarianism, an offer they accepted with enthusiasm—the personal, professional, and financial connections to the military-industrial complex fueling their narratives.

Media outlets played an important role in perpetuating and expanding the MMIC during this period, but the process of integrating media corporations with the military-industrial complex began much earlier. In an extensive historical analysis of the ties between the U.S. military, media, and financial industries since World War II, John Bellamy Foster and Robert W. McChesney reveal an extensive network of revolving doors between corporate executives and the military that have encouraged executives to move back and forth between the private sector and the DoD, setting up profitable partnerships as they go. The development of ARPANET (the precursor to today's internet), for example, was initiated by the former General Electric vice president Roy Johnson, who was appointed by President Eisenhower to be the first director of the Advanced Research Projects Agency (ARPA)—the agency that birthed the internet (Foster and McChesney 2014, 11). APRPANET partnered with the Army during the 1970s to surveil, compile, computerize, and then transmit millions of files about U.S. citizens—many of whom were war protestors—to the National Security Agency (14). The digitization of surveillance that originated with this Army-ARPA project became a model for data-broker corporations and social media platforms such as Facebook that today sell "dossiers" on hundreds of millions of U.S. residents to other corporations to be used for marketing, advertising, and online tracking purposes.[2] The largest of these, the Acxiom corporation, "keeps on average some 1,500 data points on more than 200 million Americans" and shares the data it collects with the Department of Homeland Security, the FBI, and the Pentagon (19).

Others have profited from these revolving doors, as well. For example, in 2012, the director of the Defense Advanced Research Projects Agency (DARPA), Regina Dugan, resigned to work for Google, to which she brought her knowledge of drone development. Two years later, Google acquired a U.S. corporation that builds drones with the ability to "cruise at the very edge of the atmosphere" (Foster and McChesney 2014, 24). Amazon has been refining its drone technology, as well, and, like Google, is a behemoth digital-tech corporation that utilizes fine-tuned surveillance to market its products. In 2013, Amazon's founder, Jeff Bezos, bought the *Washington Post* corporation, bringing some of these same digital surveillance and marketing algorithms to its operations in order to "reinvent the paper as a 'media and technology company,'" boosting its profitability as it simultaneously employs the sorts of CRM technologies that catapulted Amazon to corporate Valhalla (E. Kim 2016).

As is clear from these examples and those from the preceding chapters, the media piece of the MMIC creates synergies with other components in multiple ways, resulting in a profitable, self-perpetuating assemblage of mutually beneficial relationships. Because this system is lucrative for those who participate in it, it is unlikely to disappear anytime soon. But because it effectively prevents the civilian press corps from performing as a watchdog over war making and therefore unable to fulfill its most important function for a democratic society, we would be wise to encourage a diminution of its power or, better yet, eliminate it altogether.

Silencing Sexual Violence

At the same time that TV news discourses constructing women as competent warriors were proliferating across broadcast and cable TV outlets over fifteen years, the subject of military sexual violence was receiving the converse treatment. With the exception of covering two topics—numerous Air Force Academy cadets reporting sexual assaults and legislative dramas emerging as Congress crafted and debated bills to remedy MST—TV news outlets showed disinterest on the subject of sexual violence, remaining mainly silent until prompted by external events. When faced with the success of *The Invisible War*, a film documenting the prevalence and horrors of military sexual violence, for example, news outlets took notice and substantially increased reporting on the issue. But in this case, increased volume did not translate into improvements in quality: these new outlets failed to engage in investigations of conditions that produce the rape culture exposed by *The Invisible War* and repeatedly failed to draw on lessons from the extensive research conducted on the subject of sexual violence produced by feminist scholars over four decades. In this way, they again adopted a postfeminist stance—in this case, one that left intact both the patriarchal military hierarchy and structural toxic masculinity that fuel and maintain rape cultures. And although I am not naïve enough to believe that a media campaign to tackle military sexual violence would be enough to solve it, I am hopeful that it could be a part of a campaign to investigate, diagnose, and remedy this rape culture by illuminating the mind-set and structures that cause and perpetuate it.

• • •

When considered together, chapters 3 and 4 paint a picture of a discursive regime that on the one hand emphasized perceived benefits of combat for women while on the other minimized or rendered invisible experiences that would likely cause women to think twice before enlisting or considering a military career. Although TV news stories were sympathetic toward survivors of sexual assault and castigated ineffectual administrators and measures, they laid blame on individual perpetrators and systems for reporting and prosecuting these crimes rather than on the gendered power structures that institutionalize sexual violence. That is, while news narratives cast MST as an occupational hazard, they shied away from examining whether the occupation itself is to blame for creating and maintaining rape culture. The contrast between such subtle recruitment rhetoric and that from veterans opposed to war, such as Iraq Veterans Against the War (IVAW), is stark.

The Iraq War veteran and MST survivor Emily Yates (2016), for example, recounts attending a high-school job fair in Pittsburg, California, at which she and two other veterans staffed an information table for the Full Picture Coalition, a group whose members are "dedicated to bringing students the truth about military recruitment." Her experiences during two deployments to Iraq, which included PTSD, alcohol abuse, and a sexual assault perpetrated by two of her friends, had inspired Yates's determination to challenge and educate other young people about "deceptive claims" made by military recruiters like the one who had convinced her to enlist.

After two hours and numerous conversations with the students, Yates and her compatriots were asked to leave by two women representing the city's Chamber of Commerce, who could not believe they were speaking negatively about the military. One of the women tells them that her husband had served in the military and that her daughter had recently enlisted as well. "I hope she doesn't get raped!" Yates snaps as a parting shot while exiting the fair. She immediately regrets her tone (but not her comment), continuing, "I replied with too much anger, the indignant anger I'd been struggling to overcome for years, but which still surfaced when prodded by ignorance such as this. It was clear they were uninterested in hearing anything 'negative' about the military. . . . Their denial was deep and untouchable" (2016).

MST such as that fueling Yates's retort became one of the many topics addressed by veterans during the Winter Soldier hearings of 2008 organized by the IVAW and documented by Nan Levinson (2014). Winter Soldier events had been modeled on the 1971 Winter Soldier inquiry initiated by Vietnam Veterans Against the War and provided a venue to veterans from both the Afghanistan and Iraq wars to testify about horrors they had witnessed and perhaps participated in. The rationale for the event was to correct civilians' perceptions of the war in Iraq, which were, Levinson explains, "limited largely to 'strategic mistakes' and the headline-grabbing barbarity of 'a few bad apples.' Winter Soldier could provide evidence of something different and, to the nation's shame, something more typical: wrongdoing that was systemic, pervasive, and the result of official policies" (2014, 218–219). Held at the National Labor College in Maryland, Winter Soldier comprised topical panels designed to explore incidents that haunted these veterans. "Moral ambiguity could be these wars' middle name, but many here admit to doing irredeemable acts that can't be excused or forgiven. Most have not forgiven themselves, and that is one of the reasons they're here, telling what they are most ashamed of. They talk of courage and duty and truth-telling, but perhaps the worst truth they have learned is that under enough pressure, ordinary people will do horrible things to other human beings" (Levinson 2014, 231). Emily Yates and her compatriots in Iraq Veterans Against the War and the Full Picture Coalition, as well as many other individuals and groups, have struggled to get this message into the mainstream,[3] but with little apparent success. The Chamber of Commerce members who expelled Yates from the job fair did so in 2016, thus suggesting that even after a fifteen-year period of mounting human, economic, and physical damages, U.S. audiences may still be unreceptive to any criticism of the military or of war.

Accounting for the Costs of War

One of the few mainstream media representations touching on the adverse effects of military service, albeit obliquely, appeared in a *CBS This Morning* segment from November 2016 and introduced viewers to the Ms. Veteran America pageant. Ms. Veteran America originated with Major Jas Boothe, who wanted to illuminate "the woman beyond the uniform." The pageant awards a tiara and spokesperson status to one of twenty-five veteran finalists who best exhibits grace, poise, beauty, and service in competitions that include both evening gown and talent shows and physical endeavors such as push-up contests. The competition raises money for a charity also founded by Boothe, Final Salute, which helps homeless female veterans—the fastest growing homeless population, according to *CBS This Morning*. Many of these women are single parents suffering from PTSD, and although the program does not mention it, 25 percent or more are likely to be experiencing MST as well. A voice-over narrating a scene of the contestants wearing black evening dresses and combat boots assembling onstage announces that "together these veterans have found a new mission and a new definition of beauty." "What makes a woman beautiful?" Boothe asks the correspondent Dana Jacobson. Answering her own question, Boothe concludes the interview: "I feel any woman who's willing to raise her right hand and die for it is the most beautiful woman in the world" (CBS 2016).

During the course of the story, Ms. Veteran America contestants relate stories both poignant and commonplace. The winner of 2016's pageant, Molly Mae Potter, explains that along with her dog Bella, involvement in the competition helped her out of a bout of paralyzing depression and PTSD after she returned from a deployment to Afghanistan. When queried by Jacobson about what she learned while healing, Potter asserts, "I'm a lot stronger than I ever thought, and the military doesn't define me." Another finalist featured in the story had been homeless with her two young children after "gathering the strength to leave an abusive relationship"; Ingrid Rosado tells Jacobson that her work with Final Salute allows her to "be a voice . . . [for] . . . other military women who are going through the same thing that [she] did. . . . They'll have somebody there" (CBS 2016).

Potter's, Rosado's, and Boothe's own experiences with PTSD, depression, intimate-partner violence, and homelessness are so common among military women that they inspired Boothe to design a charity for aiding women in similar circumstances. And although Final Salute's work is admirable for its attempt to solve seemingly intractable problems, it is also limited by its status as a private organization: it raises funds through charitable donations made mainly in conjunction with Ms. Veteran America and from its website, which allows visitors to donate via PayPal. Jacobson tells viewers that the competitions have raised a little over $300,000, a figure surely dwarfed by the enormous financial costs of remedying homelessness and poverty.

Although Ms. Veteran America and Final Salute foreground some of the threats women face during and after military service, they do so in a depoliticizing fashion. Attempting to raise money for veterans with a charity event focuses audience attention on the event—a pageant competition in this case—and not on political decisions to reduce spending on veterans and military social services that therefore make veterans' lives more precarious. Jennifer Mittelstadt's history of the military welfare state shows that reducing social services for military personnel has been occurring since the 1990s, as the DoD fell sway to the market fundamentalism that afflicts civil society as well (2015, 226–228).

Pageant-style fund-raising is also problematic from a feminist standpoint. Not the least of its flaws is its objectification of women as a means of helping them to regain confidence and health after they leave the service. Though participants in Ms. Veteran America choose to compete in it, they reinscribe the sexist power relations of civilian pageants. About one of these, the Miss America pageant, Bonnie Dow argues that contestants challenge feminist critics by emphasizing that they are "clear-headed, ambitious contenders who have chosen to play this game and are intent on playing it to win. . . . The logic of this kind of discourse is that these women are hardly being exploited; indeed it is almost the reverse. . . . The potential for exploitation is soundly trumped by [the contestants'] belief in their individual agency and the worthiness of their goals" (2003, 139). Dow continues by elucidating a problem at the heart of this postfeminist pageant refashioning: "What gets lost here," she argues, "is the possibility that continued feminist activism dedicated to expanding women's opportunities might be a better solution" to entrenched patriarchy than the "perpetuation of the pageant system" (141–142). Expanding civilian and military women's opportunities to obtain meaningful, well-compensated jobs along with good health care, child care, and retirement benefits, for example, would probably obviate the need for pageants or any other charity taking up the work of strengthening the social safety net.

Following Dow, I would argue that Ms. Veteran America, although well intentioned, masks serious flaws in how the U.S. defense budget is allocated. As Rosa Brooks (2016b) observed during her stint working at the Pentagon, Congress wants to generously fund weapons programs—even well beyond levels requested by the DoD—but tends to overlook and therefore underfund the Veterans Administration and other service providers within the DoD's purview. Mittelstadt adds that the military welfare state is currently undergoing the same privatization and outsourcing that the DoD has been forcing onto food service, mercenary forces, and hospitals—and often with disastrous consequences (the terrible conditions at Walter Reed Army Medical Center exposed by Priest and Hull in the *Washington Post* in 2007 resulted from a private contractor, IAP Worldwide Services, taking over services it was not qualified to handle [Mittelstadt 2015, 225]).[4]

A charge that military families be encouraged toward greater self-reliance took hold during the 1990s and paralleled civilian welfare-to-work programs generated by President Clinton's weakening of the welfare system in 1996. After 9/11, the DoD continued to urge families to extricate themselves from the military safety net when troops started their deployments to Afghanistan and then Iraq. Once troops started to return home, however, the personal, physical, psychological, and social consequences of these wars for military personnel and their families overwhelmed the DoD's stripped-down social service system. It and Congress responded with increased funding for soldiers' health services and family support yet continued to rely on an Army spawned and perpetuated mantra about the need for self-reliance. However, despite the privatization pushed by the Pentagon and Congress proving "inadequate to meet key tests of the wars of the 2000s," Mittelstadt observes that the DoD is "nevertheless continuing on this path and considering the rapid acceleration of both privatization and self-support for the future." As a result of influence from the right-wing Heritage Foundation, programs currently being targeted for privatization include health care, retirement, and pensions (2015, 226).

Ms. Veteran America is a rational response to the VA's decreasing support and increasing privatization. But it is more than a little distressing that military personnel who have risked life and limb in service to their country find themselves without the safety net they need as they readjust to life after active duty. Perhaps it is this treatment that partially explains results from a Pew Research Center survey showing that female veterans express a more critical viewpoint of the wars in Iraq and Afghanistan than do their male counterparts: 63 percent of female veterans polled say the Iraq War was not worth fighting, and 54 percent report the same about the war in Afghanistan (compared with 47 percent and 39 percent of male veterans, respectively). By contrast, among the general public, there are no significant gender differences in the share who say the post-9/11 wars were not worth fighting (Patten and Parker 2011, 2–3). Compounding female veterans' concerns is a sense that the public has overlooked their contributions and even their existence. According to a 2015 poll conducted by the Iraq and Afghanistan Veterans of America, only 15 percent of female veterans believed that the civilian public recognized their extensive military labor (Jaslow 2017).

The costs of war for women are high indeed. In addition to homelessness, MST, PTSD, physical ailments, and frayed relationships with their children and romantic partners, women with active-duty or veteran partners face high rates of intimate-partner violence—behaviors that the military refers to as the "new normal" in brochures given to spouses in preparation for their partners' return from deployments, according to the survivor Stacy Bannerman (2017). Bannerman notes that over the course of the wars' sixteen-year time span, there has been a "catastrophic rise in the rates of domestic violence, murder, and child abuse and neglect in families of post-9/11 veterans." As the rates of these forms of violence rise, the severity of the violence increases along with them. Bannerman reports that between 2006 and 2014, calls from people with military connections to the National Domestic Violence Hotline saw a threefold-plus increase.

Dangerous and sometimes fatal consequences may befall children or partners of service members and manifest as self-destructive behaviors among service members themselves. To wit, the rate of suicide for women veterans is two and a half times higher than that among civilian women, according to a study of data collected by the VA over thirteen years (U.S. Department of Veterans Affairs 2016). One epidemiologist and suicide researcher in a 2015 report on female veterans' suicide rates described them as "staggering" and "obscenely" high (Zarembo 2015). The main factor that emerges in what little research has been conducted on gender differences in military suicides puts MST at the top of the list for women (J. Moore 2017). Alan Zarembo (2015) reports that one VA epidemiologist's research shows that many of the women and men who enlist have survived childhood sexual and emotional abuse. For military personnel and their families, then, the post-9/11 context of life is fraught with difficulties, though these are most often buried under media representations designed to deflect civilian attention from them.

• • •

Because the role of corporate U.S. media outlets is to inform the U.S. public about issues affecting our lives, they train their attention on U.S. troops and military operations (some aspects of them, anyway). But what of the people living in countries invaded and occupied by U.S. military forces since 9/11? Discussions about their fates are virtually absent from the accounts I reviewed for this book, yet their deaths and devastation matter if for no other reason than the United States' responsibility for the violence and militarism ruining their lives and homelands. Brown University's Costs of War Project tracks multiple categories of costs in the aftermath of the United States' 2001 and 2003 invasions that spurred the GWOT. As of April 2017, over 370,000 civilians, U.S. troops, contractors, and "allied security forces" had died from *direct* war violence in Afghanistan, Iraq, and Pakistan; 800,000 more and counting have died from indirect violence related to these wars, which includes "dislocation and loss of livelihood and the destruction of health care and sanitation systems, each of which have led to higher rates of disease, malnutrition, and resulting higher mortality rates" (Costs of War Project 2017).

These costs are borne intergenerationally as well as having a profound impact now. Writing in *The Nation*, Michelle Chen notes that wars across the Middle East—including in Afghanistan and Iraq—have been extremely destructive for the children living through them: "the trauma will likely continue to affect them decades from now, haunting the bodies, minds, and families of what scientists call a 'lost generation'" (2017). The University of Washington study that Chen cites from the Institute for Health Metrics and Evaluation (2017) reports that such "intractable and endemic violence" includes high rates of suicide, homicide, and sexual violence. This trauma-inducing violence is compounded by sharp increases in communicable diseases and noncommunicable disorders. Depression and anxiety lead the list, though bipolar disorder and schizophrenia are common as well.

These figures represent only a partial account of the fatalities that follow from post-9/11 wars, conditions enabled and obscured by banal militarism and the MMIC. Partial as it is, this account points to an urgent need to demilitarize social structures and institutions, media organizations among them. A Vietnam War veteran, West Point graduate, and member of the National Defense University, Gregory D. Foster advises that to prevent further devastation of the type I have just presented, civilians must reassert control over the military to, in effect, demilitarize it. The "American Way of War," he explains, consists of "killing people and breaking things as lethally, destructively, and overwhelmingly as possible" (2016). Whereas the U.S. military could be more of a constructive global force, it is not now and unlikely to become such without a dramatic intervention.[5] Foster suggests a long-shot, "paradigm-shattering" solution: to transform "a cumbersome, stagnant, obsolescent, irrelevant warfighting force—with its own inbuilt self-corrupting qualities—into a peacekeeping, nation-building, humanitarian-assistance, disaster-response force far more attuned to a future it helps shape and far more strategically effective than what we now have. Translated, counterintuitive as it might sound, this would mean seeking to demilitarize the military, an overarching strategic imperative if bona fide lasting peace is ever to be achieved on this planet" (2016).

Foster's suggestion is both provocative and plausible given his military credentials. I find myself drawn to it, and not only because I have spent six years (and counting) researching and writing about war, militarism, and media—a process that has left me feeling pessimistic and even hopeless more than once. This work has certainly affected my views by deepening my understanding of and appreciation for the women who choose military service or surrender their children to it. As well, it has solidified my commitment to peace and resisting militarism using whatever means I have at my disposal.

Civic literacy about war and militarism is part of what Foster recommends to demilitarize the military, an effort I believe can and should include media representations that challenge conventional martial wisdom. But I also recognize the difficulty of implementing such a program after years of being immersed in a martial regime of representation composed of formulaic treatments of military women. Lemmon's description of a woman training to become part of a Cultural Support Team, Rigby Allen, exemplifies this formula:

> All Rigby has ever wanted was to be a soldier. She grew up in Michigan playing "army" in the woods with her older brother and sister, and dreamed of leading a real maneuver one day. Her grandfather had served in the 82nd Airborne Division and her dad was a navy photographer for three years during Vietnam. Without them ever explicitly pushing the children to serve, both men had made it clear that being in the military and serving your country was the most important and patriotic work an American could do. After the Navy Rigby's father

took a job as an engineer at the defense contractor Northrop Grumman. On "Take Your Kids to Work" day she and her siblings would scamper through the helicopters he designed. (2015, 45)

Allen's family lionizes military service, and I suspect many other military families do the same.[6] Any media or civic literacy program with demilitarization as its goal will have to take on the misguided notion that military service is the best way to show patriotism and dedication to one's country, as Rigby Allen and so many others have been taught.

But we should not have to rely only on family alone to provide lessons in citizenship. Because U.S. media organizations tout themselves for providing the information necessary for citizens to engage in democratic governance (for example, the *Washington Post*'s masthead motto is "democracy dies in darkness") *and* they constitute the meanings of war and military service that most civilians rely on, it is on them I focus my attention, starting with representations of women infused with martial postfeminism. One significant aspect of hybrid, news, and documentary media representations of women in and around the military is that they legitimate the MMIC under the guise of advancing gender equality. Such equality might be a laudable goal in the abstract, but in this context, it is unclear whether it actually and concretely benefits women as a whole, premised as it is on a transaction that awards promotions on the basis of participation in combat. Does the world need more war just so women can achieve combat parity with service men? A martial postfeminist regime of representation tacitly answers this in the affirmative as it obscures the sexual violence, PTSD, racism, increased risk of suicide, and war violence that military women are likely to encounter during active duty. Far from bringing about equality, war and militarism work together to maintain systems of inequality and oppression, no matter how fervently producers of media representations suggest otherwise.

Demilitarizing this system will not come about quickly or easily—especially now that the Trump administration has committed itself to eliminating regulations of all kinds, including on media. However, it may be possible to effect some small changes now on the way to bigger, structural changes in the future. First, we can push to require media corporations to disclose their ties to the military-industrial complex as part of all war coverage. Among other things, this would entail at least the following from each media organization that reports on war: identifying what retired officers stand to gain from war strategies they recommend on TV news programs when they appear as military analysts; naming defense contractors with any ownership stakes before or as part of war reporting (perhaps using a chyron, as CNN does when calling out President Trump's falsehoods); describing any partnerships between it and the DoD; and revealing which of its stories have incorporated PR materials such as VNRs, press releases, or Astroturf tactics that attempt to create favorable impressions of war-maker clients. In short, any relationships with the MMIC that compromise the integrity of the information that media organizations convey should be illuminated by the brightest light possible.

Judith Butler asserts that "if war is to be opposed, we have to understand how popular assent to war is cultivated and maintained, in other words, how war waging acts upon the senses so that war is thought to be an inevitability, something good, or even a source of moral satisfaction" (2010, ix). *Postfeminist War* shows that civilian media employ women acting in various capacities to manufacture such popular assent within a representational regime that affirms their place in martial culture as it intensifies the warrior mystique.

Further challenges to representations that constitute this mystique could take the form of appealing to female veterans who hold or are running for elected office to reshape their campaign rhetoric so that it emphasizes nurturance and compassion for the body politic over militarism. For example, Amy McGrath promises in her "Told Me" campaign video to support a health care system fair to all—a position that her opponent, Andy Barr, opposes, as evinced by his vote to repeal the Affordable Care Act in summer 2017. More federal funding would be available for McGrath's commendable goal if more of the discretionary budget were allocated to social welfare programs and far less to military and national security concerns (currently 68 percent of total discretionary spending goes to military and security, according to the Costs of War Project [2017]). McGrath could make that argument credibly from her standpoint as a veteran, and it would be a powerful statement about how demilitarizing the budget strengthens the social safety net.

Along these same lines, it would behoove us to rearticulate national security and heroism to images of a healthy and prosperous populace. Military homegrown heroes celebrated by the Minnesota Lynx and so many other sports franchises are not the only heroic actors around. Homegrown heroes are also feminist, antiracist, and social justice activists. Homegrown heroes work to protect immigrant children and their families from predatory policies and politicians. Homegrown heroes promote peaceful solutions to domestic and international conflicts. If we take the late Stuart Hall's words to heart about the necessity for political groups to remake problematic representations by contesting them from within, we may be able to start making a regime change that demilitarizes the media by repoliticizing representations of war. Interrogating media representations such as those that fill the preceding chapters and revealing the political and financial stakes of their producers is important work that moves us just a bit closer to social justice. And if we cannot fully demilitarize our media system, at least we can demilitarize our own imaginations and lives. While quixotic, this is also worthwhile, life-affirming work. May it continue to be so. Peace.

Acknowledgments

Every book project is the culmination of the efforts of multiple people, and this one is no exception. I am grateful for the generosity and patience of the family members, friends, and reviewers who kindly listened to me talk endlessly about this book, read portions of it and offered feedback, or both. I am responsible for the book's errors, of course, but the verbal and written comments I received along the way have improved the quality of the prose and encouraged me to reconsider some of what I thought I knew about war and the military. Thanks especially for thoughtful suggestions from the editors at Rutgers University Press: Daniel Bernardi, Leslie Mitchner, Nicole Solano, and Jasper Chang. And I am immensely grateful for Andrew Katz's careful and meticulous copyediting, which has refined my writing considerably.

My World War II veteran father, Gus Vavrus, was until his death in 2016 a wellspring of information about war and propaganda. Because he was a member of the Army Radio Signal Corps, he was required to stay in Europe after the war had ended to rebuild communication infrastructure; it was there he witnessed firsthand the devastating aftermath of the bombing, violence, and genocide that marked that war. These experiences gave Dad insights that he was always ready to share with his children (and anyone else who would listen), and I learned much from his musings. That he was a part of the European Theater of Operations and therefore served under General Dwight D. Eisenhower was a point of lifelong pride, even more so after President Eisenhower called out the military-industrial complex—a cause of continuing social, political, and economic damage about which Dad shared Eisenhower's grave concerns.

But war could not be waged without the support of those who stay behind. Throughout my life, my mother, Hallie Vavrus, told my siblings and me tales of life from the World War II home front—and especially how she felt as a young person waiting for news about the fate of deployed friends and family

195

members. These memories remain vivid: even into her nineties, Mom is able to recite the names of friends whose brothers were killed, wounded, or captured during the war and how all of this affected her hometown of Marshall, Texas. Her memories and wonderful talent for storytelling have illuminated the agony that families and friends endure when their loved ones are deployed to war zones.

Conversations I've had over the course of my life with my siblings, Fran and Steve Vavrus, have been helpful to my thinking beyond measure. With me, they grew up during the Vietnam War, raised by antiwar parents. To say that our parents' views were in the minority in our conservative Indiana hometown is to understate the situation considerably, but that experience showed us how and why we could be conscientious objectors to war. Fran's wisdom is directly reflected in the following chapters, as she has read and offered excellent feedback on several of them. My extended family, too, has shaped my thinking about war, from my aunt Mildred Vavrus, who often wore a gold pendant necklace stating that "war is not healthy for children and other living things," to cousin Mike Vavrus, who became a conscientious objector during the Vietnam War, to my aunt Katy Banyai, who served in the Women's Army Corps during World War II, to my cousin Patrice Banyai, who relayed stories and provided me with postcards and other artifacts from Katy's time in the service. My entire extended family—which, fortunately for me, includes a large clan of Jahns—has contributed to the knowledge about war and the military that infuses this book.

I'm also indebted to my family of colleagues and friends who have read drafts of parts of this book or talked with me about them: Shawny Anderson, Lesley Bartlett, Susan Douglas, Linda Buturian, Valerie Fabj, Grant Farred, Lisa Gatzke, Jennifer Gunn, Meg Howlett, Jane Juffer, Sharon Mazzarella, Emily Newman, Mark Pedelty, Roozbeh Shirazi, Susannah Smith, Catherine Squires, Roger Stahl, Shayla Thiel-Stern, Steve Vaughn, Emily Witsell, the women of the Big Yellow House, and a group too big to name individually—my cohort of Spring 2017, faculty members in the Institute for Advanced Study's (IAS) fellowship program. In addition to them, I've been fortunate to have worked with wonderful, smart, kind graduate students while I toiled over this project. Individually and collectively, they have provided copious amounts of interpersonal, pedagogical, and intellectual support. Thank you, Carolina Fernandez Branson, Mia Fischer, Mel Hoffmann, Chani Marchiselli, Tony Nadler, Pam Nettleton, Dana Schowalter, Sarah Wolter, and the members of the Angry Feminist Collective—Joy Hamilton, Bree Trisler, Jules Wight, and Megan Yahnke—for all you have done to alert me to media examples, lighten my grading load, cheer me up, and humor me as I subject you to yet another breakfast meeting at Modern Times Café. The kindness you all have extended to me has been more nourishing to me than you'll ever know.

In addition to interpersonal generosity, I am grateful for the institutional support I received from various quarters of the University of Minnesota that has enabled me to write this book. The Imagine Grant, Donald Hawkins Research Professorship, CLA research sabbatical, and faculty fellowship with the Institute for Advanced Study provided me with the funding, teaching releases, and collegial support I needed to finish this project.

Finally, boatloads of thanks and love go to the people who have lived with and near me while I was writing and, more times than I care to count, losing my mind over the distressing nature of this book's subject matter. Words are wholly inadequate to recognize everything Chuck Jahn, Anton Jahn-Vavrus, Alex Juffer, Fran Vavrus, and Abi Cerra have done for me to make this book possible. For everything from offering encouraging words to listening to reassuring to letting me yell to carrying in food so that I didn't have to cook, I thank you. You all are the best! I can't imagine why you didn't abandon me, but I am eternally grateful that you did not. I hope I can return the favor someday soon.

I published portions of this book in other venues, and I want to recognize those instances:

- Part of chapter 1 appeared as "Lifetime's *Army Wives*, or I Married the Media-Military-Industrial Complex," in *Women's Studies in Communication* 36, no. 1 (2013): 92–112. It is being reprinted by permission of the Organization for Research on Women and Communication (ORWAC), www.orwac.org.
- Another part of chapter 1 appeared as "Feminizing Militainment: Post/Post-Politics on *Army Wives*," in *The Lifetime Network: Essays on "Television for Women" in the 21st Century*, edited by Emily L. Newman and Emily Witsell, © 2016, and is being reprinted with permission of McFarland & Company, Inc., Box 611, Jefferson, NC 28640, www.mcfarlandpub.com.
- One part of chapter 2 appeared as "Marketing Militarism to Moms: News and Branding after September 11th," in *The International Encyclopedia of Media Studies*, vol. 3, *Content and Representation*, edited by Angharad Valdivia and Sharon Mazzarella, © 2013.

Notes

Introduction

1 Although *Postfeminist War* focuses on U.S. women's involvement in post-9/11 wars and the military, I have been influenced by the work of scholars and activists who examine how the United States has justified its Global War on Terror, in part, as a liberation effort for Muslim/Arab women, especially those living in Afghanistan and Iraq (e.g., Al-Mahadin 2011; Brohi 2008; Lemish 2005; Macdonald 2006; and Taylor and Zine 2014).

2 As a hybrid series that brings together male- and female-identified genres and fuses non- and fictionalized accounts of news-making issues about military issues, *Army Wives* is important for how it extends the cultural terrain on which media audiences negotiate meanings about gender and the military. Additionally, the program illustrates the profitability of strategic partnerships between media corporations, the military, and military support organizations.

3 This is not to suggest that only women are gendered. Gender is a social construct and refers to all those human behaviors and practices that relate to biological sex— the configuration of reproductive organs and hormones that all of us possess. And although contemporary feminist theory understands gender to be fluid and arrayed on a spectrum rather than binary, by far most discussions of gender in military coverage use a binary understanding of gender. Indeed, as Mia Fischer (2016) shows, binary thinking about gender vis-à-vis service members was partially responsible for the trans woman Chelsea Manning's brutal treatment during and after her court martial on espionage charges.

4 A postgraduate educational institution, National Defense University describes its purpose as "Educating, Developing and Inspiring National Security Leaders" (National Defense University, n.d.).

5 I use "collusion" advisedly as the term that best describes this relationship. For example, in a scene from the documentary film *Why We Fight* (2006)—which details the contemporary military-industrial complex—"collusion" is the term used by a representative of the defense contractor Kellogg, Brown & Root (KBR) to describe that corporation's relationship with the military.

Chapter 1. Lifetime's *Army Wives*, or, I Married the Media-Military-Industrial Complex

1 Although the program's title implies that it is about wives, one of the main cast members is a husband: psychiatrist Roland Burton, married to Lieutenant Colonel Joan Burton (later promoted to colonel). Following the program's title, I use the term "wives," but this should be understood to include Roland Burton as well. The main cast of wives consists of Claudia Joy Holden (wife of Brigadier General Michael Holden, later promoted to general), Denise Sherwood (wife of Major Frank Sherwood, later promoted to lieutenant colonel), Pamela Moran (wife, ex-wife, and then wife again of Chase Moran, Delta Force), and Roxy LeBlanc (wife of Private First Class Trevor LeBlanc, later promoted to sergeant).

2 There are a couple of important exceptions to this heteronormativity across the seasons of *Army Wives*. One of the ongoing narrative arcs of season 6, for example, is based on a lesbian couple, Charlie and Nicole, who challenge Army and family prejudice to legitimate their relationship, eventually marry, and adopt a child.

3 I use "serial drama" and "soap opera" interchangeably based on a description by Christine Geraghty, who points out that contemporary TV research relies on an expansive definition of soap opera narratives as "extended, complex, and interweaving stories; a wide range of characters, allowing for different kinds of identification; the delineation of an identifiable community, paying attention to domestic and familial relationships; and an emphasis, often expressed melodramatically, on the working through of good and evil forces within a family or community" (2005, 313). *Army Wives* fits this definition to a T.

4 Lotz (2006) notes that such postfeminism is recurrent in Lifetime's serial dramas.

5 Operation Homefront's website explains that it provides relief to military families during "difficult financial times"; aids in the recovery of "wounded warriors"; and, through celebrations throughout the year, recognizes the sacrifices of military family members (n.d.).

6 ELO reports capitalize on pro-Army themes that liaison officers believe are present in particular programs and episodes of *Army Wives* (along with other TV programs and films that the office assesses).

7 This episode preceded by a few months the rollout of Jill Biden and Michelle Obama's initiative to support military families (Sherr and Murphy 2011).

8 I am grateful to an anonymous *Women's Studies in Communication* reviewer for making this important point.

9 Tina Managhan (2012) attributes this modification to the work of peace activists, especially the military mother Cindy Sheehan (whom I discuss in chapter 2).

10 An important exception to this pattern appears in season 5, when Denise and Frank Sherwood's son, Jeremy, is killed during battle in Iraq. As the Sherwoods grieve their son's death, they learn that he died honorably and even sacrificially, fighting to prevent other casualties. Although this does not eliminate the Sherwoods' deep feelings of loss, it appears to ease their grief somewhat. Noteworthy here is how the program also uses Jeremy's death to steer Denise and Frank away from having a Cindy Sheehan experience and transforming their grief into antiwar activism. To wit, at a group grief-counseling session, another mother whose son is killed in battle expresses anger toward the Army and the senselessness of the war that killed her son. Frank storms out of the session, refusing to empathize either with this mother or with where she chooses to place blame for her son's death.

11　The toxic-waste-dump episode was probably a reference to the contamination of Camp Lejeune, a Marine base in North Carolina where toxic volatile organic compounds (VOCs) infused the water supply between the mid-1950s and late 1980s, leading to numerous health problems and even deaths of the base's residents. This episode perhaps serves as a reminder that, in this instance at least, the Army bests the Marines.

12　For an analysis of *Army Wives*' postgay politics, see Elias 2016.

13　As *The Invisible War* and some other accounts make clear, men are also the victims of sexual assault. Assaults on men are "quite common" and extremely underreported. The Government Accountability Office notes that the DoD has been unprepared to respond to male victims as well (Olson 2015).

14　Several weeks after nine African Americans were gunned down by a white supremacist in the historically black Emanuel African Methodist Church in Charleston in June 2015, Governor Haley signed a law that removed the Confederate flag from the South Carolina statehouse (Schuppe 2015).

15　While the show was airing, the Lifetime website touted its good works in this regard with a guide to all the episodes that dealt with difficult subjects, along with methods for helping veterans who were experiencing psychological and physical distress. The guide is no longer in existence.

16　Reflexive submission to the Army performed by spouses in the program is a departure from the activism of "real-world" Army wives. The historian Jennifer Mittelstadt (2015) shows that since the 1970s, feminist Army wives have been responsible for pushing the Army to enact important changes to family life, such as implementing domestic-violence-prevention programs and making numerous improvements to both the housing system and child-care services.

Chapter 2. Counterintuitive Mothering in the Media-Military-Industrial Complex

1　See John Stauber and Sheldon Rampton (1995) for a detailed explanation of this sort of public relations campaign, which appears to arise organically as if from the grass-roots of a group rather than from professionals paid to mobilize populations.

2　Although news stories about soldier mothers are scattered around news coverage in the period that my sample covers, they are nowhere near as common as the others and typically appear in stories about women serving in combat. For this reason, I discuss these in chapter 3.

3　Word Spy defines a Security Mom as a "woman with children who believes the most important issue of the day is national security, particularly the fight against terrorism" ("Security Mom").

4　Despite the organization's name, the IWF is a right-wing front group formed to support Clarence Thomas when he was a Supreme Court nominee and accused of sexual harassment by the law professor Anita Hill during his confirmation hearings in the Senate (Graves 2016). Since its founding, the IWF has aligned itself with a number of right-wing causes and groups, such as the National Rifle Association (NRA), to gain women's support when it might otherwise not be forthcoming (Walsh 2016).

5　Using National Election Study data from the 2004 campaign to investigate the Security Mom and NASCAR Dad constructions, the political scientists Laurel Elder and Steven Greene conclude that there is "no support whatsoever for the idea of 'Security Moms'" (2007, 10–11). Their data show, moreover, that, "in 2004, women were significantly less likely than men to support increases in defense spending and spending on 'the war on terror,' . . . [that] women were less likely than men to think the Iraq War and the war in Afghanistan were worth it and less likely to think that the Bush Administration had made the country more secure. Thus, the 'Security Mom' label was not only inaccurate, but misrepresented the position of mothers to some extent. Mothers, like women overall, were distinctive in being less supportive than men on most defense and war-related issues in 2004" (11). Their study affirms the Security Mom's propaganda function as one attempting to push women to adopt Bush administration policies and the Republican National Committee's agenda as Bush (and Republicans before him since Ronald Reagan) faced the prospect of a large gender gap in the November 2004 election (Center for American Women and Politics 2004). That four years later, in 2008, these brand qualities and values could be condensed into one high-profile person—vice presidential candidate Sarah Palin, who went on to almost single-handedly energize her party's conservative evangelical base—shows Security Moms' value lying primarily in their ability to showcase and glorify the ideology of the GOP, whose policies had grown unpopular (to say nothing of disastrous) over the preceding eight years of its dominance.

6 The conventional elements in this clip are followed by an inclusion that is unusual for such stories: local residents—including two veterans—criticizing the war in Iraq and Donald Rumsfeld, who had just resigned as secretary of defense (Comcast Cable News 2006). Only on the rarest of occasions do holiday honorific stories go beyond these pro forma elements to air criticism of the wars—especially that made by veterans.

7 A Gold Star Mother receives this title when her child is killed during military service.

8 U.S. news-consuming publics probably became familiar with Sheehan and her protest through easily procured, national sources, so my sample consists mostly of TV news stories. Sheehan appeared frequently in TV news, which is not surprising given her telegenic protest and resonant message of maternal distress after the death of a child. These are ideal pegs for TV news, a genre that since the 1990s has been criticized for sensationalistic, superficial, context-free coverage of world, national, and local events of public importance (e.g., see McChesney 2015).

9 Managhan points out that Sheehan was advised by the PR agency Fenton Communications, "known to sponsor left wing advocacy groups like MoveOn.org" (2012, 115). Despite whatever role the firm had in shaping Sheehan's messaging, I found scant evidence that its advice paid off in positive responses to Sheehan's politics; instead, in both quantity and quality, news coverage favored military mothers with a pro-Bush, prowar message.

10 Worth noting is that another militaristic organization, the National Rifle Association (NRA), uses the term "bad guys" prolifically across its many marketing discourses intended to reach women (see Vavrus and Leinbach 2016).

11 For a book-length treatment of how PR shapes news coverage and public discussions of pressing issues, see Wendell Potter's *Deadly Spin*—a case study of how the Affordable Care Act and related health-care reporting have been influenced by public relations campaigns.

Chapter 3. "No Longer Women, but Soldiers"

1 Both World War II groups, WAC stands for Women's Army Corps and WAVES is an acronym for the Navy's Women Accepted for Volunteer Emergency Service. The

Air Force, too, had a women's auxiliary force: the Women's Air Force Service Pilots, or WASPs.

2   Throughout the book, I capitalize when referring to the name of the regime—in other words, when it is a proper noun, as in Warrior Women regime of representation. When referring to women warriors as people acting in martial settings, I use lowercase letters.

3   The six documentaries are *Lioness* (2008), *Sisters in Arms* (2010), *Service: When Women Come Marching Home* (2012), *The Invisible War* (2012), and two public television programs that aired in 2014, PBS's "Women in War" (2014—an episode in the *Makers* series) and Twin Cities Public Television's (TPT) program *Women Serving in War* (2014).

4   According to the DoD, DACOWITS is an advisory group composed of civilian men and women whose focus is "matters and policies relating to the recruitment and retention, treatment, employment, integration, and well-being of highly qualified professional women in the Armed Forces. Historically, DACOWITS' recommendations have been very instrumental in effecting changes to laws and policies pertaining to military women" (Defense Advisory Committee on Women in the Services, n.d.).

5   A study of women veterans' wages in the civilian labor force shows that regardless of combat experience, military service gives women a significant boost to their civilian wages. Women of color "show the greatest gains in the civilian labor market after their military service," mainly because their military labor makes them more likely to be brought on board in higher-earning categories than those of their civilian counterparts (Padavic and Prokos 2017, 382).

6   Established in 1988, the DoD's Risk Rule prohibited women from serving in noncombat capacities if risks of being in "direct combat, hostile fire, or capture were equal to or greater than the risk in the combat units they supported." Each branch of the service set its own standards in applying the rule to its missions (U.S. General Accounting Office 1998, 2).

7   Laura Sjoberg points out that feminist scholars refer to this narrative as a "protection racket" that justifies wars with the "chivalric pretension of protecting women (who are not actually protected by them)" (2014, 30).

8   Such treatment appears exclusive to TV news accounts. Print media and the documentaries I have examined explore the conflicts that soldier mothers experience with more nuance and depth than television does. Yet, because the majority of news consumers get their news from television, this suggests that they are exposed to a glorified perspective on women warriors.

9   Despite Donnelly's multiple appearances, anticombat views have long been in the minority among DACOWITS members, according to Francke (1997) and Enloe (1994).

10   In 2016, Duckworth was elected to the Senate, where she currently represents Illinois. Duckworth appears many more times in these news stories than does Gabbard, most likely owing to Duckworth's combat injuries: she lost both of her legs below the knees when the helicopter she was flying was attacked during a mission in Iraq. Her combat credentials make Duckworth an ideal guest for news stories that take up the subject of women's suitability for combat.

11   Across fifteen years of news programs, the words "fighting" and "dying" are almost always uttered together as if they form a compound term: "fighting-and-dying." "Fighting-and-dying" is uttered automatically in newscasts to describe some service women's experiences in Afghanistan and Iraq, thus making them recognizable. This

term works much as "womenandchildren" does—a compound that Enloe notes is used prolifically in public discourse to justify U.S. military interventions around the globe: the need to protect these innocents (see Gordon 2014, for example).

12 Hegar's combat experiences inspired a memoir, the 2017 book *Shoot like a Girl*.

13 Despite the rhetoric of equality found in recruiting ads, military compensation parallels civilian pay disparities in one respect: "cost-conscious [military] managers realize that women's labor is cheaper than men's labor of equivalent quality," according to Goldstein, a factor that makes them happy to recruit women (2001, 93). Because of policies governing military salary parity, women and men earn the same amount for most jobs, although women tend to come into the military having completed more education than men, thus making women's salaries incommensurate with their education level.

14 As recently as 1994, some NATO countries' combat policies for women were dictated by concerns about motherhood. For example, in 1994, France's policy governing women in combat was summarized in a NATO document this way: "A woman's role is to give life and not death. For this reason alone it is not desirable for mothers to take direct part in battle" (quoted in Goldstein 2001, 85).

Chapter 4. "This Wasn't the Intended Sacrifice"

The quotation in this chapter's title is drawn from comments made by Darchelle Mitchell, a former Navy aviation commander, as she related the story of her sexual assault to the NBC reporter Natalie Morales (NBC 2012).

1 Rosa Brooks (2013) argues that although military sexual assault occurs at unacceptably high levels, it has not reached the level of an epidemic and is lower in rates than in "comparable civilian populations," such as those on and around college campuses. She cautions further that "when remarks about 'epidemics' and 'crises' are carelessly made, they can discourage young women from pursuing military careers and play into the hands of those who would prefer to keep the 'no girls allowed' sign on the door."

2 "Toxic masculinity" refers to a misogynistic gender performance that at the very least normalizes and legitimates intimate-partner violence and sexual assault. At its most extreme, the performance includes acting violently as a means of subordinating and punishing individuals whom these perpetrators perceive to be feminine.

3 During the 2016 U.S. presidential campaign, a few outlets took note but then shrugged off a 2013 Donald Trump tweet about military sexual assault: "What did these geniuses expect when they put men and women together?" (CNN 2016).

4 Leora Rosen and Lee Martin's study of the relationship between sexual harassment, cohesion, and combat readiness in mixed-gender Army units shows that sexual harassment within them negatively correlates with both group cohesion and combat preparedness (1997, 235).

5 Starting in 2007, SAPRO was tasked with compiling data and reporting on sexual harassment and violence in the Air Force, Military (West Point), and Naval Academies. For the 2016–2017 academic year, the report shows that across all three, eighty-six assaults were reported, down from ninety-one the previous year (DoD SAPRO 2016, 6). The Air Force Academy was the only one that saw a drop in the number of reports (10).

6 Stories about the Air Force Academy assault are not the only ones to use the "sex scandal" frame. Several segments appearing later in the fifteen-year period use an identical frame for their coverage—particularly those about the arrests of officers in

charge of sexual assault prevention who were themselves being charged with sexual assault or domestic violence.

7   Like the many TV news segments aired on the subject of women in combat, these segments about sexual assault cycled sometimes in identical form through other programs on the same network and across sibling networks' programming as well. In tallying up the voluminous coverage in this two-year period, I counted as different segments those that did not duplicate a story/segment in recycling it. For example, if the same video clip appeared in more than one segment, I counted it as different only if the story of which it was a part changed. If a segment and the story surrounding it were duplicated across programs or networks, it did not count as different. Thus, seventy-nine of the ninety-one sexual assault stories aired in 2013 were different from one another; twenty-nine of the thirty-one stories aired in 2014 were different from one another in this way.

8   The film also includes accounts of men assaulted during their service and emphasizes that the greater proportion of men to women in the military means that more men are sexual assault victims.

9   A very abbreviated list of feminist research on this subject includes Barker-Plummer 2010; Byerly and Ross 2006; Gill 2007; Vavrus 2002, 2012. On the subject of news coverage of rape and sexual assault and feminism, see Benedict 1992; Cuklanz 1996, 2000; and Projansky 2001.

Conclusion

1   As I write this, the mother of all military tributes—a massive military parade on Veterans Day 2018—is in the planning stages. Proposed by President Trump, the parade is apparently intended to showcase U.S. military strength by featuring service members marching amid military equipment along an as-yet-undetermined parade route. While the stated rationale for such a parade, according to Secretary of Defense James Mattis, is to highlight Trump's "affection and respect for the military" (Gibbons-Neff 2018), it would also serve as a means of paying homage to the weapons manufacturers to which the Trump administration is funneling billions of dollars. The parade's other tribute, in other words, is to the military-industrial complex.

2   The social media platforms Facebook and Twitter, especially, have been implicated for allowing Russia's Internet Research Agency and two other Russian firms to interfere in political communication around the time of the 2016 U.S. presidential campaign, exploiting users' profiles (in some cases using stolen identities) and tailoring mainly false messages to them that ginned up support for Donald Trump as they demonized Hillary Clinton. In February 2018, Special Counsel Robert Mueller indicted thirteen individuals and three Russian organizations for this social-media-based interference in the U.S. electoral system (Graff 2018).

3   One full-length documentary film should be considered a part of this attempt. Released as part of the Women Make Movies series in 2012, Marcia Rock and Patricia Lee Stotter's *Service: When Women Come Marching Home* follows female veterans who encounter multiple problems after they return home from deployments in Afghanistan and Iraq, including MST, PTSD, homelessness, difficulty getting adequate treatment from the VA, and struggles to fit into civilian life again.

4   Rajiv Chandrasekaran's book *Imperial Life in the Emerald City* (2006) explores how poorly this worked in the Green Zone, the U.S. military's Iraq outpost for GOP party loyalists, diplomats, and military strategists during the Iraq War's early years.

5 For an example of such a positive effort, witness the work taking place in Puerto Rico, where U.S. troops have provided all manner of aid after the island was nearly destroyed by Hurricanes Irma and Maria in 2017.

6   Mine is likely one of few military families that has seen its warriors became peace activists after completing their service. Both of my grandfathers as well as my great-aunt, Mary Lea Johnson, served in World War I. Mary Lea was one of about three hundred women the Marines enlisted, and she did so both as a youthful expression of patriotism and because she needed to support her family after her father died, leaving Mary Lea responsible for seven siblings and an ailing mother. Her war experiences radicalized her politically and fueled her lifelong peace and social justice activism. My father, his brothers Joe and Tony, and his sister Katy were all World War II veterans. Katy was a member of the WAC and served in Europe; like Mary Lea, she became a peace activist who regularly protested the Vietnam War and nuclear weapons, being arrested at the Nevada Test Site more than once.

   After my father had seen the devastation of France and Germany during and after the war as he worked in the Army's Signal Corps, he, too, became an outspoken opponent of war. Although he endangered personal and familial relationships with his vocal and unyielding stance against the Vietnam War, Dad maintained his opposition to war throughout his life.

References

ABC. 2003a. *20/20*, February 28.
——. 2003b. *World News Tonight with Peter Jennings*, February 28.
——. 2003c. *World News Tonight with Peter Jennings*, April 17.
——. 2005a. *Nightline*, May 25.
——. 2005b. *World News Tonight with Peter Jennings*, May 19.
——. 2007. *Top Priority*, January 23.
——. 2012. *World News Tonight with Diane Sawyer*, February 8.
——. 2013a. *Good Morning America*, June 5.
——. 2013b. *World News Tonight with Diane Sawyer*, January 23.
——. 2013c. *World News Tonight with Diane Sawyer*, May 15.
——. 2014. *World News Tonight with Diane Sawyer*, March 6.
——. 2015a. *Good Morning America*, August 18.
——. 2015b. *World News Tonight with David Muir*, August 20.
African American Policy Forum. n.d. "Did You Know? The Plight of Black Girls and Women in America." Accessed May 12, 2017. http://www.aapf.org/publications/.
Alexander, Michelle. 2011. *The New Jim Crow: Mass Incarceration in the Age of Color Blindness.* Rev. ed. New York: New Press.
Alford, Matthew. 2016. "The Political Impact of the Department of Defense on Hollywood Cinema." *Quarterly Journal of Film and Video* 33 (4): 332–347.
Al-Mahadin, Salam. 2011. "Arab Feminist Media Studies." *Feminist Media Studies* 11 (1): 7–12.
Altheide, David L. 2000. "Tracking Discourse and Qualitative Document Analysis." *Poetics* 27:287–299.
Andersen, Robin. 2005. "Gendered Media Culture and the Imagery of War." *Feminist Media Studies* 5 (3): 367–370.
——. 2006. *A Century of Media, a Century of War.* New York: Peter Lang.
"*Army Wives*: Season Six Ratings." 2012. TV Series Finale. http://tvseriesfinale.com/tv-show/army-wives-season-six-ratings-22631/.
"Art of Separation, The." 2008. *Army Wives: The Complete First Season*. Written by Katherine Fugate, directed by Patrick Norris. DVD. Buena Vista Home Entertainment.
Bacevich, Andrew J. 2008. "Is Perpetual War Our Future?" ZNet, August 16. https://zcomm.org/znetarticle/is-perpetual-war-our-future-by-andrew-j-bacevich/.

Bacevich, Andrew J. 2011. "The Tyranny of Defense Inc." *Atlantic*, January–February. www .theatlantic.com/magazine/archive/2011/01/the-tyranny-of-defense-inc/308342/.

Bagdikian, Ben. 1983. *The Media Monopoly*. Boston: Beacon.

———. 2004. *The New Media Monopoly*. Boston: Beacon.

Bailey, Beth. 2009. *America's Army: Making the All-Volunteer Force*. Cambridge, MA: Harvard University Press.

Balan, Neil. 2010. "A Corrective for Cultural Studies: Beyond the Militarization Thesis to the New Military Intelligence." *Topia: Canadian Journal of Cultural Studies* 23–24:144–177.

Bannerman, Stacy. 2017. "The Fatal 'New Normal' for Wives of Veterans." Women's Media Center, March 8. www.womensmediacenter.com/news-features/the-fatal-new-normal -for-wives-of-veterans.

Barker-Plummer, Bernadette. 2010. "News and Feminism: A Historic Dialog." *Journalism and Communication Monographs* 12 (3): 144–203.

Barstow, David. 2008a. "Behind TV Analysts, Pentagon's Hidden Hand." *New York Times*, April 20. https://nyti.ms/2kfCZry.

———. 2008b. "One Man's Military-Industrial-Media Complex." *New York Times*, November 30. https://nyti.ms/2k5OZhM.

Baumgartner, Frank R., and Sarah McAdon. 2017. "There's Been a Big Change in How the News Media Covers Sexual Assault." *Washington Post*, May 11. www.washingtonpost .com/news/monkey-cage/wp/2017/05/11/theres-been-a-big-change-in-how-the-news -media-cover-sexual-assault/.

Becker, Anne. 2007. "NBC Universal to Buy Oxygen." *Broadcasting & Cable*, October 9. www.broadcastingcable.com/news/programming/nbc-universal-buy-oxygen/27999.

Bell, Margaret E., and Susan J. McCutcheon. 2015. "The Veterans Health Administration Response to Military Sexual Trauma." In *Women at War*, edited by Elspeth Cameron Ritchie and Anne L. Naclerio, 321–328. New York: Oxford University Press.

Benedict, Helen. 1992. *Virgin or Vamp: How the Press Covers Sex Crimes*. New York: Oxford University Press.

———. 2007. "The Private War of Women Soldiers." *Salon*, March 7. www.salon.com/2007/ 03/07/women_in_military/.

———. 2009. *The Lonely Soldier: The Private War of Women Serving in Iraq*. Boston: Beacon.

Bennett, Laura. 2012. "The Pentagon's Man in Hollywood: I'm a Eunuch." *New Republic*, December 21. https://newrepublic.com/article/111366/the-pentagons-man-in-hollywood -im-eunuch.

Berland, Jody, and Blake Fitzpatrick. 2010. "Introduction: Cultures of Militarization and the Military-Cultural Complex." *Topia: Canadian Journal of Cultural Studies* 23–24:9–25.

Biank, Tanya. 2006. *Under the Sabers: The Unwritten Code of Army Wives*. New York: St. Martin's.

———. 2014. *Undaunted: The Real Story of America's Servicewomen in Today's Military*. New York: New American Library.

"Big Show on Campus." 2009. *MediaWeek*, March 23, 42.

Billig, Michael. 1995. *Banal Nationalism*. London: Sage.

Birkner, Christine. 2013. "Opportunity and Sacrifice." *Marketing News*, April, 30.

Blair, Jane. 2011. *Hesitation Kills: A Female Marine Officer's Combat Experience in Iraq*. Lanham, MD: Rowman and Littlefield.

Bloch-Elkon, Yaeli, and Brigitte L. Nacos. 2014. "News and Entertainment Media: Government's Big Helpers in the Selling of Counterterrorism." *Perspectives on Terrorism* 8 (5): 18–32.

Boggs, Carl, and Tom Pollard. 2007. *The Hollywood War Machine*. Boulder, CO: Paradigm.

Bonilla-Silva, Eduardo. 2002. "The Linguistics of Color Blind Racism: How to Talk Nasty about Blacks without Sounding 'Racist.'" *Critical Sociology* 28 (1–2): 41–64.

Bonn, Scott A. 2010. *Mass Deception: Moral Panic and the U.S. War on Iraq*. New Brunswick, NJ: Rutgers University Press.

Britt, Donna. 2003. "The Mother of All Questions." *Washington Post*, March 14, B01.

Brohi, Nazish. 2008. "At the Altar of Subalternity: The Quest for Muslim Women in the War on Terror—Pakistan after 9/11." *Cultural Dynamics* 20 (2): 133–147.

Bronstein, Carolyn. 1994–1995. "Mission Accomplished? Profits and Programming at the Network for Women." *Camera Obscura* 33–34 (1–2): 213–240.

Brook, Tom Vanden. 2017. "Black Troops as Much as Twice as Likely to Be Punished by Commanders, Courts." *USA Today*, June 7. www.usatoday.com/story/news/politics/2017/06/07/black-troops-much-twice-likely-punished-commanders-courts/102555630/.

Brooks, Rosa. 2013. "Is Sexual Assault Really an 'Epidemic'?" *Foreign Policy*, July 10. http://foreignpolicy.com/2013/07/10/is-sexual-assault-really-an-epidemic/.

———. 2016a. "Civil-Military Paradoxes." In *Warriors and Citizens: American Views of Our Military*, edited by Kori Schake and Jim Mattis, 21–68. Stanford, CA: Hoover Institution Press.

———. 2016b. *How Everything Became War and the Military Became Everything: Tales from the Pentagon*. New York: Simon and Schuster.

Brown, Melissa T. 2006. "'A Woman in the Army Is Still a Woman': Recruiting Women into the All-Volunteer Force." Paper presented at the meeting of the International Studies Association, San Diego, CA, March.

———. 2012. "'A Woman in the Army Is Still a Woman': Representations of Women in US Military Recruiting Advertisements for the All-Volunteer Force." *Journal of Women, Politics & Policy* 33:151–175.

Brubaker, Sarah Jane. 2009. "Sexual Assault Prevalence, Reporting and Policies: Comparing College and University Campuses and Military Service Academies." *Security Journal* 22 (1): 56–72.

Bryant, Susan, and Brett Swaney. 2017. "Deconstructing the 'Warrior Caste': The Beliefs and Backgrounds of Senior Military Elites." *Strategic Insights: A Forum for Concise Analyses of Critical Policy Issues* (blog), July 5. https://stratblog.sites.usa.gov/deconstructing-the-warrior-caste-the-beliefs-and-backgrounds-of-senior-military-elites/.

Buchwald, Emilie, Pamela R. Fletcher, and Martha Roth. 2005. Introduction to *Transforming a Rape Culture*, rev. ed., edited by Emilie Buchwald, Pamela R. Fletcher, and Martha Roth, xiii–xviii. Minneapolis, MN: Milkweed Editions.

Bumiller, Elizabeth, and Thom Shanker. 2013. "Pentagon Is Set to Lift Combat Ban for Women." *New York Times*, January 23. https://nyti.ms/2k7oObp.

Burke, Carol. 2004. *Camp All-American, Hanoi Jane, and the High-and-Tight: Gender, Folklore, and Changing Military Culture*. Boston: Beacon.

Burston, Jonathan. 2013. "The Slippery Slopes of 'Soft Power': Production Studies, International Relations, and the Military Industrial Media Complex." In *The International Encyclopedia of Media Studies*, edited by Angharad N. Valdivia, vol. 2, *Media Production*, edited by Vicki Mayer, 83–104. Malden, MA: Blackwell.

Butler, Judith. 1990. *Gender Trouble: Feminism and the Subversion of Identity*. New York: Routledge.

———. 2004a. *Precarious Life: The Powers of Mourning and Violence*. London: Verso.

———. 2004b. *Undoing Gender*. New York: Routledge.

———. 2010. *Frames of War: When Is Life Grievable?* New York: Verso.

Butler, Smedley D. 2013. *War Is a Racket (The Profit That Fuels Warfare)*. N.p.: Stellar Books.

Buying the War. 2007. Written by Bill Moyers and directed and produced by K. Hughes. DVD. Public Broadcasting Service.

Byars, Jackie, and Eileen R. Meehan. 1994–1995. "Once in a Lifetime: Constructing 'the Working Woman' through Cable Narrowcasting." *Camera Obscura* 33–34 (1–2): 13–41.

Byerly, Carolyn, and Karen Ross. 2006. *Women and Media: A Critical Introduction* Malden, MA: Blackwell.

Carden, James. 2018. "A New Poll Shows the Public Is Overwhelmingly Opposed to Endless US Military Interventions." *The Nation*, January 9. www.thenation.com/article/new-poll -shows-public-overwhelmingly-opposed-to-endless-us-military-interventions/?print=1.

Carney, Tiffany. 2009. "Support Group Helps Local Military Moms Deal with Worry, Grief." *San Jose Mercury News*, July 30. LexisNexis Academic.

Carter, April. 1998. "Should Women Be Soldiers or Pacifists?" In *The Women and War Reader*, edited by Lois Ann Lorentzen and Jennifer Turpin, 33–37. New York: NYU Press.

CBS. 2004. *The Early Show*, October 8.

———. 2005a. *The Early Show*, June 30.

———. 2005b. *KCAL 9 News*, August 23. KCAL, Los Angeles.

———. 2005c. "The Longest Wait: Agony of a Soldier's Mother Is as Old as War." *Sunday Morning*, May 8.

———. 2005d. *Morning News 5:00 AM*, August 11. KLAS, Las Vegas.

———. 2006. *CBS Evening News*, August 22.

———. 2007. *News Channel 5 Morning Report*, October 3. WTVF, Nashville, TN.

———. 2011. *8 News Now*, June 22. KLAS, Las Vegas.

———. 2013. *CBS Evening News*, January 25. www.cbsnews.com/videos/female-vet-men-will -resist-women-in-ground-combat/.

———. 2014. *CBS Evening News*, April 8.

———. 2015. *CBS This Morning*, May 25.

———. 2016. *CBS This Morning*, November 23. www.cbsnews.com/news/ms-veteran -america-competition-female-service-women-final-salute-charity/.

Center for American Women and Politics. 2004. "Gender Gap Persists in the 2004 Election." November 5. www.cawp.rutgers.edu/sites/default/files/resources/pressadvisory _gg2004_11-05-04.pdf.

Chandrasekaran, Rajiv. 2006. *Imperial Life in the Emerald City: Inside Iraq's Green Zone*. New York: Vintage Books.

Chen, Michelle. 2017. "The Middle East's Wars Are Creating a Lost Generation." *The Nation*, August 22. www.thenation.com/article/the-middle-easts-wars-are-creating-a-lost -generation/.

Cieply, Michael. 2011. "States Weigh Cuts in Hollywood Subsidies." *New York Times*, January 19. www.nytimes.com/2011/01/20/business/media/20incentives.html?pagewanted=all.

Cloud, Dana. 1994. "Operation Desert Comfort." In *Seeing through the Media: The Persian Gulf War*, edited by Susan Jeffords and Lauren Rabinovitz, 155–170. New Brunswick, NJ: Rutgers University Press.

CNN. 2001. *CNN Tonight*, November 3.

———. 2003. "Interview with Alan Carlson, Wilma Vaught." *Live from . . .* , April 25.

———. 2004. *Paula Zahn Now*, September 23.

———. 2005a. *American Morning*, August 16.

———. 2005b. *American Morning*, August 25.

———. 2005c. *Anderson Cooper 360 Degrees*, August 24.

———. 2005d. *CNN Live Sunday*, October 16.

———. 2005e. "Women in Combat." *American Morning*, January 14.

———. 2005f. "Women in Combat." *CNN Evening News*, June 30.

———. 2005g. "Women in Combat: Senate Showdown." *CNN Live Today*, May 18.

———. 2012. *CNN Newsroom*, November 28.

———. 2013a. "Pentagon's Move to Lift Restrictions for Women in Combat." *Starting Point*, January 24.

———. 2013b. *State of the Union*, May 12.

———. 2016. *CNN Newsroom*, September 8.

CNN.com. 2008. "Senate Report Slams Bush over Prewar Intelligence." June 5. www.cnn. com/2008/POLITICS/06/05/senate.iraq/index.html.

CNNFN. 2003. "A New Role for Women in Military Combat." *Market Call*, April 9.

———. 2004. "Do Women Get Special Treatment in the U.S. Military?" *The Flipside*, May 26.

Codinha, Alessandra. 2017. "Armed Forces." *Vogue*, March 8. www.vogue.com/projects/ 13528881/american-women-in-the-military-female-soldiers/.

Collins, Patricia Hill, and Sirma Bilge. 2016. *Intersectionality*. Cambridge, UK: Polity.

Comcast Cable News. 2006. *8 NEWS*, November 11. Hagerstown, MD. LexisNexis Academic.

Cooper, Christopher, and Greg Jaffe. 2004. "Army's Recruiters Miss Target for Enlistees in Latest Month." *Wall Street Journal*, October 20. www.wsj.com/articles/SB1098233856 01950158.

Costs of War Project. 2017. "The Costs of War Project." Watson Institute for International & Public Affairs, Brown University, April. http://watson.brown.edu/costsofwar/.

Crenshaw, Kimberlé. 1991. "Mapping the Margins: Intersectionality, Identity Politics, and Violence against Women of Color." *Stanford Law Review* 43 (6): 1241–1299.

Crowley, Kacy, and Michelle Sandhoff. 2016. "Just a Girl in the Army: U.S. Iraq War Veterans Negotiating Femininity in a Culture of Masculinity." *Armed Forces & Society*, 1–17. DOI: 10.1177/0095327X16682045.

Cuklanz, Lisa M. 1996. *Rape on Trial: How the Mass Media Construct Legal Reform and Social Change*. Philadelphia: University of Pennsylvania Press.

———. 2000. *Rape on Prime Time: Television, Masculinity, and Sexual Violence*. Philadelphia: University of Pennsylvania Press.

D'Amico, Francine. 1998. "Feminist Perspectives on Women Warriors," in *The Women and War Reader*, edited by Lois Ann Lorentzen and Jennifer Turpin, 119–125. New York: NYU Press.

Dao, James. 2011. "Black Women Enlisting at Higher Rates in the U.S. Military." *New York Times*, December 22. http://nyti.ms/1Hc2LEV.

Defense Advisory Committee on Women in the Services. n.d. Home page. Accessed January 13, 2017. http://dacowits.defense.gov/.

Dempsey, Jason K., and Robert Y. Shapiro. 2009. "The Army's Hispanic Future." *Armed Forces & Society* 35 (3): 526–561.

Der Derian, James. 2009. *Virtuous War*. 2nd ed. New York: Routledge.

de Volo, Lorraine Bayard, and Lynn K. Hall. 2015. "'I Wish All the Ladies Were Holes in the Road': The US Air Force Academy and the Gendered Continuum of Violence." *Signs* 40 (4): 865–889.

Dick, Kirby. 2013. "Don't Trust the Pentagon to End Rape." *New York Times*, June 3. https:// nyti.ms/1oMQ2Uk.

DiMaggio, Anthony. 2009. *When Media Goes to War: Hegemonic Discourse, Public Opinion, and the Limits of Dissent*. New York: Monthly Review Press.

"Dirty Laundry." 2007. *Army Wives*, August 5. Directed by Joanna Kerns. Television series. ABC Television Studio.

DoD SAPRO (Department of Defense, Sexual Assault Prevention and Response). 2016. *Annual Report on Sexual Harassment and Violence at the Military Service Academies:*

Academic Program Year 2015–2016. Washington. DC: Department of Defense. http://sapr.mil/public/docs/reports/MSA/APY_15-16/APY_15_16_MSA_Report_v2.pdf.

DoD SAPRO. 2017. *Department of Defense Annual Report on Sexual Assault in the Military: Fiscal Year 2016.* Washington. DC: Department of Defense. www.sapr.mil/public/docs/reports/FY16_Annual/FY16_SAPRO_Annual_Report.pdf.

Douglas, Susan J., and Meredith W. Michaels. 2004. *The Mommy Myth: The Idealization of Motherhood and How It Has Undermined All Women.* New York: Free Press.

Dow, Bonnie J. 2003. "Feminism, Miss America, and Media Mythology." *Rhetoric & Public Affairs* 6 (1): 127–160.

Dowler, Lorraine. 2002. "Women on the Frontlines: Rethinking War Narratives Post 9/11." *GeoJournal* 58: 159–165.

"Duty to Inform." 2010. *Army Wives: The Complete Third Season.* Written by T. D. Mitchell, directed by Emile Levisetti. DVD. Buena Vista Home Entertainment.

Eager, Paige Whaley. 2014. *Waging Gendered Wars: U.S. Military Women in Afghanistan and Iraq.* Burlington, VT: Ashgate.

Edwards, David. 2014. "SC Governor Defends Confederate Flag at Statehouse: Not 'a Single CEO' Has Complained." *Raw Story*, October 15. www.rawstory.com/rs/2014/10/sc-governor-defends-confederate-flag-at-statehouse-not-a-single-ceo-has-complained/.

Eggerton, John. 2008. "Obama, McCain Tape *Army Wives* Spots." *Broadcasting & Cable*, June 4. www.broadcastingcable.com/article/print/114003-Obama_McCain_Tape_Army_Wives_Spots.php.

Eisenhower, Dwight D. 1961. "Farewell Address." www.eisenhower.archives.gov/research/online_documents/farewell_address/Reading_Copy.pdf.

Eisenstein, Zillah. 2007. *Sexual Decoys: Gender, Race and War in Imperial Democracy.* London: Zed Books.

Elder, Laurel, and Steven Greene. 2007. "The Myth of 'Security Moms' and 'NASCAR Dads': Parenthood, Political Stereotypes, and the 2004 Election." *Social Science Quarterly* 88 (1): 1–19.

Elias, Liora P. 2016. "Lesbian and Gay Civil Rights in a Post-Gay Era: 'Don't Ask, Don't Tell' and Its Repeal as Seen in Lifetime's *Army Wives* (2007–2013)." In *American Militarism on the Small Screen*, edited by Anna Froula and Stacy Takacs, 261–274. New York: Routledge.

Ellul, Jacques. 1965. *Propaganda: The Formation of Men's Attitudes.* New York: Vintage Books.

Elshtain, Jean Bethke. 1987. *Women and War.* Chicago: University of Chicago Press.

Enloe, Cynthia. 1994. "The Politics of Constructing the American Woman Soldier." In *Women Soldiers: Images and Realities*, edited by Elizabetta Addis, Valeria Russo, and Lorenza Sebesta, 81–110. New York: St. Martin's.

———. 1998. "All the Men Are in the Militias, All the Women Are Victims: The Politics of Masculinity and Femininity in Nationalist Wars." In *The Women and War Reader*, edited by Lois Ann Lorentzen and Jennifer Turpin, 50–62. New York: NYU Press.

———. 2000. *Maneuvers: The International Politics of Militarizing Women's Lives.* Berkeley: University of California Press.

———. 2007. *Globalization and Militarism: Feminists Make the Link.* Lanham, MD: Rowman and Littlefield.

FAIR (Fairness and Accuracy in Reporting). 2003. "In Iraq Crisis, Networks Are Megaphones for Official Views." March 18. http://fair.org/article/in-iraq-crisis-networks-are-megaphones-for-official-views/.

Faludi, Susan. 1999. *Stiffed: The Betrayal of the American Man.* New York: William Morrow.

———. 2007. *The Terror Dream: Fear and Fantasy in Post-9/11 America.* New York: Metropolitan Books.

Fang, Lee. 2014. "Who's Paying the Pro-War Pundits?" *Nation*, September 16. www.thenation .com/article/whos-paying-pro-war-pundits/.

Favara, Jeremiah. 2016. "Combat Feminism: Women, Military Recruiting, and a Gender-Equal Military." Paper presented at the Annual Meeting of the National Communication Association, Philadelphia, PA, November.

Fejes, Fred. 2001. "Advertising and the Political Economy of Lesbian/Gay Identity." In *Sex and Money: Feminism and Political Economy in the Media*, edited by Eileen R. Meehan and Ellen Riordan, 196–208. Minneapolis: University of Minnesota Press.

Fenner, Lorry M. 1998. "Either You Need These Women or You Do Not: Informing the Debate on Military Service and Citizenship." *Gender Issues*, Summer, 5–32.

Fischer, Mia Louisa. 2016. "Terrorizing Gender: Transgender Visibility and the Surveillance Practices of the U.S. Security State." PhD diss., University of Minnesota.

Fleischer, Jeff. 2004. "Operation Hollywood: How the Pentagon Bullies Movie Producers into Showing the U.S. Military in the Best Possible Light." *Mother Jones*, September 20. http://motherjones.com/politics/2004/09/operation-hollywood.

Foster, Gregory D. 2016. "A Case for Demilitarizing the Military." *TomDispatch* (blog), March 15. www.tomdispatch.com/blog/176115/.

Foster, John Bellamy, and Robert W. McChesney. 2014. "Surveillance Capitalism: Monopoly-Finance Capital, the Military-Industrial Complex, and the Digital Age." *Monthly Review*, July–August, 1–31.

Foucault, Michel. (1972) 2010. *The Archaeology of Knowledge and the Discourse on Language*. New York: Vintage Books.

———. 1977. "The Political Function of the Intellectual." *Radical Philosophy* 17:12–14.

———. 1978. *The History of Sexuality, Volume One*. New York: Pantheon Books.

Fox News Channel. 2003. *Special Report with Brit Hume*, May 20.

———. 2004. *Special Report with Brit Hume*, September 28.

———. 2006. *Fox News*, September 16.

———. 2013a. *Fox News Sunday*, January 27.

———. 2013b. *Lou Dobbs Tonight*, June 4.

Francke, Linda Bird. 1997. *Ground Zero: The Gender Wars in the Military*. New York: Simon and Schuster.

Fugate, Katherine. 2008. "'Wives' Puts a Face on Military's Unsung Heroes." *Television Week*, August 11, 12.

Funk, Rus Ervin. 1997. "Men Who Are Raped: A Profeminist Perspective." In *Male on Male Rape: The Hidden Toll of Stigma and Shame*, by Michael Scarce, 221–231. New York: Plenum.

Garrett, Sheryl, and Sue Hoppin. 2009. *A Family's Guide to the Military for Dummies*. Hoboken, NJ: Wiley.

Garrett-Peltier, Heidi. 2017. "Job Opportunity Cost of War." Costs of War, Watson Institute of International & Public Affairs, Brown University, May 24. http://watson.brown.edu/costsofwar/files/cow/imce/papers/2017/Job%20Opportunity%20Cost%20of%20War%20-%20HGP%20-%20FINAL.pdf.

Gavey, Nicola. 2009. "Fighting Rape." In *Theorizing Sexual Violence*, edited by Renée J. Heberle and Victoria Grace, 96–124. New York: Routledge.

Geraghty, Christine. 2005. "The Study of Soap Opera." In *A Companion to Television*, edited by Janet Wasko, 308–323. Malden, MA: Blackwell.

Gerney, Arkadi, and Chelsea Parsons. 2014. *Women under the Gun: How Gun Violence Affects Women and 4 Policy Solutions to Better Protect Them*. Washington, DC: Center for American Progress.

Gibbons-Neff, Thomas. 2017. "'I'm Never Reenlisting': Marine Corps Rocked by Nude-Photo Scandal." *Washington Post*, March 5. www.washingtonpost.com/news/checkpoint/wp/2017/03/05/im-never-reenlisting-marine-corps-rocked-by-nude-photo-scandal/?utm_term=.5f1ea65cfb89.

———. 2018. "Trump Wants a Military Parade. But Not Everyone Is in Step." *New York Times*, February 7. https://nyti.ms/2BM82bi.

Gibbs, Nancy. 2010. "Sexual Assaults on Female Soldiers: Don't Ask, Don't Tell." *Time*, March 8. www.servicewomen.org/wp-content/uploads/2011/01/3.8.10-Sexual-Assaults-on-Female-Soldiers-Dont-Ask-Dont-Tell.pdf.

Gill, Rosalind. 2007. *Gender and the Media*. Cambridge, UK: Polity.

Giroux, Henry A. 2013. "The Disimagination Machine and the Pathologies of Power." *symplokē* 21 (1–2): 257–269.

Glenn, Cheryl. 2004. *Unspoken: A Rhetoric of Silence*. Carbondale: Southern Illinois University Press.

Gold Star Families for Peace. n.d. Home page. Accessed February 12, 2011. https://web.archive.org/web/20050805073328/http://www.gsfp.org:80/.

Goldstein, Joshua S. 2001. *War and Gender: How Gender Shapes the War System and Vice Versa*. New York: Cambridge University Press.

Goodman, Ellen. 2007. "Spying Parents: When Worrying Becomes Stalking." Alternet, November 8. www.alternet.org/story/66846/spying_parents%3A_when_worrying_becomes_stalking.

Gordon, Linda. 2014. "Innocent Womenandchildren." ZNet, September 14. https://zcomm.org/znetarticle/innocent-womenandchildren/.

Gorman, Bill. 2011. "Sunday Cable Ratings." *TV by the Numbers*, June 14. http://tvbythenumbers.zap2it.com/2011/06/14/sunday-cable-ratings-game-of-thrones-real-housewives-kardashians-in-plain-sight-army-wives-more/95543/.

Graff, Gerald. 2018. "A Blockbuster Indictment Details Russia's Attack on US Democracy." *Wired*, February 16. www.wired.com/story/mueller-indictment-russia-attack-us-democracy/.

Graves, Lisa. 2016. "Confirmation: The Not-So-Independent Women's Forum Was Born in Defense of Clarence Thomas and the Far Right." Center for Media and Democracy, April 21. www.prwatch.org/news/2016/04/13091/confirmation-how-not-so-independent-womens-forum-was-launched-aid-clarence.

Gray, Herman. 2013. "Subject(ed) to Recognition." *American Quarterly* 65 (4): 771–798.

Grewal, Inderpal. 2006. "'Security Moms' in the Early Twenty-First Century United States: The Gender of Security in Neoliberalism." *Women's Studies Quarterly* 34 (1–2): 25–39.

Grossberg, Lawrence. 2010. *Cultural Studies in the Future Tense*. Durham, NC: Duke University Press.

Hajjar, Remi M. 2014. "Emergent Postmodern US Military Culture." *Armed Forces & Society* 40 (1): 118–145.

Hall, Stuart. 1997. "The Work of Representation." In *Representation: Cultural Representations and Signifying Practices*, edited by Stuart Hall, 13–74. London: Sage.

———. 2001. "The Spectacle of the 'Other.'" In *Discourse Theory and Practice: A Reader*, edited by M. Wetherell, S. Taylor, and S. J. Yates, 324–343. London: Sage.

Hardin, Marie, and Erin Whiteside. 2013. "From Second-Wave to Poststructuralist Feminism: Evolving Frameworks for Viewing Representations of Women's Sports." In *The International Encyclopedia of Media Studies*, edited by Sharon Mazzarella, 116–136. Malden, MA: Blackwell.

Harding, Kate. 2015. *Asking for It: The Alarming Rise of Rape Culture—and What We Can Do about It*. Boston: Da Capo.

Harris, John F., and Christopher Muste. 2004. "56 Percent in Survey Say Iraq War Was a Mistake." *Washington Post*, December 21, A4. www.washingtonpost.com/wp-dyn/articles/A14266-2004Dec20.html.

Hartung, William D. 2017. "The Wrong Diagnosis on Defense: More Money Won't Solve the Military's Readiness Problems." *U.S. News & World Report*, September 29. www.usnews.com/opinion/world-report/articles/2017-09-29/the-pentagon-needs-better-budget-discipline-not-more-money.

———. 2018. "Trump Is on His Way to Record-Setting Defense Spending in 2018." *Nation*, January 11. www.thenation.com/article/trump-is-on-his-way-to-record-setting-defense-spending-in-2018/?print=1.

Hasian, Marouf, Jr. 2013. "*Zero Dark Thirty* and the Critical Challenges Posed by Populist Postfeminism during the Global War on Terrorism." *Journal of Communication Inquiry* 37 (4): 322–343.

Hay, James. 2006. "Designing Homes to Be the First Line of Defense: Safe Households, Mobilization, and the New Mobile Privatization." *Cultural Studies* 20:349–377.

Hegar, Mary Jennings. 2017. *Shoot like a Girl: One Woman's Dramatic Fight in Afghanistan and on the Home Front*. New York: Berkley.

Herdy, Amy, and Miles Moffeitt. 2004. "Betrayal in the Ranks." Digital newsbook. Denver, CO: Denver Post.

Holm, Jeanne. 1982. *Women in the Military: An Unfinished Revolution*. Novato, CA: Presidio.

Holmstedt, Kristen. 2007. *Band of Sisters: American Women at War in Iraq*. Mechanicsburg, PA: Stackpole Books.

Hoskins, Andrew, and Ben O'Loughlin. 2010. *War and Media: The Emergence of Diffused War*. Cambridge, UK: Polity.

Hoy, Anita. 2016. "A Soldier's Mom." Army Mom Strong, February 21. http://armymomstrong.com/a-soldiers-mom/.

Human Rights Watch. 2015. *Embattled: Retaliation against Sexual Assault Survivors in the US Military*. New York: Human Rights Watch. www.hrw.org/report/2015/05/18/embattled/retaliation-against-sexual-assault-survivors-us-military.

Hundley, Heather. 2002. "The Evolution of Gendercasting: The Lifetime Television Network—'Television for Women.'" *Journal of Popular Film and Television* 29 (4): 174–181.

"Incoming." 2009. *Army Wives*, June 28. Directed by Chris Peppe. Television series. ABC Television Studio.

"Independence Day." 2007. *Army Wives*, July 1. Directed by John T. Kretchmer. Television series. ABC Television Studio.

Independent Lens Blog. 2013. "*Invisible War* Director Kirby Dick on the Healing Power of Film." May 9. PBS. www.pbs.org/independentlens/blog/invisible-war-filmmaker-kirby-dick.

Institute for Health Metrics and Evaluation. 2017. "Mental Illness, Suicide, and 'Intractable Violence' Creating 'Lost Generation' in Middle East." University of Washington, August 2. www.healthdata.org/news-release/mental-illness-suicide-and-%E2%80%98intractable-violence%E2%80%99-creating-%E2%80%98lost-generation%E2%80%99-middle.

Invisible War, The. 2012. Written by Kirby Dick, produced by Kirby Dick and Amy Ziering. Film. Chain Camera Pictures.

Jaslow, Allison. 2017. "The VA Has a Woman Problem. It Starts with Its Motto." *Washington Post*, May 29. www.washingtonpost.com/posteverything/wp/2017/05/29/va-motto/?utm_term=.2e6be91b01b8.

Jauregui, Beatrice. 2015. "World Fitness: US Army Family Humanism and the Positive Science of Persistent War." *Public Culture* 27 (3): 449–485. DOI: 10.1215/08992363-2896183.

Jeffords, Susan. 1991a. "Performative Masculinities, or, 'After a Few Times You Won't Be Afraid of Rape at All.'" *Discourse* 13 (2): 102–118.

———. 1991b. "Rape and the New World Order." *Cultural Critique* 19: 203–215.

JAMRS. n.d. "Welcome to Joint Advertising, Market Research & Studies." U.S. Department of Defense. February 16, 2016. http://jamrs.defense.gov/.

———. 2008. *Influencer Poll Wave 10: Overview Report.* June. Arlington, VA: Department of Defense. http://jamrs.defense.gov/Portals/20/Documents/Influencer_Poll_10.pdf.

JAMRS Marketing Communications. n.d. "*FUTURES* Magazine." Accessed February 16, 2016. http://jamrs.defense.gov/Marketing-Communications/Media-Gallery/.

Jeffreys, Sheila. 2007. "Double Jeopardy: Women, the US Military and the War in Iraq." *Women's Studies International Forum* 30:16–25.

Johnson, Chalmers. 2008. "The Pentagon Bailout Fraud." *TomDispatch* (blog), September 28. www.tomdispatch.com/blog/174982/.

———. 2009. "Chalmers Johnson, Dismantling the Empire." *TomDispatch* (blog), July 30. www.tomdispatch.com/post/175101/chalmers_johnson_dismantling_the_empire.

Katz, Cindi. 2001. "The State Goes Home: Local Hyper-vigilance of Children and the Global Retreat from Social Reproduction." *Social Justice* 28 (3): 47–56.

Katz, Jackson. 2006. *The Macho Paradox: Why Some Men Hurt Women and How All Men Can Help.* Naperville, IL: Sourcebooks.

———. 2011. "Advertising and the Construction of Violent White Masculinity." In *Gender, Race, and Class in Media: A Critical Reader*, 3rd ed., edited by Gail Dines and Jean M. Humez, 261–269. Los Angeles: Sage.

Keeter, Scott. 2007. "Trends in Public Opinion about the War in Iraq, 2003–2007." Pew Research Center, March 15. www.pewresearch.org/2007/03/15/trends-in-public-opinion -about-the-war-in-iraq-20032007/.

Keller, Jared. 2017. "Thousands of Troops Have Had Their Explicit Photos Shared without Consent, DoD Report Finds." *Task & Purpose*, May 1. http://taskandpurpose.com/ military-sexual-assault-report-2016/?utm_content=bufferbd3da&utm_medium=social &utm_source=twitter&utm_campaign=tp-buffer.

Kellner, Douglas. 1992. *The Persian Gulf TV War.* Boulder, CO: Westview.

———. 2004. "Media Propaganda and Spectacle in the War on Iraq: A Critique of U.S. Broadcasting Networks. *Cultural Studies<—>Critical Methodologies* 4 (3): 329–338.

———. 2005. "Foreword: The Bush Administration's March to War." In *Bring 'Em On: Media and Politics in the Iraq War*, edited by Lee Artz and Yahya R. Kamalipour, vii–xvii. Lanham, MD: Rowman and Littlefield.

———. 2010. *Cinema Wars: Hollywood Film and Politics in the Bush-Cheney Era.* Malden, MA: Wiley-Blackwell.

Kim, Eugene. 2016. "How Amazon CEO Jeff Bezos Reinvented The Washington Post, the 140-Year Old Newspaper He Bought for $250 Million." *Business Insider*, May 15. www .businessinsider.com/how-the-washington-post-changed-after-jeff-bezos-acquisition -2016-5/#bezos-initially-wasnt-sure-if-he-wanted-buy-the-post-but-after-a-couple -meetings-with-former-owner-don-graham-bezos-became-intrigued-1.

Kim, Jonathan. 2012. "ReThink Interview: Kirby Dick and Amy Ziering on *The Invisible War*." YouTube, June 18. www.youtube.com/watch?v=mHcuF7w3CQc.

Kimmel, Michael. 2005. "Men, Masculinity, and the Rape Culture." In *Transforming a Rape Culture*, rev. ed., edited by Emilie Buchwald, Pamela R. Fletcher, and Martha Roth, 139–157. Minneapolis, MN: Milkweed Editions.

Koshgarian, Lindsay. 2017. "The Militarized Budget: How the U.S. Funds Force." National Priorities Project, April 4. https://media.nationalpriorities.org/uploads/publications/ militarized_budget.pdf.

Krakauer, Jon. 2009. *Where Men Win Glory: The Odyssey of Pat Tillman*. New York: Doubleday.

Kucinich, Jackie. 2014. "Next Mission for Female Vets: Storming the Halls of Congress. *She the People* (blog), *Washington Post*, March 20. www.washingtonpost.com/blogs/she-the -people/wp/2014/03/20/next-mission-for-women-vets-storming-the-halls-of-congress/.

Kumar, Deepa. 2004. "War Propaganda and the (Ab)uses of Women: Media Constructions of the Jessica Lynch Story." *Feminist Media Studies* 4 (3): 297–313. DOI: 10.1080/ 1468077042000309955.

Lafayette, Jon. 2007. "Andrea Wong's Lifetime Project." *Television Week*, September 3. *EBSCOhost*.

———. 2008. "Ford Deal Drives 'Wives' Storyline." *Television Week*, June 2. *EBSCOhost*.

Lamothe, Dan. 2017. "Frustrated with Misogyny, Hundreds of Female Marines Have Joined a Group Pressuring Male Colleagues to Change." *Washington Post*, April 11. www .washingtonpost.com/news/checkpoint/wp/2017/04/11/frustrated-with-misogyny -hundreds-of-female-marines-have-joined-a-group-pressuring-male-colleagues-to -change/?utm_term=.4cb9b12f95c2.

"Last Minute Changes." 2008. *Army Wives*, November 11. Directed by Stephen Gyllenhaal. Television series. ABC Television Studio.

Lee, Felicia R. 2007. "Watching Army Wives Watching 'Army Wives.'" *New York Times*, June 28, E1, E8.

Lemish, Dafna. 2005. "Guest Editor's Introduction." *Feminist Media Studies* 5 (3): 275–280.

Lemmon, Gayle Tzemach. 2015. *Ashley's War: The Untold Story of Women Soldiers on the Special Ops Battlefield*. New York: Harper Perennial.

Levinson, Nan. 2014. *War Is Not a Game: The New Antiwar Soldiers and the Movement They Built*. New Brunswick, NJ: Rutgers University Press.

Lewis, Justin. 2008. "The Role of the Media in Boosting Military Spending." *Media, War & Conflict* 1 (1): 108–117. DOI: 10.1177/1750635207087631.

Lifetime. n.d.-a. "About Lifetime." Accessed March 2, 2010. www.mylifetime.com/about-us/ about-lifetime.

———. n.d.-b. "Coming Home Episode Guide." Accessed March 20, 2011. www.mylifetime .com/shows/coming-home/episodes.

———. 2008. "Heroes at Walter Reed." http://www.mylifetime.com/about-us/heroes-walter -reed.

"Lifetime Orders More Army Wives: Women Focused Cabler Picks Up Future Season of Popular Drama." 2009. *Broadcasting & Cable*, February 24. www.broadcastingcable.com/ article/179784-Lifetime_Orders_More_Army_Wives_.php.

"Lifetime's 'Army Wives' Averages 4.2 Million Viewers in Season Five Premiere." 2011. *The Futon Critic*, March 7. www.thefutoncritic.com/ratings/2011/03/07/lifetimes-army-wives -averages-42-million-total-viewers-in-season-five-premiere-427315/20110307lifetime01/.

Lioness. 2008. Directed and produced by Meg McLagan and Daria Sommers. DVD. Room 11 Productions.

Lotz, Amanda D. 2006. *Redesigning Women: Television after the Network Era*. Urbana: University of Illinois Press.

Low, Setha. 2003. *Behind the Gates: Life, Security, and the Pursuit of Happiness in Fortress America*. New York: Routledge.

Lutz, Catherine. Forthcoming. "Militarization." In *The International Encyclopedia of Anthropology*, edited by Hilary Callan. Hoboken, NJ: Wiley.

Macdonald, Myra. 2006. "Muslim Women and the Veil." *Feminist Media Studies* 6 (1): 7–23.

MacKenzie, Megan. 2015. *Beyond the Band of Brothers: The US Military and the Myth That Women Can't Fight*. Cambridge: Cambridge University Press.

MacLeish, Kenneth T. 2013. *Making War at Fort Hood: Life and Uncertainty in a Military Community*. Princeton, NJ: Princeton University Press.

Malkin, Michelle. 2004. "Candidates Ignore 'Security Moms' at Their Peril." *USA Today*, July 21, 11A.

Maltby, Sarah. 2012. *Military Media Management: Negotiating the "Front Line" in Mediatized War*. New York: Routledge.

Managhan, Tina. 2012. *Gender, Agency and War: The Maternalized Body in US Foreign Policy*. New York: Routledge.

Marcus, Ruth. 2014. "The Challenge of 'Leaning In' within the Military." *Washington Post*, April 25. www.washingtonpost.com/opinions/ruth-marcus-sheryl-sandberg-pitchs-lean -in-at-the-naval-academy/2014/04/25/07dd9fa8-cc94-11e3-95f7-7ecdde72d2ea_story .html.

Martin, David. 2017. "Marines Nude Photos Scandal Expands to All Branches of Military." *CBS News*, March 9. www.cbsnews.com/news/marines-nude-photo-scandal-expands-to -military-wide-explicit-message-board/.

Mazzetti, Mark, and Scott Shane. 2008. "Senate Panel Accuses Bush of Iraq Exaggerations." *New York Times*, June 5. www.nytimes.com/2008/06/05/washington/05cnd-intel .html?_r=0.

McCaughey, Martha. 2008. *The Caveman Mystique: Pop-Darwinism and the Debates over Sex, Violence, and Science*. New York: Routledge.

McChesney, Robert W. 2008. *The Political Economy of Media: Enduring Issues, Emerging Dilemmas*. New York: Monthly Review Press.

———. 2015. *Rich Media, Poor Democracy: Communication Politics in Dubious Times*. New York: New Press.

McCoy, Alexander. 2017. "More than Just Marines Behaving Badly." *New York Times*, March 9. https://nyti.ms/2m2jp3f.

McLaren, Peter, and Gregory Martin. 2004. "The Legend of the Bush Gang: Imperialism, War, and Propaganda. *Cultural Studies<—>Critical Methodologies* 4 (3): 281–303.

McRobbie, Angela. 2009. *The Aftermath of Feminism: Gender, Culture and Social Change*. Los Angeles: Sage.

Medzian, Myriam. 2005. "How Rape Is Encouraged in American Boys and What We Can Do to Stop It." In *Transforming a Rape Culture*, rev. ed., edited by Emilie Buchwald, Pamela R. Fletcher, and Martha Roth, 159–172. Minneapolis, MN: Milkweed Editions.

Meehan, Eileen R., and Jackie Byars. 2000. "Telefeminism: How Lifetime Got Its Groove, 1984–1997." *Television & New Media* 1 (1): 33–51.

Mesok, Elizabeth. 2016. "Sexual Violence and the US Military: Feminism, US Empire, and the Failure of Liberal Equality." *Feminist Studies* 42 (1): 41–69.

Meyer, Leisa D. 1996. *Creating GI Jane: Sexuality and Power in the Women's Army Corps during World War II*. New York: Columbia University Press.

Meyers, Marian. 1997. *News Coverage of Violence against Women: Engendering Blame*. Thousand Oaks, CA: Sage.

MikieSherrill.com. n.d. "Mikie Sherrill: U.S. Congress." Accessed September 2, 2017. http:// mikiesherrill.com/#meet-mikie.

Military Families Speak Out. n.d. "FAQ." Accessed February 10, 2011. www.militaryfamilies speakout.com/faq.

Miller, Laura L. 1998. "Feminism and the Exclusion of Army Women from Combat." *Gender Issues*, Summer, 33–64.

Mirrlees, Tanner. 2016. *Hearts and Mines: The US Empire's Culture Industry*. Vancouver: UBC Press.

Mitchell, Amy. 2014. *State of the News Media 2014*. Pew Research Journalism Project. March. http://assets.pewresearch.org/wp-content/uploads/sites/13/2017/05/30142556/state-of -the-news-media-report-2014-final.pdf.

Mitchell, Billie. 1996. "The Creation of Army Officers and the Gender Lie: Betty Grable or Frankenstein?" In *It's Our Military, Too! Women and the U.S. Military*, edited by Judith Hicks Stiehm, 35–59. Philadelphia: Temple University Press.

Mittelstadt, Jennifer. 2015. *The Rise of the Military Welfare State*. Cambridge, MA: Harvard University Press.

Mohanty, Chandra Talpade. 2003. "'Under Western Eyes' Revisited: Feminist Solidarity through Anticapitalist Struggles." *Signs* 28 (2): 499–535.

Moniz, Dave. 2005. "Army Misses Recruiting Goal." *USA Today*, March 2. www.usatoday .com/news/washington/2005-03-02-army-goal_x.htm.

Moore, Brenda L. 1996. "From Underrepresentation to Overrepresentation: African American Women." In *It's Our Military, Too! Women and the U.S. Military*, edited by Judith Hicks Stiehm, 115–135. Philadelphia: Temple University Press.

———. 2017. "Introduction to Armed Forces & Society: Special Issue on Women in the Military." *Armed Forces & Society* 43 (2): 191–201. DOI: 10.1177/0095327X16652610.

Moore, Jack. 2017. "Women Vets Have More than Double the Suicide Rate of Civilian Women." *Newsweek*, September 21. www.newsweek.com/women-vets-have-more-double -suicide-rate-civilian-women-668732.

Morris, William, ed. 1981. *The American Heritage Dictionary of the English Language*. Boston: Houghton Mifflin.

MSNBC. 2003. *Hardball*, June 27.

———. 2013a. *Andrea Mitchell Reports*, November 19.

———. 2013b. *MSNBC Special*, January 30.

———. 2013c. *The Rachel Maddow Show*, January 23.

Mulrine, Anna. 2014. "Sexual Harassment in the Military: What Female Cadets Have to Say." *Christian Science Monitor*, January 10. www.csmonitor.com/USA/Military/2014/ 0110/Sexual-harassment-in-the-military-what-female-cadets-have-to-say.

Nadler, Anthony, and Mary Vavrus. 2015. "Critical Voices in the Future of News Debates." *Communication Review* 18:71–81.

National Defense University. n.d. "Vision and Mission." Accessed May 13, 2017. www.ndu .edu/About/Vision-Mission/.

National Priorities Project. 2017. "The Militarized Budget 2017." April 3. www.national priorities.org/analysis/2017/militarized-budget-2017/.

Nayak, Meghana. 2009. "Feminist Interrogations of Democracy, Sexual Violence, and the US Military." In *Theorizing Sexual Violence*, edited by Renée J. Heberle and Victoria Grace, 147–175. New York: Routledge.

NBC. 2003a. *The Today Show*, February 19.

———. 2003b. *The Today Show*, May 14.

———. 2004a. *Meet the Press*, September 26.

———. 2004b. *NBC Nightly News*, January 10.

———. 2004c. *NBC Nightly News*, September 20.

———. 2004d. *NBC Nightly News*, September 28.

———. 2005a. *NBC Nightly News*, May 18.

———. 2005b. *NBC Nightly News*, June 25.

———. 2006. *NBC Nightly News*, October 3.

———. 2012. *Rock Center*, September 27.

———. 2013a. *NBC Evening News*, May 15.

NBC. 2013b. *The Today Show*, January 24.

———. 2014. *The Today Show*, March 7.

———. 2016. *NBC Nightly News*, April 15.

NCES. n.d. "United States Military Academy." Accessed June 3, 2017. https://nces.ed.gov/collegenavigator/?q=united+states&s=all&id=197036#enrolmt.

"Need to Know Basis." 2010. *Army Wives: The Complete Third Season*. Written by Elizabeth Jacobs, directed by Allison Liddi-Brown. DVD. Buena Vista Home Entertainment.

Nettleton, Pamela Hill. 2011. "Domestic Violence in Men's and Women's Magazines: Women Are Guilty of Choosing the Wrong Men, Men Are Not Guilty of Hitting Women." *Women's Studies in Communication* 34 (1): 139–160.

Neuman, Scott. 2015. "First Female Soldiers Graduate from Army Ranger School." *The Two-Way: Breaking News from NPR*, August 21. National Public Radio. www.npr.org/sections/thetwo-way/2015/08/21/433482186/first-female-soldiers-graduate-from-army-ranger-school.

Newman, Emily, and Emily Witsell. 2016. Introduction to *The Lifetime Network: Essays on "Television for Women" in the 21st Century*, edited by Emily Newman and Emily Witsell, 1–17. Jefferson, NC: McFarland.

Newport, Frank. 2014. "More Americans Now View Afghanistan War as a Mistake." Gallup, February 19. www.gallup.com/poll/167471/americans-view-afghanistan-war-mistake.aspx.

NOW Foundation. 2014. "Will Military Sexual Assault Survivors Find Justice? (Issue Advisory)." March 19. http://now.org/resource/will-military-sexual-assault-survivors-find-justice-issue-advisory/.

NPR. 1992. "Women Vets Testify to Senate about Sexual Harassment." *Morning Edition*, July 1.

———. 2005. *Day to Day*, August 17.

Nye, Joseph S., Jr. 2008. *The Powers to Lead*. New York: Oxford University Press.

O'Connor, Seamus. 2008. "Charleston Airmen Become TV Series Extras." *Army Times*, May 8. www.armytimes.com/news/2008/05/airforce_armywives_charleston_050808w/.

Oliver, Kelly. 2007. *Women as Weapons of War: Iraq, Sex, and the Media*. New York: Columbia University Press.

Olson, Wyatt. 2015. "Federal Watchdog: DOD Slow in Addressing Sexual Assault of Men." *Stars and Stripes*, March 19. www.stripes.com/news/federal-watchdog-dod-slow-in-addressing-sexual-assault-of-men-1.335600.

Ono, Kent. 2010. "Postracism: A Theory of the 'Post'- as Political Strategy." *Journal of Communication Inquiry* 34 (3): 227–233.

"Onward Christian Soldier." 2009. *Army Wives*, July 19. Directed by Carl Lawrence Ludwig. Television series. ABC Television Studio.

"Operational Intelligence: Getting the Army's Support." 2009. *Army Wives: The Complete Second Season*. DVD bonus feature. Buena Vista Home Entertainment.

Operation Homefront. n.d. "Our Mission." Accessed July 3, 2009. www.operationhomefront.net/about.aspx.

Operation Mom. n.d. "Military Family Support." Accessed July 20, 2018. www.operationmom.org/about/.

Outback Steakhouse. 2010. "Outback Steakhouse to Support U.S. Troops and Their Families with $1 Million Donation." Press release. March 3. http://multivu.prnewswire.com/mnr/outback/42752/.

———. 2011a. "Outback Steakhouse Presents $1 Million Donation in Support of U.S. Troops through Operation Homefront." Press release. June 22. www.prnewswire.com/

news-releases/outback-steakhouse-presents-1-million-donation-in-support-of-us-troops
-through-operation-homefront-124376793.html.

———. 2011b. "Real Army Wives Surprise Part 2." YouTube, March 22. www.youtube.com/
watch?v=tW8NYf9vp2c/.

Padavic, Irene, and Anastasia Prokos. 2017. "Aiming High: Explaining the Earnings
Advantage for Female Veterans." *Armed Forces & Society* 43 (2): 368–386. DOI: 10.1177/
0095327X16682044.

Parker, Kathleen. 2017. "The Few, the Proud, the Sharing of Nude Photos of Fellow Marines."
Washington Post, March 7. www.washingtonpost.com/opinions/the-few-the-proud
-the-sharing-of-nude-photos-of-fellow-marines/2017/03/07/15c1329c-0387-11e7-b9fa
-ed727b644a0b_story.html?tid=ss_mail.

Pason, Amy. 2010. "Cindy Sheehan and the Peace Movement: Networks of Care and Rhetorical Exploits." PhD diss., University of Minnesota.

Patten, Eileen, and Kim Parker. 2011. *Women in the U.S. Military: Growing Share, Distinctive
Profile*. Pew Research Center: Social & Demographic Trends, December 22. www.pew
socialtrends.org/files/2011/12/women-in-the-military.pdf.

"Payback." 2009. *Army Wives: The Complete Second Season*. Written by Tanya Biank and
Katherine Fugate, directed by John Kretchmer. DVD. Buena Vista Home Entertainment.

PBS. 2003. *Washington Week*, May 30.

———. 2006. *PBS NewsHour*, October 6. Access World News NewsBank, Inc.

Peach, Lucinda Joy. 1996. "Gender Ideology in the Ethics of Women in Combat." In *It's Our
Military, Too! Women and the U.S. Military*, edited by Judith Hicks Stiehm, 156–194.
Philadelphia: Temple University Press.

Pew Research Center. 2008. "Public Attitudes toward the War in Iraq: 2003–2008."
March 19. www.pewresearch.org/2008/03/19/public-attitudes-toward-the-war-in-iraq
-20032008/.

———. 2013. "Broad Support for Combat Roles for Women." January 29. www.people-press
.org/files/legacy-pdf/1-29-13%20Women%20in%20Combat%20Release.pdf.

Potter, Wendell. 2010. *Deadly Spin*. New York: Bloomsbury.

Priest, Dana, and Anne Hull. 2007. "Soldiers Face Neglect, Frustration at Army's Top Medical Facility." *Washington Post*, February 18. www.washingtonpost.com/wp-dyn/content/
article/2007/02/17/AR2007021701172.html.

Projansky, Sarah. 2001. *Watching Rape: Film and Television in Postfeminist Culture*. New
York: NYU Press.

Protect Our Defenders. n.d. "Protect Our Defenders to Continue the Work of #NotInvis-
ible." Accessed June 6, 2017. www.protectourdefenders.com/invisiblewar/.

———. 2017a. "Facts on United States Military Sexual Violence." May. www.protectour
defenders.com/factsheet/.

———. 2017b. *Racial Disparities in Military Justice: Findings of Substantial and Persistent
Racial Disparities within the United States Military Justice System*. June. www.protectour
defenders.com/disparity/.

Purdum, Todd. 2003. "The Nation: Focus Groups? To Bush, the Crowd Was a Blur." *New
York Times*, February 23. www.nytimes.com/2003/02/23/weekinreview/the-nation-focus
-groups-to-bush-the-crowd-was-a-blur.html.

Rakow, Lana. 2010. "The Politics of Identity Work." In *Key Concepts in Critical Cultural
Studies*, edited by Linda Steiner and Clifford Christians, 128–141. Urbana: University of
Illinois Press.

Rampton, Sheldon, and John Stauber. 2001. *Trust Us, We're Experts! How Industry Manipu-
lates Science and Gambles with Your Future*. New York: Jeremy Tarcher.

Right Web. 2012. "Family Security Matters." Last updated January 27. http://rightweb.irc
-online.org/profile/Family_Security_Matters/.

Riordan, Ellen. 2002. "Intersections and New Directions: On Feminism and Political
Economy." In *Sex and Money: Feminism and Political Economy in the Media*, edited by
Eileen R. Meehan and Ellen Riordan, 3–15. Minneapolis: University of Minnesota Press.

Risen, James, and Eric Lichtblau. 2005. "Bush Lets U.S. Spy on Callers without Courts." *New
York Times*, December 16. https://nyti.ms/2k9ozpQ.

Rivers, Caryl. 1996. *Slick Spins and Fractured Facts: How Cultural Myths Distort the News*.
New York: Columbia University Press.

Robb, David L. 2004. *Operation Hollywood: How the Pentagon Shapes and Censors the Movies*. New York: Prometheus Books.

Rodino, Michelle. 2005. "War Mothering." *Feminist Media Studies* 5:380–385.

Rose, Nikolas. 1996. *Inventing Our Selves: Psychology, Power, and Personhood*. Cambridge:
Cambridge University Press.

Rosen, Leora N., and Lee Martin. 1997. "Sexual Harassment, Cohesion, and Combat Readiness in U.S. Army Support Units." *Armed Forces & Society* 24 (2): 221–244.

"Safe Havens." 2009. *Army Wives: The Complete Second Season*. Written by Tanya Biank and
Katherine Fugate, directed by Lloyd Ahern. DVD. Buena Vista Home Entertainment.

Sahadi, Jeanne. 2017. "The U.S. Already Spends More on Defense than Any Other Country."
CNN Money, February 28. http://money.cnn.com/2017/02/28/news/economy/trump
-defense-spending/index.html.

Sakuma, Amanda. 2014. "Vast Majority of Americans Feel Iraq War Wasn't Worth It."
MSNBC.com, June 24. www.msnbc.com/msnbc/poll-majority-americans-feel-war-iraq
-wasnt-worth-it.

Scarce, Michael. 1997. *Male on Male Rape: The Hidden Toll of Stigma and Shame*. New York:
Plenum.

Schafer, Amy. 2017. "The Warrior Caste." *Slate*, August 2. www.slate.com/articles/news
_and_politics/politics/2017/08/the_warrior_caste_of_military_families_that_fight
_america_s_wars.html.

Schiller, Dan. 2011. "The Militarization of US Communications." In *The Handbook of Political Economy of Communications*, edited by Janet Wasko, Graham Murdock, and Helena
Sousa, 264–282. Malden, MA: Wiley-Blackwell.

Schuppe, Jon. 2015. "South Carolina Gov. Nikki Haley Signs Bill Removing Confederate
Flag." NBCNews.com, July 9. www.nbcnews.com/storyline/confederate-flag-furor/
gov-haley-sign-bill-removing-confederate-flag-n389231.

Secker, Tom, and Matthew Alford. 2017. "New Evidence for the Surprisingly Significant
Propaganda Role of the Central Intelligence Agency and Department of Defense
in the Screen Entertainment Industry." *Critical Sociology*, 1–13. DOI: 10.1177/
0896920517739093.

"Security Mom." n.d. Word Spy. Accessed October 7, 2008. http://wordspy.com/index.php
?word=security-mom.

Service: When Women Come Marching Home. 2012. Directed by Marcia Rock and Patricia
Lee Stotter. DVD. Women Make Movies.

Sheehan, Cindy. 2005. *Not One More Mother's Child*. Kihai, Maui, HI: Koa Books.

Sherr, Lynn, and Maggie Murphy. 2011. "America's First Moms." *Parade*, April 24, 9–11, 13.

Simerman, John. 2009. "Military Mothers' Groups Grow as Wars Continue." *Contra Costa
Times*, March 18. LexisNexis Academic.

Singer, P. W. 2010. "Meet the Sims . . . and Shoot Them: The Rise of Militainment." *Foreign
Policy*, March–April, 91–95. www.foreignpolicy.com/articles/2010/02/22/meet_the
_sims_and_shoot_them.

Sisters in Arms. 2010. Directed, written, and produced by Beth Freeman. Film. Women Make Movies.

Sjoberg, Laura. 2007. "Agency, Militarized Femininity and Enemy Others: Observations from the War in Iraq." *International Feminist Journal of Politics* 9 (1): 82–101.

———. 2014. *Gender, War, and Conflict.* Cambridge, UK: Polity.

Smith, Steven Donald. 2006. "Hollywood, Military Cooperation Often Mutually Beneficial." U.S. Department of Defense, August 21. http://archive.defense.gov/news/news article.aspx?id=516.

Smith, Tim. 2010. "Are Shows Such as 'Army Wives' Worth Incentives?" *Post and Courier*, May 27. www.postandcourier.com/news/2010/may/27/rebate-debate/?print.

Snow, Nancy. 2002. *Propaganda, Inc.: Selling America's Culture to the World.* New York: Seven Stories.

Solomon, Norman. 2005. *War Made Easy: How Presidents and Pundits Keep Spinning Us to Death.* Hoboken, NJ: Wiley.

Source Watch. 2008. "Family Security Matters." Last edited September 11. www.sourcewatch .org/index.php/Family_Security_Matters.

Squires, Catherine R. 2014. *The Post-Racial Mystique: Media and Race in the Twenty-First Century.* New York: NYU Press.

Stabile, Carol A. 1994. *Feminism and the Technological Fix.* Manchester: Manchester University Press.

Stahl, Roger. 2009. "Why We 'Support the Troops': Rhetorical Evolutions." *Rhetoric & Public Affairs* 12 (4): 533–570. DOI: https://doi.org/10.1353/rap.0.0121.

———. 2010. *Militainment, Inc.: War, Media, and Popular Culture.* New York: Routledge.

Stauber, John. 2007. "Pro-war PR Front, Move America Forward, Caravanning to DC." PR Watch, July 20. www.prwatch.org/news/2007/07/6270/pro-war-pr-front-move-america -forward-caravanning-dc.

Stauber, John, and Sheldon Rampton. 1995. *Toxic Sludge Is Good for You: Lies, Damn Lies, and the Public Relations Industry.* Monroe, ME: Common Courage.

Stiehm, Judith Hicks. "Just the Facts, Ma'am." In *It's Our Military, Too! Women and the U.S. Military*, edited by Judith Hicks Stiehm, 60–70. Philadelphia: Temple University Press.

Strub, Phil. 2010. "Pentagon's Military Entertainment Office Brings Military Science to Hollywood." *Armed with Science*, May 20. http://science.dodlive.mil/2010/05/20/ pentagons-entertainment-office-brings-military-science-to-hollywood.

Sussman, Gerald. 2010. "A Regime of Propaganda: The Systemic Bases of Promotional Political Culture." In *The Political Economy of Media and Power*, edited by Jeffery Klaehn, 113–140. New York: Peter Lang.

Tanklefsky, David. 2009. "Lifetime Prepares 'Army Wives' Mini-Marathon: Holiday-Themed 'Give Back' Segment Slated as Part of Programming." *Broadcasting & Cable*, November 18. www.broadcastingcable.com/article/389764-Lifetime_Prepares_Army_Wives_Mini _Marathon.php.

Tasker, Yvonne. 2011. *Soldiers' Stories: Military Women in Cinema and Television since World War II.* Durham, NC: Duke University Press.

Taylor, Lisa K., and Jasmin Zine. 2014. *Muslim Women, Transnational Feminism and the Ethics of Pedagogy: Contested Imaginaries in Post-9/11 Cultural Practice.* New York: Routledge.

Terry, Don. 2015. "In the Crosshairs." *SPLC Hatewatch*, June 9. Southern Poverty Law Center. https://medium.com/hatewatch-blog/in-the-crosshairs-3700fbf2203d#.g6ibgnmeq.

Thomas, Tanja. 2009. "Gender Management, Popular Culture, and the Military." In *War Isn't Hell, It's Entertainment: Essays on Visual Media and the Representation of Conflict*, edited by Rikke Schubert, Fabian Virchow, Debra White-Stanley, and Tanja Thomas, 97–114. Jefferson, NC: McFarland.

Thomas, Tanja, and Fabian Virchow. 2005. "Banal Militarism and the Culture of War." In *Bring 'Em On: Media and Politics in the Iraq War*, edited by Lee Artz and Yahya R. Kamalipour, 23–36. Lanham, MD: Rowman and Littlefield.

Thompson, Marie. 2014. "Military Sexual Trauma: Bridging the Chasm between Trauma and Support." *Women & Language* 37 (1): 131–136.

Thorpe, Helen. 2014. *Soldier Girls: The Battles of Three Women at Home and at War*. New York: Scribner.

Thorpe, Rebecca U. 2014. *The American Warfare State: The Domestic Politics of Military Spending*. Chicago: University of Chicago Press.

Today's Military. n.d. "Parents' Stories." Accessed February 20, 2016. http://todaysmilitary .com/guidance/parents-stories.

"Told Me." 2017. Amy McGrath for Congress announcement video (KY-6). YouTube, August 1. www.youtube.com/watch?v=CcjG2fK7kNk&feature=youtu.be&app=desktop.

Tough Guise 2. 2013. Created by Jackson Katz, and directed and produced by Jeremy Earp. Film. Media Education Foundation.

Treichler, Paula A. 1999. *How to Have Theory in an Epidemic: Cultural Chronicles of AIDS*. Durham, NC: Duke University Press.

Tumulty, Karen, and Viveca Novak. 2003. "Goodbye, Soccer Mom. Hello, Security Mom." *Time*, June 2. www.time.com/time/printout/0,8816,1004926,00.html.

Turse, Nick. 2008. *The Complex: How the Military Invades Our Everyday Lives*. New York: Metropolitan Books.

U.S. Air Force Academy. n.d. "Academy Releases Class of '16 Stats." Accessed May 27, 2017. www.usafa.af.mil/News/Article-Display/Article/788557/academy-releases-class-of-16 -stats/.

U.S. Army. 2015. FA-15-0157. Redacted Responsive Documents. Response to Freedom of Information Act request by Tom Secker and Matthew Alford. May 29.

U.S. Department of Veterans Affairs. 2016. *Suicide among Veterans and Other Americans 2001–2014*. Washington, DC: U.S. Department of Veterans Affairs. www.mentalhealth .va.gov/docs/2016suicidedatareport.pdf.

U.S. General Accounting Office. 1998. *Gender Issues: Information on DOD's Assignment Policy and Direct Ground Combat Definition*. Washington, DC: U.S. General Accounting Office.

U.S. Marine Corps. 2017. "U.S. Marine Corps Commercial: Battle Up." YouTube, May 12. www.youtube.com/watch?v=yotXRoLxFdY&feature=player_embedded.

U.S. Military Academy. 2017. "Simone Askew Selected First Captain." Public Affairs Office, August 3. www.army.mil/article/191821.

van Zoonen, Liesbet. 1994. *Feminist Media Studies*. London: Sage.

Vavrus, Mary Douglas. 2002. *Postfeminist News: Political Women in Media Culture*. Albany: State University of New York Press.

———. 2007. "The Politics of NASCAR Dads: Branded Media Paternity." *Critical Studies in Media Communication* 24 (3): 245–261.

———. 2012. "Postfeminist Redux?" *Review of Communication* 12 (3): 224–236.

———. 2017. "The Challenge of Warrior Women: Gender, Race, and Militarism in Media." In *Race and Gender in Electronic Media: Content, Context, Culture*, edited by Rebecca Ann Lind, 72–88. New York: Routledge.

Vavrus, Mary Douglas, and August Leinbach. 2016. "Postfeminism at the Shooting Range: Vulnerability and Fire-Empowerment in the Gun Women Network." In *Dangerous Discourses: Feminism, Gun Violence, and Civic Life*, edited by Catherine R. Squires, 180–212. New York: Peter Lang.

Walsh, Joan. 2016. "Meet the 'Feminists' Doing the Koch Brothers' Dirty Work." *The Nation*, August 18. www.thenation.com/article/meet-the-feminists-doing-the-koch-brothers -dirty-work/.

Ward, Alex. 2017. "The Marine Corps Has a 'Toxic Masculinity' Problem." *Vox*, May 29. www.vox.com/world/2017/5/29/15619574/marine-corps-women-sexual-harassment.

Warren, Catherine Annette. 1996. "First, Do Not Speak: Errant Doctors, Sexual Abuse, and Institutional Silence." PhD diss., University of Illinois.

West, Candace, and Don Zimmerman. 1987. "Doing Gender." *Gender and Society* 1 (2): 125–151.

"Who We Are." 2007. *Army Wives*, July 8. Directed by Allison Liddi-Brown. Television series. ABC Television Studio.

Why We Fight. 2006. Written and directed by Eugene Jarecki. Film. Sony Pictures Classic.

Wikipedia. n.d. "A&E Television Networks." Accessed December 19, 2010. http:// en.wikipedia.org/wiki/A%26E_Television_Networks.

Williams, Alex T. 2014. "The Growing Pay Gap between Journalism and Public Relations." *Fact Tank: News in the Numbers*, August 11. Pew Research Center. www.pewresearch.org/ fact-tank/2014/08/11/the-growing-pay-gap-between-journalism-and-public-relations/.

"Women in War." 2014. Episode in *Makers: Women Who Make America*, October 21. Directed and produced by Rachel Grady and Heidi Ewing. Public Broadcasting Service.

Women Serving in War. 2014. Aired November 9. Directed and produced by Sherece Lamke, produced by Stephanie Halleen. Television program. Twin Cities PBS, St. Paul, MN.

"Wong Polishes Lifetime's Brand." 2008. *Broadcasting & Cable* 16 (3): 23.

WREI (Women's Research and Education Institute). 2013. *Women in the Military: Where They Stand*. 8th ed. Washington, DC: WREI.

WVTM. 2005. *News NBC 10:00 PM*, August 13. NBC, Tuscaloosa, AL.

Yates, Emily. 2016. "Thanks for Your Service, but Don't Tell the Kids about It (We Need Them to Enlist)." *Truthout*, June 15. www.truth-out.org/opinion/item/36397-thanks-for -your-service-but-don-t-tell-the-kids-about-it-we-need-them-to-enlist.

Zarembo, Alan. 2015. "Suicide Rate of Female Military Veterans Is Called 'Staggering.'" *Los Angeles Times*, June 8. www.latimes.com/nation/la-na-female-veteran-suicide-20150608 -story.html#page=1.

Zine, Jasmin. 2006. "Between Orientalism and Fundamentalism: Muslim Women and Femi- nist Engagement." In *(En)Gendering the War on Terror: War Stories and Camouflaged Politics*, edited by Krista Hunt and Kim Rygiel, 27–49. Aldershot, UK: Ashgate.

Zremski, Jerry. 2014. "Gillibrand's Stature in Capital Skyrockets." *Buffalo News*, February 9. http://buffalonews.com/2014/02/09/gillibrands-stature-in-capital-skyrockets/.

Index

Actionable Change, 177
Advanced Research Projects Agency
(ARPA), 184–185
affluencers, 50–51
Affordable Care Act, 179–180, 194, 202n11
Afghanistan war, 190; *Army Wives* promot-
ing, 29–30, 31; Gold Star Families for
Peace against, 49; MFSO against, 49, 62;
military mothers on, 86–87; Ms. Veteran
America pageant and, 188; polling of public support on, 2; third-gender concept
and, 183
Air Force Academy, 149, 150–153, 155,
204nn5–6
Alexander, Michelle, 175
all-volunteer military forces (AVF), 2, 80–81
Amazon, 185
Andersen, Robin, 4, 61, 180
Army Ranger school: training at, 130;
women graduates from, 104
Army Wives, 8, 199n2; affluencers and,
50–51; banal militarism produced with,
31–32; cast members, 200n1; domestic-
violence portrayal in, 52–53; ELO working with, 34, 43, 44, 45, 200n6; friendly
fire deaths in, 40–41, 49–50; Give Back
program, 48; heteronormativity exceptions in, 200n2; marriage portrayal in,
36–38; as militainment, 47; Obama and
McCain interest in, 34, 35; organizations
in contrast to, 49; postfeminism in,
52–56; postpolitics of, 51–52; post-racial

mystique in, 13; postracism in, 57–62;
propaganda in, 20, 27, 29–30, 31, 38–42,
181–182; rape culture and, 53–55; regime
of representation and, 33; as soap opera /
serial drama, 30, 32, 62, 200n3; soft-power
activities' portrayal in, 36, 41, 42; *Under
the Sabers: The Unwritten Code of Army
Wives* as base for, 33, 41
Astroturf campaign: by Bush, 182; gender
gap in relation to, 70; regarding Security
Moms, 73, 93

banality: fatalities of, 178–181; of Lifetime
network, 32–36; of militarism, 31–32
banal militarism: *Army Wives* producing,
31–32; militarization linked to, 22–23;
women and, 5
banal nationalism, 22
band-of-brothers mythology: combat-
exclusion policy maintained by, 108–109;
proven false, 123–124
Benedict, Helen: on feminism and rape
culture, 165–166; *The Lonely Soldier: The
Private War of Women Serving in Iraq* by,
143–144; on rape myths, 154
Biank, Tanya, 33, 41
Biden, Jill, 200n7; on *Army Wives*, 34; of
Joining Forces, 84
biopower: Foucault on, 97; regime of representation and, 66
Blue Star Mothers, 80, 82, 86, 97
Boothe, Jas, 187–188

Britt, Donna, 98–99
Brooks, Rosa: on benefits of women's military service, 136; on costs of war, 189; on sexual violence, 204n1; on soft-power activities, 5
Bush, George W.: Astroturf campaign by, 182; campaign propaganda, 79; Kerry compared to, 68, 74–75; military families met by, 94; patriotism as support for, 64; psy-ops activities of, 18; Security Moms support of, 68, 72; Sheehan letter to, 89
Butler, Judith: on gender performance, 11–12, 31; on media representations of war, 8–9, 119–120; on solicitation, 118; on trajectories of affect, 8–9; on war opposition, 194
Butler, Smedley D., 15, 16

Canadian military, 131
Center for Media and Democracy, 73
Chandrasekaran, Rajiv, 205n4
civic literacy, 192, 193
Clinton, Bill: Soccer Moms in relation to, 70; welfare system and, 71, 189
Cold War, 65
collusion, 17–18, 199n5
combat: celebration of, 183–185; Duckworth injuries in, 203n10
combat-exclusion policy: band-of-brothers mythology maintaining, 108–109; Donnelly on, 114–115; Duckworth and, 115, 120–121; equality from eliminating, 125; media treatment of, 126, 129–130; paradox of, 116; polling on elimination of, 136; sexual violence in relation to, 145; Vaught on, 115–116; for women, 102
combat readiness, 204n4; gender equality and, 124–128; gender equivalence and, 121–123; gender neutrality and, 123–124; physical strength and, 129–130; soldier mothers and, 132–134; unit cohesion and, 131
Complex, The: defined, 19; marriage to, 42–51. See also military-industrial complex
Confederate flag, 57, 201n14
Congress: military spending promoted by, 16–17; sexual violence legislation and, 142–143, 163–164; sexual violence victims

testifying to, 141; women veterans running for, 179–180
conscription, 4–5; end of, 7, 24
costs of war: demilitarization in relation to, 192, 193, 194; Ms. Veteran America pageant and, 187–188, 189; for women, 190–191
Costs of War Project, 16, 17, 191, 194
Crenshaw, Kimberlé, 12
Cultural Support Teams (CSTs): DoD creation of, 9; Lemmon on training for, 192–193; third-gender concept and, 183–184

D'Amico, Francine: on MST, 147; on warrior mystique, 110
Defense Advisory Committee on Women in the Services (DACOWITS), 106, 203n4; member views on women in combat, 203n9
defense contractors: KBR, 199n5; media influenced by, 17–18, 99–100
Defense Equal Opportunity Management Institute (DEOMI), 106–107
demilitarization: civic literacy and, 192, 193; of media, 194
Department of Defense (DoD): FETs and CSTs created by, 9; IO employment by, 18–19; reality television and, 45–46; Risk Rule, 108, 203n6; SAPRO of, 142; sexual violence silenced by, 56
Dick, Kirby: director of The Invisible War, 145; on investigative journalism, 160; on sexual violence, 160; on viewer involvement, 162
discursive formation, 24–25
domestic violence: Army Wives and, 52–53; as cost of war, 190; prevention of, 201n16
Donnelly, Elaine, 114–115
Duckworth, Tammy: combat-exclusion policy and, 115, 120–121; combat injuries, 203n10; on MST, 147; on rape culture, 154–155

Eisenhower, Dwight D.: ARPA and, 184; on military-industrial complex, 15–16
enlistment: of women in military, 4–5; women of color, 107; Women's Armed

Services Act (1948) for, 106; women's reasons for, 121

Enloe, Cynthia: on military mothers, 64, 75; on sexual violence, 168–169; on "women-andchildren," 203n11

Entertainment Liaison Office (ELO): *Army Wives* working with, 34, 43, 44, 45, 200n6; films' and television shows' approval from, 20; Lifetime network alliance with, 30; reality television and, 45–47; Strub of, 43

equivalence, gender, 121–123

families. *See* military families

Family Security Matters (FSM), 73

Female Engagement Teams (FETs): DoD creation of, 9; launch of, 157

feminism: Benedict on rape culture and, 165–166; liberal, 136; Ms. Veteran America pageant and, 189. *See also* postfeminism

feminist analysis: of *Army Wives*, 36; goal of, 11

"fighting-and-dying" term, 203n11

films/television: documentary list, 203n3; ELO approval of, 20; reality television, 45–47; Robb on military influence of, 43–44; *Saving Private Lynch*, 19; *Service: When Women Come Marching Home*, 147, 205n3; *Tough Guise*, 2, 166–167; warrior women portrayal in, 9; *Why We Fight*, 199n5. See also *Army Wives*; *Invisible War, The*

Final Salute charity, 188

foreign policy, 2

Fort Bragg, 33

Fort Snelling State Park, 1

Foster, Gregory D., 192

Foucault, Michel: on biopower, 97; discursive formation concept by, 24–25; regime of truth concept by, 7

friendly fire, 40–41, 49–50

Fugate, Katherine: *Army Wives* executive producer, 30, 181; military families' praise for, 35

Full Picture Coalition, 186–187

Gabbard, Tulsi: on rape culture, 154–155; on Silver Star recipients, 117

Gavey, Nicola, 172–173

gender: equivalence, 121–123; neutrality, 123–124; sexual violence and, 166–168; as social construct, 199n3; warrior caste regarding, 13

gender equality, 4; for combat readiness, 124–128; MMIC and, 193; third-gender concept promoting, 183–184

gender gap: Astroturf campaign in relation to, 70; regarding war, 79

genderization: propaganda and, 181–182; of war, 108–110

gender performance: Butler on, 11–12, 31; masculinity and, 166–167; militarization in relation to, 21; propaganda in *Army Wives*, 20, 38–42; Security Moms influencing, 74, 78; sexual violence and, 167–168

GI Bill: college benefits from, 59–60, 81; for women, 33

Gillibrand, Kirsten, 161, 163–164; *The Invisible War* and, 162; Military Justice Improvement Act and, 153

Glenn, Cheryl, 171

Global War on Terror (GWOT), 2, 199n1; deaths from, 191; homefront fear from, 76–77; as Orwellian nightmare, 120; Security Moms influence from, 21–22

Gold Star Families for Peace, 49, 89

Gold Star Mothers, 202n7; grievability of, 87, 98; Sheehan as, 183

Goldstein, Joshua, 107, 204n13; on WAC, 105; *War and Gender* by, 102

Google, 185

Gray, Herman, 181

grievability: in *Army Wives*, 200n10; Butler on, 9; of Gold Star Mothers, 87, 98; precariousness in relation to, 9, 118; warrior women and, 118, 145, 173

Grossberg, Lawrence, 6–7

Haley, Nikki: on *Army Wives*, 34–35; on Confederate flag, 57, 201n14

Hall, Stuart, 6, 8, 24, 62, 135

Hegar, Mary Jennings, 126, 204n12

homegrown heroes, 178, 194

identities, social, 9–12

ideology: of gender performance, 11; of martial postfeminism, 4; prowar, 42–43

Imperial Life in the Emerald City (Chandrasekaran), 205n4
Independent Women's Forum (IWF), 73, 201n4
infidelity, 61–62
information operations (IO), 18–19
intersectionality, 12
intertextual activities, 51–52
Invisible War, The: awards for, 160; Dick director of, 145; media failure with, 185–186; MST accounts by, 148; release of, 26, 55; sexual violence prevention influenced by, 143, 160–163
Iraq and Afghanistan Veterans of America, 190
Iraq Veterans Against the War (IVAW), 186–187
Iraq War, 8; *Army Wives* promoting, 29–30, 31; Blue Star Mothers on, 86; false narratives for starting, 91; Gold Star Families for Peace against, 49; MFSO against, 49, 62; polling of public support on, 2; propaganda for, 18–19, 112–113; Sheehan critic of, 26, 27, 67, 82–83; warrior women in, 116–117; women of color views on, 98–99
Islamic State in Iraq and Syria (ISIS), 2

Joining Forces, 84
Joint Advertising, Market Research & Studies (JAMRS), 80–81, 82, 83, 87, 97–98, 124

Keane, Jack, 18
Kellogg, Brown & Root (KBR), 199n5
Kerry, John, 68, 74–75

Lemmon, Gayle Tzemach: on CST training, 192–193; third-gender concept by, 183
liberal feminism, 136
Lifetime network, 200n4; affluencers and, 50–51; banality of, 32–36; military-industrial complex partnership with, 29–30; Outback Steakhouse alliance with, 47–48; for support of women, 32, 48–49
Lonely Soldier, The: The Private War of Women Serving in Iraq (Benedict), 143–144

Lynch, Jessica, 19; fame of, 102–103; media story on, 112–113

Mackey, Dorothy: rape victim, 153; on reporting of sexual violence, 159
Malkin, Michelle, 72, 76
Managhan, Tina: on Persian Gulf War, 66, 67; on Sheehan, 90, 200n9, 202n9
Manning, Chelsea, 199n3
Marine Corps: masculine mythology in, 124; rape culture in, 156, 157–158; toxic masculinity in, 141
MarineParents.com, 93
Marines United: Actionable Change response to, 176–177; Facebook group, 141; military justification of, 169
marketing: JAMRS program for, 80–81, 82, 83, 87, 97–98, 124; of militarism, 2; for military mothers, 182–183; Security Moms label for, 69
marriage: *Army Wives* portrayal of, 36–38; to The Complex, 42–51
martial postfeminism: combat and, 120, 136; danger of, 15; defined, 4; importance of, 179; warrior mystique and, 137, 143, 176
masculinity: combat as form of, 108–109; Enloe on acceptable form of, 64; gender performance and, 166–167; sexual violence and downplaying, 158–159; sexual violence and military, 168–172; warrior mystique promoting, 110; warrior women as threat to, 111. *See also* toxic masculinity
McCain, John: *Army Wives* interest from, 34, 35; Security Moms' support of, 68
McCaskill, Claire, 161, 163–164
McGrath, Amy: demilitarization and, 194; running for Congress, 179–180
media: Butler on war representations by, 8–9, 119–120; Center for Media and Democracy, 73; combat-exclusion policy and, 126, 129–130; defense contractors influencing, 17–18, 99–100; demilitarization of, 194; discourses of militarism, 6–9; fear of feminism, 165–166; gender equality strategy by, 124–128; gender equivalence strategy by, 121–123; gender neutrality strategy by, 123–124; identities generated by, 69–70; interrogation of representations by, 24–28; Lynch story

in, 112–113; marketing of militarism by, 2; militarism and political economy, 21–24; military-industrial complex connection to, 15, 17–20; military-industrial complex integration of, 184–185; on physical strength, 129–130; post-9/11 and, 3, 5–6; postfeminism and postracism portrayal by, 12–14; rape survival stories by, 154–158; regime of representation and, 8, 178–179; Security Moms labeled by, 69; sexual violence disregarded by, 144–145, 147–148; Sheehan discredited by, 90–96; silence on sexual violence, 185–186; social, 82, 85, 141, 184–185, 204n3, 205n2; on soldier mothers, 132–134; on unit cohesion and women, 131; WAC attacked by, 110–111; warrior women representations by, 110–113. *See also* films/television

media-industrial complex, 17

media-military-industrial complex (MMIC), 6; expansion of, 184–185; gender equality and, 193; militarism as product of, 21; military mothers and, 63–68

meritocracy, postracial, 58

militainment: *Army Wives* as, 47; defined, 44; Stahl on, 23, 44, 134

militarism: banality of, 31–32; media discourses of, 6–9; political economy and media, 21–24; political economy of, 15–20; social identities of, 9–12; women's roles in, 1–2. *See also* banal militarism

militarization: banal militarism linked to, 22–23; of federal budget, 17; gender performance in relation to, 21; of mothers, 63–68, 79–83, 182–183; Security Moms as result of, 21–22; of women, 6

military: approach to pregnancy, 114; Canadian, 131; as career path, 124–125; demilitarization of, 192, 193, 194; as escape from poverty, 59–60; films/television influence from, 43–44; homegrown heroes, 194; Marines United justification by, 169; masculinity and sexual violence, 168–172; as paterfamilias, 58, 67; patriarchy regarding women, 104–105, 135–136; punishment and postracism, 175–176; racial and gendered hierarchy within, 13; rape culture in, 148–149; soap opera / serial drama as

strategy of, 62; spending, 16–17; spouses and infidelity, 61–62; Trump tribute to, 205n1; Uniform Code of Military Justice, 155, 164; women enlistment in, 4–5; women tribute by WNBA, 178

military families: *Army Wives* portrayal of, 31–32, 33–34; Bush meeting with, 94; Fugate praise from, 35; Gold Star Mothers and Families, 49, 87, 88, 89, 98, 183, 202n7; as peace activists, 206n6; welfare system and, 189–190

Military Families Speak Out (MFSO): against Afghanistan and Iraq wars, 49, 62; military mothers and, 96

military-industrial complex: Eisenhower warning of, 15–16; Lifetime network partnership with, 29–30; media connection to, 15, 17–20; media integration into, 184–185

Military Keynesianism, 16

military mothers: on Afghanistan war, 86–87; biopower paradoxes and, 66; Blue Star Mothers, 80, 82, 86; Enloe on, 64, 75; Gold Star Mothers, 87, 92, 98, 183, 202n7; holidays and, 84–88; JAMRS and, 80–81, 82, 83, 87, 97–98; marketing for, 182–183; MFSO and, 96; MMIC and, 63–68; Operation Mom support group, 87–88; regime of representation and, 98; Security Moms compared to, 79–80; troop-supporting rhetoric and, 85–86; warrior women as, 132–134. *See also* Sheehan, Cindy

military sexual trauma (MST): defined, 146; *The Invisible War* accounts of, 148; threats toward victims of, 147, 161; VA treatment for, 146; Yates survivor of, 186–187. *See also* rape culture; sexual violence

Mittelstadt, Jennifer, 188–189, 201n16

Mother of All Bombs (MOAB), 3

mothers. *See* military mothers; Security Moms; Soccer Moms

Move America Forward (MAF), 93, 94

Ms. Veteran America pageant: Boothe founder of, 187–188; feminist critique of, 189; VA in relation to, 190

NASCAR Dads, 201n5; as media-generated identity, 69; Security Moms' counterpart as, 73

National Defense University, 13; Foster of, 192; purpose of, 199n4

National Rifle Association (NRA), 201n4, 202n10

neutrality, gender, 123–124

New Jim Crow, The (Alexander), 175

NOW Foundation, 142, 149

Obama, Barack: *Army Wives* interest from, 34, 35; ISIS airstrikes by, 2; postracism in relation to, 57, 174

Obama, Michelle, 84, 200n7

Office of the Chief of Public Affairs (OCPA-West). *See* Entertainment Liaison Office (ELO)

Oliver, Kelly, 10

Operation Homefront: Outback Steakhouse donations to, 47–48; purpose of, 200n5

Operation Mom, 87–88

Oprah Winfrey Network (OWN), 46

Ortiz, Jacqueline: sexual violence survivor, 140–141; VA treatment and, 146

Outback Steakhouse, 47–48

paterfamilias, military as, 58, 67

patriarchy: *Army Wives* refusal to confront, 53–55; of military culture regarding women, 104–105, 135–136; narratives regarding post-9/11, 71–72; rape culture fueled by, 28

patriotism: Bush support as, 64; Sheehan accusations regarding, 89–90; women's military service as, 121

pedagogy, warrior women, 172–177

Pentagon: combat-exclusion policy for women, 102; JAMRS program of, 80–81, 82, 83, 87, 97–98, 124; Youth Attitude Tracking Survey conducted by, 45. *See also* Department of Defense (DoD)

Pentagon Entertainment Office, 20. *See also* Entertainment Liaison Office (ELO)

Persian Gulf War: Managhan on, 66, 67; military mothers and, 64, 65; troop-supporting rhetoric and, 37; yellow ribbon campaign during, 65–66

physical strength, 129–130

policy: public support on foreign, 2;

Security Moms on, 77. *See also* combat-exclusion policy

political economy: media militarism and, 21–24; of militarism, 15–20

polling: on elimination of combat-exclusion policy, 136; by Iraq and Afghanistan Veterans of America, 190; of public support on foreign policy, 2

postfeminism: *Army Wives* and, 52–56; combat-exclusion policy and, 136; depoliticization of, 138–139; Gabbard and, 155; media portrayal of, 12–14; sexual violence and, 56, 128, 173–174. *See also* martial postfeminism

post-9/11: media and, 3, 5–6; patriarchy narratives regarding, 71–72; public support polling and, 2; Security Moms in, 68–79; women's roles and, 4

postpolitics, 51–52

postracial meritocracy, 58

post-racial mystique: defined, 13; warrior women and, 137

postracism: *Army Wives* and, 57–62; as color blind, 175; media portrayal of, 12–14; military punishment and, 175–176; Obama in relation to, 57, 174; regarding warrior women, 137–138

poverty: Final Salute charity helping fight, 188; military as escape from, 59–60

power: domains of, 12; masculinity and, 167; sexual violence as, 169–170; soft-power activities, 5, 36, 41, 42; truth as, 7

precariousness, 9, 118

propaganda: in *Army Wives*, 20, 27, 29–30, 31, 38–42, 181–182; Bush campaign, 79; definitions of, 38–39; genderization and, 181–182; for Iraq War, 18–19, 112–113; Security Moms, 201n5; yellow ribbon campaign as, 65–66

prosecution, 174–175

psychological operations (psy-ops), 18

public support: for elimination of combat-exclusion policy, 136; polling on foreign policy, 2; regime of truth regarding, 7–8

Puerto Rico, 206n5

Rakow, Lana, 69

Rand Corporation, 25–26

rape culture: at Air Force Academy, 149,
150–153, 155, 204nn5–6; *Army Wives*
hinting at, 53–55; Benedict on feminism
and, 165–166; defined, 148; Gabbard and
Duckworth on, 154–155; Mackey victim
of, 153; in military, 148–149; patriarchy
fueling, 28; protection of accused within,
56; Russo victim of, 156, 157–158
reality television, 45–47
recognizability: *Vogue* magazine and, 134–
135; of warrior women, 9, 117–118, 134
recruitment ads: evolution of, 126–127;
women of color and, 113
regime of representation concept: *Army
Wives* and, 33; biopower and, 66; by
Hall, 6, 8, 62, 135; media and, 8, 178–179;
military mothers and, 98. *See also* Warrior
Women regime
regime of truth concept: by Foucault, 7;
regarding military mothers, 64, 83;
regarding public support, 7–8
Reserve Officers' Training Corps (ROTC):
hazing in, 149; scholarship, 59
Risk Rule, 108, 203n6
Robb, David, 43–44
Russia, 205n2
Russo, Claire, 156, 157–158

Saving Private Lynch, 19
Scarce, Michael, 169–170
Security Moms: Bush support from, 68, 72;
defined, 21–22, 201n3; FSM representing,
73; gender performance influenced by, 74,
78; Malkin as head of, 72, 76; as media-
generated identity, 69–70; military
mothers compared to, 79–80; in post-
9/11, 68–79; propaganda, 201n5; Soccer
Moms compared to, 68, 71, 98
*Service: When Women Come Marching
Home*, 147, 205n3
Sexual Assault Prevention and Response
Office (SAPRO): annual reports, 172,
204n5; DEOMI working with, 106–107;
of DoD, 142; study by, 150–151
sexual violence, 27; Actionable Change for
ending, 176–177; *Army Wives'* absence of,
52, 56; Brooks on, 204n1; Congress and
legislation on, 142–143, 163–164; Dick
on, 160; education methods contributing

to, 151, 152–153; Enloe on, 168–169; as
epidemic, 142; Gavey on, 172–173; gender
and, 166–168; *The Invisible War*'s influence on prevention of, 143, 160–163; *The
Lonely Soldier: The Private War of Women
Serving in Iraq* on, 143–144; male victims
of, 148, 165, 167–168, 201n13, 205n8;
media disregard of, 144–145, 147–148;
media silence on, 185–186; military masculinity and, 168–172; NOW Foundation
on, 142, 149; obstacles with reporting
system, 158–159, 161–162; Ortiz survivor
of, 140–141; as patriarchal oppression,
55; postfeminism and, 56, 128, 173–174;
prosecution improvements regarding,
174–175; silence regarding, 56, 170, 171;
survival stories of, 154–158; training in,
149–154; traumas of, 146–148; Trump
on, 204n3; warrior mystique and, 146;
women interviewed regarding, 109.
See also rape culture
Sheehan, Cindy, 202n8; face of antiwar
movement, 88; Gold Star Families for
Peace founded by, 49; as Gold Star
Mother, 183; Iraq War critic, 26, 27, 67, 80,
82–83; letter to Bush, 89; Managhan on,
90, 200n9, 202n9; media discrediting,
90–96; as media exception, 68
Sherrill, Mikie, 180
Shoot like a Girl (Hegar), 204n12
silence: DoD and, 56; media and, 185–186;
as strategy, 171; Warren on institutional,
170
Sjoberg, Laura, 112, 203n7
soap opera / serial drama: *Army Wives* as, 30,
32, 62, 200n3; as military strategy, 62
Soccer Moms: Clinton in relation to, 70;
as media-generated identity, 69; Security
Moms compared to, 68, 71, 98; tips on, 63
social identities, 9–12
social media: ARPA as model for, 184–185;
JAMRS influence through, 82; Marines
United Facebook group, 141; for military
mother connection, 85; Russia and,
205n2; Trump on, 204n3
soft-power activities: *Army Wives* portraying, 36, 41, 42; Brooks on, 5
soldier mothers, 132–134, 204n14
Squires, Catherine, 13, 137

Stahl, Roger: on militainment, 23, 44, 134; on troop-supporting rhetoric, 37; on yellow ribbon campaign, 65–66
Strub, Phil, 43

Tasker, Yvonne, 10; on military mothers, 132; on warrior women, 111, 135
television. See films/television
terrorism, 64. See also Global War on Terror (GWOT)
third-gender concept, 183–184
Tough Guise, 2, 166–167
toxic masculinity: defined, 204n2; in Marine Corps, 141; sexual violence roots in, 143, 149; transformation of, 176–177
toxic volatile organic compounds (VOCs), 201n11
training: at Army Ranger school, 130; The Invisible War for sexual violence prevention, 172; ROTC, 59, 149; in sexual violence, 149–154
trajectories of affect, 8–9
trauma. See military sexual trauma (MST)
Treichler, Paula, on truth as power, 7
troop-supporting rhetoric: military mothers and, 85–86; Stahl on, 37
Trump, Donald: MOAB and, 3; on social media, 204n3; tribute to military, 205n1
Turse, Nick: on The Complex, 19; on JAMRS, 81

Under the Sabers: The Unwritten Code of Army Wives (Biank), 33, 41
Uniform Code of Military Justice, 155, 164
unit cohesion, 131
U.S.-Dakota war, 1

Vaught, Wilma: on combat-exclusion policy, 115–116; on soldier mothers, 132–133
veterans: on demilitarization, 192; Iraq and Afghanistan Veterans of America, 190; IVAW, 186–187; Ms. Veteran America pageant, 187–188, 189, 190; running for Congress, 179–180
Veterans Health Administration (VA): MST treatment from, 146; Ms. Veteran America pageant in relation to, 190; on women veterans' suicide, 191

Vietnam War: troop-supporting rhetoric and, 37; veteran on demilitarization, 192
Vogue magazine, 134–135

war: accounting for costs of, 187–194; Andersen on promotion of, 61, 180; Butler on media representations of, 8–9, 119–120; Butler on opposition to, 194; Cold War, 65; gender gap regarding, 79; genderization of, 108–110; Persian Gulf War, 37, 64, 65–66, 67; profiteering, 15; as safety from terrorism, 64; U.S.-Dakota war, 1; Vietnam War, 37, 192; World War II, 101–102. See also Afghanistan war; Global War on Terror (GWOT); Iraq War
War and Gender (Goldstein), 102
Warren, Catherine: brotherhood of silence case study, 171; on institutional silence, 170
warrior caste, 13
warrior mystique: defined, 110; martial postfeminism and, 137, 143, 176; sexual violence and, 146
Warrior Women regime, 27–28, 203n2; construction strategies of, 103; as equals, 114; gender equality of, 124–128; gender equivalence of, 121–123; gender neutrality of, 123–124; grievability and, 118, 173; history of, 104–108; in Iraq War, 116–117; liberal feminism and, 136; masculinity threatened by, 111; media representations of, 110–113; pedagogy of, 172–177; physical strength of, 129–130; postcracism regarding, 137–138; recognizability of, 9, 117–118, 134; soldier mothers in, 132–134; unique role of, 128–129; unit cohesion of, 131; in Vogue magazine, 134–135
welfare system, 71, 189–190
Why We Fight, 199n5
Winter Soldier hearings, 187
WNBA, 178
women: Army Ranger school graduates, 104; costs of war for, 190–191; enlistment of military, 4–5; evaluations as individuals, 129–130; Final Salute charity for veteran, 188; GI Bill promotion for, 33; interviews regarding sexual violence, 109; IWF for, 73, 201n4; Kerry impressions

from, 74; Lifetime network for support of, 32, 48–49; militarism roles of, 1–2; militarization of, 6; military hierarchy opportunities for, 127–128; military patriarchy regarding, 104–105, 135–136; as patriotic, 121; Pentagon combat-exclusion policy for, 102; post-9/11 and roles of, 4; VA on suicides of veteran, 191; veterans running for Congress, 179–180; WNBA tribute to military, 178; yellow ribbon campaign appealing to, 65–66. *See also* military mothers; Security Moms; Soccer Moms; Warrior Women regime
women of color, 203n5; enlistment, 107; intersectionality and, 12; Iraq War views from, 98–99; recruitment ads and, 113

Women's Armed Services Act (1948), 106
Women's Army Corps (WAC), 202n1; Goldstein on, 105; media attacks on, 110–111; in World War II, 101–102
Women's Research and Education Institute (WREI): on enlistment, 107; warrior women and, 105–106
World War II, 101–102

Yates, Emily, 186–187
yellow ribbon campaign, 65–66
Youth Attitude Tracking Survey, 45

Zinni, Anthony, 18

About the Author

MARY DOUGLAS VAVRUS is an associate professor of Communication Studies at the University of Minnesota. She teaches media studies courses and conducts research in the areas of feminist media studies, political economy of media, and media militarism. Her work has appeared in numerous anthologies and journals, including *Critical Studies in Media Communication*, *Journal of Communication Inquiry*, *Political Communication*, and *Women's Studies in Communication*. She is also the author of the book *Postfeminist News: Political Women in Media Culture*.